# Lecture Notes in Computer Science        8395

*Commenced Publication in 1973*
Founding and Former Series Editors:
Gerhard Goos, Juris Hartmanis, and Jan van Leeuwen

Stefan Göbel   Josef Wiemeyer (Eds.)

# Games for Training, Education, Health and Sports

4th International Conference on Serious Games,
GameDays 2014
Darmstadt, Germany, April 1-5, 2014
Proceedings

 Springer

Volume Editors

Stefan Göbel
Technische Universität Darmstadt
Electrical Engineering and Information Technology
Multimedia Communications Lab - KOM
Rundeturmstr. 10
64283 Darmstadt, Germany
E-mail: stefan.goebel@kom.tu-darmstadt.de

Josef Wiemeyer
Technische Universität Darmstadt
Human Sciences, Sport Science
Magdalenenstr. 27
64289 Darmstadt, Germany
E-mail: wiemeyer@sport.tu-darmstadt.de

ISSN 0302-9743            e-ISSN 1611-3349
ISBN 978-3-319-05971-6     e-ISBN 978-3-319-05972-3
DOI 10.1007/978-3-319-05972-3
Springer Cham Heidelberg New York Dordrecht London

Library of Congress Control Number: 2014934312

LNCS Sublibrary: SL 3 – Information Systems and Application,
incl. Internet/Web and HCI

*Typesetting:* Camera-ready by author, data conversion by Scientific Publishing Services, Chennai, India

Printed on acid-free paper

Springer is part of Springer Science+Business Media (www.springer.com)

# Preface

Games play an important role in everyone's life. Humans play games for fun, entertainment and other intrinsic reasons. Thus, playing games is part of human culture. Despite negative side effects like addiction, emotional dysfunctions and psychophysical strain, this holds also for digital games. Some years ago, a new kind of digital games entered the stage combining entertainment and fun on the one hand and training, education, science etc. on the other hand: Serious Games. Since then, Serious Games have passed a history of continuous improvement and scientific substantiation. Numerous application fields have been addressed, for example, learning in academia and school, health education, emergency training, rehabilitation and health training, to name but a few. In the meantime, activities in development and research have exploded. For example, Google scholar research using the search item "Serious Games" evoked more than 18,000 hits.

In Darmstadt, Germany, the great potential of digital games and in particular Serious Games were addressed early by scientific work. As a symbol of these activities, the GameDays were established in 2005 as a "Science meets Business" workshop in the field of Serious Games, taking place on an annual basis in Darmstadt. The principle aim of this initiative is to bring together academia and industry and to discuss the current trends and practices, grand challenges, and potentials of Serious Games for different application domains.

Since 2010, the academic part has been emphasized resulting in a first International Conference on Serious Games for Sports and Health. In 2011, the GameDays spectrum of topics was broadened and the different facets, methods, concepts and effects of game-based learning and training have been covered as well. In 2012, the Third International Conference of the GameDays was organised in conjunction with the 7th international Edutainment conference. In 2013, due to a time-shift from September to April, no international conference took place, but a round table and research community workshop "Serious Games – Quo Vadis" among selected German and European game researchers was initiated.

This year, 2014, the 10th GameDays including the 4th International Conference on Serious Games takes place. Again, all scientific papers were reviewed by 4 reviewers on average; the overall acceptance rate is ∼40% (compared to ∼50% in 2012).

The topics of the papers are settled in the fields of (game-based) training, teaching and learning, authoring tools, mobile gaming, health and rehabilitation, and citizen science. The papers address a broad scope of issues, including mechanisms and effects of (Serious) Games, adaptation and personalization, local, mobile, and internet learning and education applications, game, reuse and evaluation, game settings, types of learners, problem solving etc.

Furthermore, workshops are offered addressing Serious Games mechanics, designing mobile games, and authoring tools (StoryTec). Practical demonstrations of systems (e.g. tools or interactive installations) and applications (games, learning environments) – ranging from ideas and concepts (posters) to prototypes and commercially available products – are provided within the exhibition space of the conference and the Serious Games (Team) Challenge at the public day of the GameDays. Here, altogether more than 20 exhibits are expected.

The editors would like to thank all PC members for their tremendous work and all institutions, associations and companies for supporting and sponsoring the GameDays 2014 conference: Technische Universität Darmstadt (Multimedia Communications Lab – KOM, Institute for Sport Science, Graduate School Topology of Technology and Forum for interdisciplinary Research – FIF), Hessen-IT, German Association of Computer Science, German Chapter of the ACM, G.A.M.E. (German game developers association), BIU (German association for interactive entertainment industry), VDE/ITG Association for Electrical, Electronic & Information Technologies, Darmstadt Marketing, Software AG, HEAG, KTX Software Development, gamearea FRANKFURTRHEINMAIN, GALA Games and Learning Alliance Network of Excellence and Springer.

Of course, special thanks goes to Springer for publishing the proceedings of the GameDays and Edutainment conference in LNCS in 2012 as well as for the support of the present LNCS, to Hessen-IT for supporting the GameDays since its early days in 2005 and to the Forum for interdisciplinary research (FiF) for bundling and supporting the wide range of Serious Games research activities at the Technische Universität Darmstadt (TU Darmstadt). The FiF forum offers space for topics, problems and projects too broad to fit within the framework of a single discipline. It proved to be the perfect partner for expanding the various Serious Games research efforts and consolidating the network of Serious Games researchers at the TU Darmstadt. The disciplines involved in the FiF Serious Games Research Group range from computer science, bioinformatics, and civil engineering to mathematics, sports science, and psychology. Further information about the interdisciplinary research in Serious Games at TU Darmstadt is available at www.serious-games.tu-darmstadt.de.

Further information about the "International Conference on Serious Games – GameDays 2014" is available on the conference website:
http://www.gamedays2014.de

April 2014                                                              Stefan Göbel
                                                                    Josef Wiemeyer

# Organization

## Conference Co-chairs

Stefan Göbel                      Technische Universität Darmstadt, Germany
Josef Wiemeyer            Technische Universität Darmstadt, Germany
Patrick Felicia                 Waterford Institute of Technology, Ireland
Florian 'Floyd' Mueller    RMIT University, Australia
Noah Wardrip-Fruin      University of California at Santa Cruz, USA

## Program Committee

Jannicke Baalsrud Hauge    Universität Bremen, Germany
Thomas Baranowski        Baylor College of Medicine, USA
Gerald Bieber                Fraunhofer Institute for Computer Graphics
                                   in Rostock, Germany
Ian Bogost                   Georgia Institute of Technology, USA
Michael Brach              University of Münster, Germany
Linda Breitlauch          Mediadesign Hochschule Düsseldorf, Germany
Maiga Chang              Athabasca University, Canada
Karin Coninx              Hasselt University, Belgium
Ralf Dörner                RheinMain University of Applied Sciences,
                                   Germany
Wolfgang Effelsberg       University of Mannheim, Germany
Lars Elbaek                University of Southern Denmark, Denmark
Abdulmotaleb El Saddik    University of Ottawa, Canada
Kai Erenli                University of Applied Sciences Vienna,
                                   Austria
Baltasar Fernández-Manjón  Comlutense University of Madrid, Spain
Mateus David Finco       Federal University of Rio Grande do Sul, Brazil
Alex Fleetwood            Hide&Seek, London, UK
Tom Gedeon               Australian National University, Australia
Paul Grimm               University of Applied Sciences Fulda,
                                   Germany
Peter A. Henning          Karlsruhe University of Applied Sciences,
                                     Germany
Markus Herkersdorf       TriCAT GmbH, Germany
M. Shamim Hossain       King Saud University, Kingdom
                                   of Saudi Arabia
Jun Hu                      Eindhoven University of Technology,
                                   The Netherlands
Wolfgang Hürst            Utrecht University, The Netherlands

Ido Iurgel                      Hochschule Rhein-Waal, Kamp-Lintfort,
                                  Germany
Pamela Kato                     University Medical Center Utrecht,
                                  The Netherlands
Harri Ketamo                    Tampere University of Technology, Finland
Fares Kayali                    Universität für angewandte Kunst Wien,
                                  Austria
Michael Kickmeier-Rust          TU Graz, Austria
Christoph Klimmt                Hochschule für Musik, Theater und Medien
                                  Hannover, Germany
Martin Knöll                    TU Darmstadt, Germany
Oliver Korn                     University of Stuttgart, Germany
Kristof van Laerhoven           TU Darmstadt, Germany
Effie Law                       ETH Zürich, Switzerland
Jimmy H.M. Lee                  The Chinese University of Hong Kong,
                                  Hong Kong
Alke Martens                    PH Schwäbisch Gmünd, University of
                                  Education, Germany
Maic Masuch                     Universität Duisburg-Essen, Germany
Robin Mellecker                 University of Hong Kong, Hong Kong
André Miede                     Hochschule für Technik und Wirtschaft des
                                  Saarlandes, Germany
Wolfgang Müller                 PH Weingarten, Germany
Jörg Müller-Lietzkow            Universität Paderborn, Germany
Wolfgang Mueller-Wittig         Nanyang Technological University, Singapore
Frank Nack                      University of Amsterdam, The Netherlands
Lennart Nacke                   University of Ontario Institute of Technology
                                  (UOIT), Canada
Zhigeng Pan                     Zhejiang University, China
Paolo Petta                     Austrian Research Institute for Artificial
                                  Intelligence, Austria
Alenka Poplin                   HafenCity University Hamburg, Germany
Eliseo Reategui                 Federal University of Rio Grande do Sul, Brazil
Rui Rodrigues                   Faculty of Engineering of University of Porto
                                  and INESC TEC, Portugal
Roman Schönsee                  Ranj Serious Games, The Netherlands
Ulrike Spierling                RheinMain University of Applied Sciences,
                                  Germany
Florian Stadlbauer              DECK13 Interactive, Germany
Ralf Steinmetz                  TU Darmstadt, Germany
Janine Sturm                    Eindhoven University of Technology,
                                  The Netherlands
Roger Tavares                   Universidade Federal do Rio Grande do Norte,
                                  Brazil

# Table of Contents

## Health Games and Effects

## Workshops

# How Computer Games Can Improve Your Health and Fitness

Rainer Malaka

TZI, University of Bremen, Germany
malaka@tzi.de

**Abstract.** Serious games became an object of research and development in the last decade. Using computer game technology for serious applications can be very beneficial for a variety of applications. In particular when it is about motivating people through gaming mechanisms, there is a great potential to use gaming technology and the psychological mechanisms that attract people to games for making them do activities that would otherwise either be not done or at least with much less enthusiasm. One such application is personal fitness. So called *exergames* aim at wrapping physical exercises into computer games. They range from rehabilitation programs to workout programs mimicking a personal trainer.

## 1   Introduction

Computer games are one of the most successful genres of Digital Media. They directly address a central human desire, namely to engage in entertaining activities. Playing has been identified an important mechanism for learning and transmitting cultural skills. It has also been seen as a driving force behind culture and society. The concept of the *homo ludens* proposed by Huizinga (1949) identifies game play not only as something that is innate to mankind but also as a principle that leads to cultural evolution. If we enter the *magic circle* of a game, we obviously follow a quite natural instinct.

Concerning computer games, the last decades have shown that the new technology brought about very popular games that some critics even consider harmful due to their addictiveness. Apart from these negative tendencies we can observe two additional trends with rather positive effects:

- Computer games had a high impact on the technological development (both hardware and software)
- It could be shown that entertainment technology can be used for serious applications

The first point is obvious. Through deployment on a mass market and due to huge investments both hardware and software became more advanced. Without game technology, graphics hardware would be much more expensive, 3D engines would be less advanced and human tracking devices (such as the Kinect) would not be low-cost off-the-shelf products.

S. Göbel and J. Wiemeyer (Eds.): GameDays 2014, LNCS 8395, pp. 1–7, 2014.

The second aspect is often overlooked by the public. Most people regard computer games as a waste of time for young (mostly male) people. However, the quite natural habit of the *homo ludens* of enjoying games has been turned into a motivational motor for involving people into activities with a serious background. Serious games address this mechanism by wrapping activities into games. Such games can have different purpose, e.g.

- games to raise awareness (e.g. for ethical issues)
- games for learning and training (so called edutainment)
- games for harvesting data (e.g. games with a purpose)
- games for health and fitness (exergames)

In particular in combination with new console technology and advanced tracking methods, games for health and fitness are just turning from a niche phenomenon to a mass market. The combination of exercising and gaming – *exergames* – together with advanced tracking of the whole human body can help people to do exercises in a motivating and playful environment and in combination with the computer feedback and the evaluation of the actual activity of the player, custom programs and personalized sessions can be designed that act as a virtual personal trainer.

With this technology not only young and healthy games can be addressed. Rehabilitation patients, elderly and people with special challenges can do custom exercises with individual monitoring and feedback. In this paper, we want to give an overview on this field of serious games and highlight some exemplary developments that address some research challenges of exergames.

## 2      Games for Serious Applications and Health

The trend of using games and entertainment technology for serious applications such as training or learning is not new [2]. Games like board games or role playing games have been used long before computer games were available. However, with computer games and the huge success of the genre, serious games also became very popular. Interactive games for learning and simulation using computer gaming technology could now become a new field of research and development [3,4,5]. There is a wide spectrum of terms and application domains ranging from game-based learning via edutainment to training applications. One particular area are games with a purpose or human computation games where the players contribute with their interactive game play data for solving complex problems [6,7]. Thus serious games can aim at having an impact on the user or outside of the user´s context to some other problem solving domain.

Besides learning and training, physical exercises are among those applications of serious games that came into focus in recent years. These games can either address just general fitness of healthy players or specific needs for people needing individual training or physiotherapy [8,9,10,11].

## 2.1    Trends in Exergames

Exergames as serious computer games are a relatively new phenomenon. In contrast to game-based learning where user feedback can just be given by mouse and keyboard, exergaming requires physiological feedback from the user. With the breakthrough of low-cost tracking methods for game consoles, games for physical exercising became more popular. Even though early products such as the Atari Puffer date back to 1982 using an exercise bike in combination with a personal computer, it was the Wii controller in 2006 that brought simple tracking for exergames to the mass market.

Today camera-based tracking including depth-sensing with IR- and stereo cameras are state-of-the-art technology for full body tracking. The Kinect-Sensor was a milestone for making advanced tracking affordable for consumers and bringing natural user interfaces (NUI) into the living room. New games using full-body interaction came on the market. Many of these console games, such as for Dance Dance Revolution, have been a commercial success and did – in fact – let the users exercise their physical fitness. The boundaries between genres are not sharp and there is rather a continuum between games that use physical, full body input, fitness programs that are not intended to be games, and exergames. Many products are actually mixing concepts and include gaming elements, physiotherapeutic elements, and fitness programs.

One general principle drives all approaches: the higher immersion through interaction and gaming technology the more it is likely to enhance a user´s motivation for doing more physical activity leading to potentially a healthier lifestyle. However, there is no guarantee for success. Like with many fitness products and programs – be it aerobic DVDs or exercising bikes – the initial enthusiasm may quickly fade away and/or wrong execution might lead to unwanted results. This brings in important challenges for the design of exergames.

## 2.2    Design Challenges for Exergames

In order to successfully design exergames, a number of goals have to be achieved that lead to quite sophisticated design challenges. The overall paradigm of exergames postulates that the motivational power of games addressing the *homo ludens* and the immersion of interactive computer software can lead to a *sustainable motivation* for doing exercises. The second challenge is to give users feedback on doing *physiologically positive movements*. Unlike ordinary computer games that sometimes even lead to negative physiological effects such as muscle tension or uni-lateral stress or normal ergonomic aspects that try to avoid strain, we want to evoke a certain amount of stress in order to train the body but we want to avoid negative effects. The third challenge is to *adapt to individual users*, which is the most difficult task. In particular when it comes to physiotherapy, many patients (users) have quite individual pre-dispositions, abilities and depending on the reason for their condition might have phases with more or less restrictions. These individual adaptions are certainly necessary between individual users. However, they can also be necessary between sessions of the same user since the physical fitness may vary in phases and can improve or degrade. Even more subtle is an in-session adaption when - after a warm-up activation exercise - the physical state of the day can be assessed.

The goals of

- sustainable motivation
- physiologically positive movements
- and adaptation to users

have to be carefully balanced. There is no straight-forward design-process guaranteeing success. In the following case studies we want to give a few examples how these aspects can be addressed.

## 3      Case Studies

In the following we want to present exergames developed in our research team in which we addressed the design challenges mentioned above.

### 3.1      Individualized Exergaming for Physiotherapy

The ageing societies of the western world lead to a high percentage of older people. Many of them are more active and physically more fit than people of the same age in the generation before. However, since there are just many more and since people get much older today, there is a rising need for physiotherapy and exercising in this age group. Moreover, some age related disorders and diseases progress such as dementia or Parkinson disease (PD). Regular physical activity helps not only to slow down the decline that comes with these progressive diseases. It also leads to a general better body feeling, prevents accidents, stimulates social activities and leads to better and more healthy ageing.

We developed a series of exergames for elderly people and for patients with PD in a participatory design process [10]. The age of our participating players was often above 60 and for the experience of exergaming was very positive. Besides the health and motivational aspects of exergaming, the virtual interaction with environments such as nature was stimulating because the radius of their everyday activities was often limited.

For our target user group it was in particular important to adapt the games to the individual (dis-)abilities [2,12]. But also aesthetics and design have to be adapted to the target group [13]. In addition, reward mechanisms [14], multiplayer and the interaction of sound, music and gameplay have to be tuned to the individual preferences of the players [15]. Even though the user-centered design process and the individual design decisions were the result of intensive user studies, the resulting games had to be simple and easy. An example of one of the resulting games is the game star-money in which a user controls a game with two arms and has to perform wide wiping movements in order to let a virtual character collect star money (Fig. 1).

For the target group of PD patients it was an important design principle to emphasize positive feedback in order to give the users more confidence. In this case the design of the games and the game mechanics differ a lot from off-the-shelf computer games. Simple mechanics, lower challenges and positive reinforcement are important since the users suffer from daily frustrations and have the continuous feeling of becoming less competent.

**Fig. 1.** Exergames examples. Left: screen shot of star-money, a game for PD patients, right: device for suspended walking interface for the SPortal game.

## 3.2 NUI-fication of AAA-Games for Exergaming

If we want to design a game for young and healthy people who just want to do more sports, simple games without challenge like star money would not raise much interest in people who play AAA computer games in their spare time.

In order to address this quite different target group (compared to older PD patients), we took took another approach. Instead of building a custom game for the audience we wanted to use an already existing game. There is no way to compete with big game studios with a small research team. In our project *Exercise My Game* (XMG) we developed a four step procedure to turn a AAA game into an exergame [9]:

1. selection of a game
2. mapping of movements to actions in the game
3. design of appropriate feedback
4. level design for custom training sessions

In our prototypical realization we selected the game Portal 2 and built the exergame SPortal in which the virtual character has to be controlled by body movements of the player. We implemented as control walking in place, jumping, crouching, jumping jacks, and turning. These actions were mapped on activities in the game. For the walking in place we used two alternatives: once just normal walking in place tracked with Kinect and Wii-Sensors and as a more immersive interface a form of suspended walking where the user is hanging in a harness and slides on the ground (Fig. 1, right). Feedback is given to the user through a visual display of a small skeletal tracking model and instructions on what movement is expected from the user. These displays are an overlay onto the Portal display. In a voice-over we add instructions in a game-like fashion for the user to explain current tasks. Additional displays can show calorie consumption, speed etc.

For customizing Portal, we used the possibility of editing custom levels in SPortal. This way, we could design levels as training session.

## 4     Discussion and Conclusions

In this paper, the focus was on the successful design of exergames. Three challenges are have to be dealt with: sustainable motivation, physiologically positive movements, and adaptation to users. We looked at a variety of users and presented a number of ideas on how to design exergames. There is no unified solution and as with all interactive software, a human-centered approach that builds on iterative prototyping with a high involvement of users is key to success. However, some solutions can be generalized.

For user motivation, we propose a combination of commercial games with exergame-specific enhancements that turn them into AAA games that can be used for exercising. Further experiments have to show to what extend the game control of other games can also be replaced by new mappings that use physical full-body input as a replacement for classical mouse or keyboard input.

How can we build user interfaces employing physiologically positive body motion? With new and cheap tracking devices, we can define completely new mappings of user input to computer systems. This interaction beyond the desktop allows for more healthy and ergonomic interaction not only for exergaming.

Consequently, we can adapt the user interaction to the individual condition of a user during a session and between session in order to compensate for changes in the user´s fitness and ability.

These three aspects –discussed here in the context of exergames – can also be expanded to the broader filed of serious games. When we talk about game-based learning, games for change or human computation games, similar problems occur: how to find a good game as basis, how to find appropriate mapping of the serious user interaction to the game mechanics and how to adapt to the individual progress/condition of the user.

**Acknowledgments.** Some project results presented in this paper were funded by Klaus Tschira Foundation and the WfB Bremen. The author thanks Marc Herrlich, Ben Walther-Franks; Jan Smeddinck, Dirk Wenig and the students of the Digital Media program at the University of Bremen for their contributions, ideas and enthusiasm on the projects presented here.

# References

1. Huizinga, J.: Homo Ludens: A Study of the Play-Element in Culture. Routledge & Kegan Paul, London (1949)
2. Abt, C.C.: Serious games. University Press of America (1987)
3. Malaka, R., Schneider, K., Kretschmer, U.: Stage-based augmented edutainment. In: Butz, A., Krüger, A., Olivier, P. (eds.) SG 2004. LNCS, vol. 3031, pp. 54–65. Springer, Heidelberg (2004)
4. Sawyer, B., Rejeski, D.: Serious games: Improving public policy through game-based learning and simulation (2002)
5. Sawyer, B., Smith, P.: Serious games taxonomy. In: Slides from the Serious Games Summit at the Game Developers Conference (2008)
6. Krause, M., Takhtamysheva, A., Wittstock, M., Malaka, R.: Frontiers of a paradigm: exploring human computation with digital games. In: Proceedings of the ACM SIGKDD Workshop on Human Computation, pp. 22–25 (2010)
7. von Ahn, L., Dabbish, L.: Labeling images with a computer game. In: CHI 2004 Proceedings of the 22nd International Conference on Human Factors in Computing Systems, pp. 319–326. ACM Press (2004)
8. Göbel, S., Hardy, S., Wendel, V., Mehm, F., Steinmetz, R.: Serious games for health: personalized exergames. In: Proceedings of the International Conference on Multimedia, MM 2010, pp. 1663–1666. ACM, New York (2010)
9. Walther-Franks, B., Wenig, D., Smeddinck, J., Malaka, R.: Exercise My Game: Turning Off-The-Shelf Games into Exergames. In: Anacleto, J.C., Clua, E.W.G., da Silva, F.S.C., Fels, S., Yang, H.S. (eds.) ICEC 2013. LNCS, vol. 8215, pp. 126–131. Springer, Heidelberg (2013)
10. Assad, O., Hermann, R., Lilla, D., Mellies, B., Meyer, R., Shevach, L., Siegel, S., Springer, M., Tiemkeo, S., Voges, J., Wieferich, J., Herrlich, M., Krause, M., Malaka, R.: Motion-Based games for parkinson's disease patients. In: Anacleto, J.C., Fels, S., Graham, N., Kapralos, B., Saif El-Nasr, M., Stanley, K. (eds.) ICEC 2011. LNCS, vol. 6972, pp. 47–58. Springer, Heidelberg (2011)
11. Ijsselsteijn, W., Nap, H.H., de Kort, Y., Poels, K.: Digital game design for elderly users. In: Proceedings of the 2007 Conference on Future Play, Future Play 2007, pp. 17–22. ACM, New York (2007)
12. Smeddinck, J., Siegel, S., Herrlich, M.: Adaptive difficulty in exergames for parkinson's disease patients. In: Proc. of Graphics Interface (GI), pp. 25:1–25:8. ACM (2013)
13. Smeddinck, J., Gerling, K.M., Tiemkeo, S.: Visual Complexity, Player Experience, Performance and Physical Exertion in Motion-Based Games for Older Adults. In: The 15th ACM SIGACCESS International Conference on Computers and Accessibility (ASSETS 2013), Bellevue, WA, USA (2013)
14. Springer, M., Herrlich, M., Krannich, D., Malaka, R.: Achievements in exergames for parkinson's patients. In: Entertainment Interfaces at Mensch und Computer. Oldenbourg Wissenschaftsverlag (2012)
15. Lilla, D., Herrlich, M., Malaka, R., Krannich, D.: The influence of music on player performance in exergames for parkinson's patients. In: Herrlich, M., Malaka, R., Masuch, M. (eds.) ICEC 2012. LNCS, vol. 7522, pp. 433–436. Springer, Heidelberg (2012)
16. Walther-Franks, B., Wenig, D., Smeddinck, J., Malaka, R.: Suspended Walking: A Physical Locomotion Interface for Virtual Reality. In: Anacleto, J.C., Clua, E.W.G., da Silva, F.S.C., Fels, S., Yang, H.S. (eds.) ICEC 2013. LNCS, vol. 8215, pp. 185–188. Springer, Heidelberg (2013)

# Game-Based IT Solutions for Active and Healthy Aging

Mario Drobics[1] and Stuart Smith[2]

[1] AIT Austrian Institute of Technology GmbH, Austria
Mario.Drobics@ait.ac.at
[2] University of Tasmania, Australia
Stuart.Smith@utas.edu.au

**Abstract.** Game-based approaches can be used to support traditional intervention schemes which enable older adults in staying active & healthy for a longer time. These techniques are especially useful as they improve the motivation of the users and thus help to improve the effectiveness of the intervention. TV-based games are often oriented along traditional video games. External sensors like video cameras can be incorporated to provide direct feedback on the activities of the user. This information can also be utilized to reassess the status of the user and monitor his/her training progress. Mobile devices and the large range of available body worn sensors offer the opportunity to design games around daily and outdoor activities. By adding a social level to the games, competition and group efforts can be initiated, giving further motivation to reach a certain goal. In this overview, we will present different approaches of game-based IT solutions to support active & healthy aging, including concrete examples from resent applications.

## 1 Motivation

There is a wide body of literature that points to the fact that to increase people's quality of life and fitness, we need to encourage them to become more physically active [6], [17]. Structured exercise training has a positive impact on older adults and may be used for the management of frailty [11], [12], [20].

Consumer driven forces for new ways to interact with videogames have led to development of sophisticated video capture and inertial sensing devices for measuring movement of the human body. Until recently, such technology could only be found in expensive and dedicated laboratory facilities. Devices such as the Microsoft Xbox Kinect are now at a price point that it is possible to relatively inexpensively deploy motion capture and feedback technologies into the lives of consumers for use in physical activity programs. Additionally, systems for tracking training physical activities such as Nike Plus, running watches and heart rate monitors like Timex Ironman, or GPS solutions as Garmin are commonly available. In the research field, commercial exergames supported by Nintendo Wii [8], [14], [19] have also been explored as an alternative approach to make young and old adults more physically active or to recover patients from stroke as a therapeutic intervention for example.

S. Göbel and J. Wiemeyer (Eds.): GameDays 2014, LNCS 8395, pp. 8–11, 2014.
© Springer International Publishing Switzerland 2014

## 2    Games for Health

Interactive videogames that combine player movement, engaging recreation, immediate performance feedback and social connectivity via competition, have been shown to promote motivation for, and increase adherence to, physical exercise amongst children and young adults [1], [2], [5], [9], [15], [21]. In older adults, videogames have also been shown to improve cognitive abilities [7], to be a feasible alternative to more traditional aerobic exercise modalities for middle-aged and older adults [10] and can be used to train stepping ability in older adults to reduce the risk of falls [18].

In partnership with Humana Inc, a large health insurance provider in the US, Ubisoft has included in the 2012 release of their Yourshape Fitness Evolved product a series of exercise routines that have been purposely designed to help older adults stay active and mobile as well as giving people of all ages tools for lowering their blood pressure. Recently Nike have also introduced Nike Kinect + Training which enables players to count activity in the videogame towards their Nike+ Fuel pool in the cloud, syncing all Nike+ services, including the new Nike FuelBand into a single measurable value of activity. Such advances will enable the capability to monitor compliance with all forms of exercise, the rate and intensity of exercise as well as progression of exercise level. This information could then be tracked by clinicians and used to deliver tailored PA training routines to individuals. PA programs are those that build exercise slowly over time and make use of behaviour change principles [4], moderate intensity activities, are inexpensive and convenient [3], are tailored [16] and can be done independently with some instruction [22] have all been shown to be highly effective in engaging people to increase their over levels of PA. In particular for females, inclusion of a social component to PA programs can be very important for maintaining adherence [13].

In addition to use of console-based game technology, the use of mobile phones as part of a lifestyle improvement is nascent. As smart phones have become more common, two parallel developments have created an easier to use interface than ever before – the large touch screen), (and significantly more complex functionality in accelerometers, compasses, GPS and other sensing devices. Additionally, third party creators of specialist sensing devices, such as Nike® Fuel Band™, Polar heart rate monitors and FitBit™ amongst others, are now supplying the feedback from these sensors into these smartphones. Globally, there has been in increase in apps which are designed to improve health through better lifestyle choice, including tracking food intake (Lose It), tracking activity (My Fitness Goal), encourage healthy food and activity replacements (Swap it, Don't Stop It), retaining mental flexibility (Brainy App) and support for giving up smoking (My QuitBuddy). In some cases, games and gamification techniques have been implemented to make the apps more likely to be used and the encourage compliance with the lifestyle changes (Eat this, Not that! The Game and My QuitBuddy).

The inclusion of gamification techniques [points, rewards, personalisation, data visualisation, levelling up, status rewards, badges, peer obligation, social currency, missions and challenges] is still a new area with early signs of great potential for lifestyle improvements.

## 3    Supportive Games

In our projects we include gamification across all the developments in new and comprehensive ways. Gamification here is useful as it automatically collects data from the user which, via the smart back end cloud based system, and can track the correlation between actual user activity and perceived user activity.

In our project iStoppFalls we use games in conjunction with traditional exercises for fall-prevention training. While the exercises are executed along an automatically determined training-plan, the schedule of the games can selected by the user. Currently three games are provided: A skiing game, which supports the balance and strength of the upper limbs. Additionally, dual-task exercises (e.g. simple mathematical calculations) are incorporated to increase difficulty and to improve postural stability. The second game is called Bistro, and aims to support the balance and coordination abilities of the user. In this game the user has to collect ingredients for a sandwich that are falling from the top of the kitchen by stepping left and right. Finally, a game called "Bees" simulates a walk through a park, where the user has to avoid bees coming by. All this games are inspired by traditional games, but aim to support specific physical abilities of the users.

A completely different approach was chosen in our project KIT-Active, where we have setup an intelligent infrastructure in Grafenwörth, a small village close to Vienna. Along a recently build fitness course, eight intelligent fitness poles have been erected. Users are provided with small RFID bracelets and can register at the pole, every time they pass by. The system then calculates distance and speed between the poles. Additionally, semi-public terminals have been set-up, where users can view their data and connect personal monitoring devices or measure their body weight.

By providing the RFID bracelets to a wide range of users, including school children, people interested in sports, and older adults, a wide variety of new applications can be set-up easily. This includes competitions between individuals or groups, but also joined efforts, e.g. for charity purposes. Finally, virtual tours and games can be implemented which utilize this infrastructure and extending it with other sensors or devices.

## 4    Summary

Games can support older adults in staying active & healthy for a longer time. The combination of ubiquitous sensing techniques and game-based approaches can increase fun and motivation of the users. By offering a wide range of possibilities ranging from direct motion feedback to social interaction, different motivation strategies can be applied. It is, however, important to constantly monitor the status of the users, to prevent excessive strain and injuries, especially when older or ill people are involved. However, if done right game-based approaches can help to overcome the digital-divide and enable also older adults to benefit from state-of-the-art technologies by providing intuitive interfaces and by being fun.

# References

1. Baranowski, T., et al.: Playing for real: Video games and stories for health-related behaviour change. Am. J. Prev. Med. 34(1), 74–82 (2008)
2. Barnett, A., et al.: Active video games for youth: a systematic review. Journal of Physical Activity and Health 8, 724–737 (2011)
3. Bawley, L.R., et al.: Promoting physical activity for older adults: the challenges for changing behaviour. Am. J. Prev. Med. 25(3), 172–183 (2003)
4. Cress, M.E., et al.: Best practices for physical activity programs and behaviour counselling in older adults. Journal of Aging and Physical Activity 13(1), 61–74 (2005)
5. Epstein, L.H., et al.: Choice of interactive dance and bicycle games in overweight and nonoverweight youth. Ann. Behav. Med. 33(2), 124–131 (2007)
6. Ferrucci, et al.: Disease severity and health-related quality of life across different chronic conditions. J. Am. Geriatr. Soc. 48(11), 1490–1495 (2000); PMID:11083330
7. Gamberini, L., et al.: Playing for a real bonus: videogames to empower elderly people. Journal of Cybertherapy and Rehabilitation 1(1), 37–47 (2008)
8. Gerling, et al.: Designing and evaluating digital games for frail elderly persons. In: Proceedings of the 8th International Conference on Advances in Computer Entertainment Technology, ACE 2011, Article No. 62. ACM, New York (2011)
9. Graves, L., et al.: Comparison of energy expenditure in adolescents when playing new generation and sedentary computer games: cross sectional study. BMJ 335, 1282–1284 (2007)
10. Guderian, B., et al.: The cardiovascular and metabolic responses to Wii Fit video game playing in middle-aged and older adults. Journal of Sports Medicine and Physical Fitness 50(4), 436–442 (2010)
11. Hess, Woollacott: Effect of high-intensity strength-training on functional measures of balance ability in balance-impaired older adults. J. Manipulative Physiol. Ther. 28(8), 582–590 (2005); PMID:16226626.
12. Heyn, et al.: The effects of exercise training on elderly persons with cognitive impairment and dementia: A meta-analysis. Archives of Physical Medicine and Rehabilitation 85(10), 1694–1704 (2004); PMID:15468033
13. Holt-Lunstad, J., et al.: Social relationships and mortality risk: A meta-analytic review. PLoS Med. 7(7), e1000316 (2010), doi: 10.1371/journal.pmed.1000316
14. Li, J., et al.: Nintendo Wii as an intervention: improving the well-being of elderly in long-term care facilities. Final year project report, Nanyang Technological University (2009)
15. Maddison, R., et al.: Energy expended playing video console games: an opportunity to increase children's physical activity. Pediatric Exercise Science 19(3), 334–343 (2007)
16. Marsh, A., et al.: Should physical activity programs be tailored when older adults have compromised function? Journal of Aging and Physical Activity 17(3), 294–306 (2009)
17. Obi, et al.: Promoting ICT innovations for the ageing population in Japan. Int. J. of Med. Inform. 82(4), e47–e62 (2012, 2013), doi:10.1016/j.ijmedinf.2012.05.004
18. Smith, S.T., et al.: A novel Dance Dance Revolution [DDR] system for in-home training of stepping ability: basic parameters of system use by older adults. British Journal of Sports Medicine 45(5), 441–445 (2011)
19. Theng, et al.: An exploratory study on senior citizens' perceptions of the Nintendo Wii: the case of Singapore. In: Proceedings of the 3rd Int. Convention on Rehabilitation Engineering & Assistive Technology, i-CREATe 2009. ACM, New York (2009)
20. Theou, et al.: The effectiveness of exercise interventions for the management of frailty: a systematic review. J. Aging Res., 569194 (2011); PMID:21584244
21. Warburton, D., et al.: The health benefits of interactive video game exercise. Appl. Physio. Nutr. Metab. 32, 655–663 (2007)
22. Yan, T., et al.: Results from the healthy moves for aging well program: changes of the health outcomes. Home Health Care Services Semiannually 28(2-3), 100–111 (2009)

# Cat King's Metamorphosis

## The Reuse of an Educational Game in a Further Technical Domain

Heinrich Söbke[1], Eva Chan[1], Raban von Buttlar[2], Jessica Große-Wortmann[3], and Jörg Londong[1]

[1] Bauhaus-Universität Weimar, Fakultät Bauingenieurwesen, Germany
`{heinrich.soebke,eva.chan,joerg.londong}@uni-weimar.de`
[2] Lernfreak UG (haftungsbeschränkt), Berlin, Germany
`hello@lernfreak.de`
[3] Universität Potsdam, Juristische Fakultät, Germany
`info@juristischer-gedankensalat.de`

**Abstract.** In general the development of educational video games is costly. Reuse of existing games is an approach which may lower development efforts in some cases. In this paper we present such a case: The original game is a mobile app which supports memorizing basic knowledge of the law domain. Starting with a description of the software architecture and the game mechanics of the mobile app we outline the necessary steps and methods to extend the software to an own, new app with content from an engineering discipline. The provided clone of the original educational game is a fully usable mobile educational game. We compare the efforts needed for the development of the original and the new app. Finally we discuss the limitations and requirements of this approach as there are legal issues, limitations to the knowledge which is transferred by the game, the systematic use of the game, change of the context and an appropriate game structure. Nevertheless our result is a generic procedure to extend that game to arbitrary further technical domains – at a considerably smaller fraction of the original effort.

**Keywords:** software reuse, educational game, mobile game, graduate education, game development.

## 1 Introduction

Software development itself is a complex and therefore often risky and costly task. Many technical and organizational difficulties have to be overcome [1]. The creation of a video game –a subtype of software - adds to that complexity the requirement to design intriguing game mechanics – game software not only has to work properly but also has to provide an attractive gaming experience. The design of such an experience needs (paper) prototypes and play test cycles with the consequence of increased complexity[1] [2]. An even greater challenge is the design of an appealing educational

---

[1] Concededly games are not required to deal with real world systems – when a real world model becomes too complex, a game can be built on a simpler model. This non-requirement mitigates the challenging task a bit.

S. Göbel and J. Wiemeyer (Eds.): GameDays 2014, LNCS 8395, pp. 12–22, 2014.
© Springer International Publishing Switzerland 2014

game: Pursuing educational goals lowers the game designers' grades of freedom as educational content has to be integrated into the game in a fun preserving manner. Habgood & Ainsworth call this 'intrinsic integration' [3]. The complexity of such a task reaches a level which has led to many failed attempts [4–6].

One approach to face that task's enormous complexity is to simply avoid it by reuse of an existing and successful game. This strategy is not very common as many limitations have been discussed in [7]. Such an attempt requires an attractive video game which offers the opportunity to add educational content. These cases may be rare, but here we describe an example that demonstrates the feasibility of this approach.

The iOS app 'JuraShooter StGB: Jagd nach dem Katzenkönig' (*Cat King app*) is a mobile serious game used by graduate students for memorizing basic knowledge of the German criminal law domain [8, 9]. It is one of the most downloaded apps in the Apple App Store in the field of German law education. The app is used as a voluntary learning aid to strengthen the students' familiarity with elementary knowledge of German law. This skill saves time in exam situations. In traditional law education it is trained in - student-paid - so called extracurricular revision courses. The initiator of this game – himself a former law student and now a lawyer - created it as a partial substitution of these costly revision courses [8].

The game's basic mechanic is the answering of multiple response questions: Correct and false answer fractions are flashing up on the screen continuously. The player has to tap the correct fractions and to ignore the false ones – not knowing how many fractions are needed to form the correct answer (cf. Fig. 1). Examples for questions from the domain of criminal law are *How is 'death' defined?* or *What are the defining characteristics of 'perfidiousness'?* The faster the correct answer is identified the higher is the reached score. Due to this basic game mechanic the app's mainly supported educational objective is *remembering factual knowledge* (cf. Bloom's Taxonomy [10])[2].

Players' engagement can be measured by means of the Apple Game Center partly. The app has an interface to it and players can share their highscores. Repeatedly we have observed the increasing highscore trajectories of certain players. Over a week we daily recorded the shared highscore of a player – identifiable by his/her nickname. We observed a steady increase of the highscore to a maximum mark. These maximal achievable points are defined by a run of play when all correct answer fractions are identified on their first appearance. In our valuation a player has memorized the correct answer at that point – so the educational aim of the game is reached at least by some players[3].

Questions and their answers carry the knowledge which should be learned by the player. Since a question is a generic construct the game is not limited to a certain technical domain. Thus the game seems to be very appropriate to work in other

---

[2] Acquisition of knowledge is not the main goal of the game although it is supported by so called 'Jokers' which reveal the correct answer. The knowledge acquisition is part of the course the game should accompany. The main goal of the game is to strengthen the player's knowledge.

[3] Efficacy of multiple choice questions in learning processes has been discussed roughly in [7].

domains also. In this article we describe the process of using this software to create another app edition supporting the technical domain of urban wastewater management. First we describe all necessary steps to create the app in Sec. 2. In the creation process of the game we employed the additional methods of play tests to gather knowledge about question design and an online survey to collect feedback for an appropriate story. Since one main motivation for reusing a game is saving costs we compare the required efforts for both the original app and the new app in Sec. 3. In Sec. 4 we discuss our experiences, prerequisites and the transferability of this approach. Sec. 5 contains the conclusions and an outlook.

**Fig. 1.** Main Screen of the Cat King App

## 2     Creating the New Game

### 2.1     Initial Situation

Our target is the provision of a new educational app in the field of urban wastewater management. This app should be based on the existing Cat King app. Its intended usage is to support the formal education of environmental engineering bachelor students. They are supposed to play it as a voluntary, extracurricular activity. The app is recommended to the students as a kind of *suggested reading* and should enable them to train basic domain knowledge which is needed in order to develop higher order knowledge about typical systems of that domain, e.g. substance flow cycles.

The base app is already designed for being extended: questions are packaged in *levels*. A set of levels can be combined to a *package*, which is the downloadable unit for distribution via Apple's App Store. Finally a *module* determines all packages used for a *JuraShooter engine*[4] powered app. After downloading the Cat King app from the App Store it is featured with basic packages (of questions). Additional packages are distributed via App Store separately.

The administration of the content is supported by a web based content management system (CMS) in the backend. The CMS also offers a possibility to configure graphics and sound effects (SFX): defining a new, so-called *Style* requires the bundling of graphic and audio resources. Although the possibility to extend the app exists it has never been utilized so far.

## 2.2    Creation Process

**Content.** The first step of content creation was the determination of the content area. We chose as a starting point a basic course of undergraduate environmental engineering education: *Urban Wastewater Management*. The existing teaching material was searched for knowledge which can be presented by using multiple response questions [11]. Since Urban Wastewater Management mainly deals with systems, we found a lot of knowledge which cannot easily be transferred in an appropriate form for the game[5]. Nevertheless after processing half of the teaching material we identified 150 questions. These questions have been arranged in 15 groups – each with a main topic and similar size of 10 questions.

The results and experiences from the process of content creation can be summarized in the following categories:

1. Selection of Content
2. Structure of Questions
3. Strategies for Creation of False Answers
4. Criteria for Level Building

The experiences have been complemented with the results of unstructured play tests and interviews. These play tests focused on additional structures of questions - taking into account that the form of trained knowledge differs slightly between original and cloned app[6]. We asked 4 scientific associates[7] and 2 students of our department to

---

[4]  We use the term *JuraShooter engine* for the generic software parts of the Cat King app, which are a base of reuse in further apps.

[5]  Iz & Fok [14] demonstrated that knowledge of all cognitive levels of Bloom's Taxonomy [15] can be used in multiple choice questions. This seems to be more a theoretic approach, but not suitable for such a game: If calculations outside of the game become necessary the game flow gets lost. However the game flow seems to be one essential element of the gaming experience of the Cat King app which has to be preserved.

[6]  As an example: In the *Cat King* app's content definitions are predominant whereas in the *Sewer Rats* app classifications are a main part of the content.

[7]  These test persons had a working knowledge of the app's content, but were not currently invented in the course.

play through the first two levels. They had been instructed to think aloud, so their impressions could be recorded by the supervising person. In interviews after the play session the test persons were asked – amongst others -about their reception of new structures of questions.

*Selection of content*: Table 1 shows candidates and examples for question generation. These are heuristics to detect possible content for the app. In general the selection of content is driven by the learning objectives. In our case those have been explicitly stated in the learning material. Thus they guided content creation as a criterion.

**Table 1.** Question candidates

| Candidate | Example |
|-----------|---------|
| Enumeration | Types of pumps: rotary pump, ram pump, ... |
| Definition | What is drinking water? |
| (Sequential) List | Steps of the water cycle |

*Structure of Questions.* Certain attributes of a question have been proven as being important for the gaming experience:

- **The ratio of correct and false answers**: Too less false answers ease the solution too much. For each correct answer part at least one false answer part is recommended, more false answers seem to be better up to a ratio of 1:2.
- **Minimum number of correct answers**: If there are only one or two correct answer parts the positive acknowledgement was reported to appear too abrupt. In that case also more false answers are necessary. In play tests the resulting small ratio of correct to false answers led to a perception of the correct answers as lost. A minimum number of three correct answers is recommended.
- **Maximum number of correct answers**: Questions with too many correct answers have been reported as confusing. A limit seems to be 5 or 6 correct answers.
- **Length of question and answer texts**: Since the game screen is limited to the size of mobile devices there is only little space available. Additionally test players complained that long texts require too much time to read. So questions and answers should be kept short. For answers a maximum length of 25 characters is recommended, questions should not be longer than 70 characters.
- **Attribute "Correct Order"**: Questions can be marked with the flag "Correct Order", which implies an additional score if correct answers are tapped in a given order. Players could not recognize this game feature easily for all questions. So it should only be used if a question requires an obvious, natural order of answers or if that order is requested explicitly in the question.

*Strategies for Creation of False Answers.* False answers are an important part of the game as they are involved in most of the player's actions in the game. By provision of wrong answers the difficulty level of the questions is controlled. Players can select correct answers easily if all false answers are obviously incorrect. The "nearer" the content of false answers seems to be to the content of correct answers the more the player is required to reflect about his choice: Reflection spurs learning. Another function of false answers brings fun and tension into the game: allusions, ambiguity and other forms of double twist can be a form of entertainment for the player. As an example the question for types of pumps in Table 1 can have the false answer "bull pump". That alludes to the correct answer "ram pump". In the following list the main strategies for creation of false answers are described[8]:

1. **Words with similar spelling:** Similarly spelt words lure the player to choose wrong answers when s/he reads carelessly.
2. **Words with similar syllables, but other meaning:** Such answers provoked a short term feeling of success when they were recognized: The spelling of the word is similar to a correct answer, but there is a large contrast in meaning.
3. **Correct answers of previous questions:** An observation of the play tests was players choosing "keywords" of the technical domain regardless of the question. This behavior does not work if domain related answers appear as false answers.
4. **Opposites of correct answers:** Opposites of correct answers are related to the technical domain and the question as well. In this way they require the player to reflect about his answer.
5. **Technical terms of other domains:** These words provide the illusion of a correct answer and increase the demand for reflection – if the correct answer is not known.
6. **Well known sentences:** Known sentences, e.g. proverbs - split into different answer parts - are often recognized by the player. This was reported as a kind of feeling of success and surprise – even if it could not contribute to progress in the game.

*Criteria for Level Building.* A level in the game is an ordered set of questions. Scores are published for levels. To complete a level the player is allowed to select at most 2 false answers[9]. Also s/he can use 3 *Jokers.* A Joker reveals the correct answer of the current question. We used two criteria in order to design a level: the first is coherence concerning the contents: The player should be able to use the game to strengthen his knowledge about a certain topic – by choosing appropriate levels. The second criterion is the number of questions: the level size. Levels consisting of 3 questions have been sensed as too short. The number of repetitions of a level is connected to the number of *lives*: the more questions there are the more difficult it becomes to finish the level successfully. Besides that more questions require longer durations of continuous game play. For this reason in our experience 10 to 15 questions per level seem to be a good size.

**Story.** The story of the game has been designed in a multi-stage procedure: the first step was a brainstorming session. This session was attended by interested members of our institute. Domain related ideas have been discussed, iterated and collected. Based on the resulting collection each of the participants came up with his/her story. Those stories have been polished and transformed into a common format. After that an online survey with these 6 stories has been created. For each story the survey asked for an assessment regarding authenticity and challenge on a 5 point Likert scale.

---

[8] The strategies have been designed in a heuristic way, a more systematic approach should be reviewed also – as previous research results provide a rich set of strategies [16].

[9] In game related terminology: The gamer has three lives.

Finally the respondent was asked to rank his/her 3 favorite stories. In order to acquire survey participants from the given target group of the game, the link to the online survey was distributed by placing it on the virtual blackboard of the faculty with the connotation "Environmental Engineers". Also it was sent to a mailing list of students and alumni of the environmental engineering course of studies. Within the duration of a week we got 46 answers.

Unfortunately there was no clear winner. Instead 3 of the stories were leaders in different categories. By a commonly made expert decision (together with the originators of the Cat King app) we have chosen the *Sewer Rat* story – as rats seem to be a natural target of a shooter game.

**Graphics/SFX**

Since the app framework (JuraShooter engine) is already given there exists a template of the needed graphics with size and functionality/expected content of each graphic. Together with the story this list was given to a scientific assistant capable of creating graphics. In a few proposal-acceptance cycles the final graphics have been created. The same approach worked for SFX – sounds seem not be as important as graphics since the game often is played with sounds turned off.

**Fig. 2.** The question answering screen of the Sewer Rats app

## 3    Consideration of Efforts

One main goal for the reuse of an existing game is effort reduction. After having created the Sewer Rats app the analysis of the effort needed is possible. We measure the effort in hours of work time. This approach excludes effects of varying hourly rates - as they may vary due to personal contacts, different contexts and locations of game production[10]. It also allows inclusion of personal contribution. Of course different work items may be accomplished by roles with specific skill sets. Each of these roles has to be charged with a specific hourly rate. Our simplifying assumption is that for the original and for the new app the relative distribution of work items (i.e. hourly rates) is roughly the same as the same work items are required. The only exception is the engine-related effort (cf. Table 2, Pos. 1). So the number of working hours can be taken as a valid measurement for the effort.

In Table 2 the needed effort for the Cat King app is listed. The effort of those work items which need additional resources has been adjusted accordingly. For example the voice effects have to be recorded in a sound studio: the pure working time of a professional dubber has been about 30 minutes. The hourly rate for such a person is much higher than the average rate. In addition the sound studio has to be rented – so altogether an effort of 10 hours has to be scheduled. The effort sums up to 1000 hours.

**Table 2.** Work items and needed effort for the *Cat King* app

| Pos. | Work item | Effort (h) |
|---|---|---|
| 1 | Implementation of JuraShooter engine and Content Editor | 800 |
| 2 | Story | 10 |
| 3 | Graphics | 50 |
| 4 | Sound effects / background music | 20 |
| 5 | Introductory video | 20 |
| 6 | Voice effects (including studio effort) | 10 |
| 7 | Content | 60 |
| 8 | Coordination of the production process | 20 |
| 9 | Technical production (Compilation and submission to the App Store) | 10 |
| | **Sum** | **1000** |

For the Sewer Rats app the effort has arisen accordingly, except for Pos. 1, the software: instead of developing an own app framework and content editor the existing software has been used. This leads to the consideration of license fees. Since there is not yet a fixed license fee rate we calculated an hourly equivalent of fictitious royalties. Our calculation approach was to get back the efforts for software

---

[10] That is the reason why we do not measure effort in absolute sums of money - as it has been done e.g. by [17], but in relative ratios of work time. The required monetary expenditures are specific to each local context with its characteristic wage level.

development after selling a certain number of licenses. This number was determined as 10: After selling 10 licenses all the costs should be covered by fees. This leads to an hourly equivalent of 800 / 10 = 80 hours.

**Table 3.** Work items and needed effort for the *Sewer Rats* app

| Pos. | Work item | Effort (h) |
|------|-----------|-----------:|
| 1 | License fees for JuraShooter engine and Content Editor | 80 |
| 2-9 | App individual work items (cf. Table 2) | 200 |
| | **Sum** | 280 |

Altogether the effort sums up to 280 h (cf. Table 3). Compared to the effort for the original app the development costs have been reduced to less than 30 percent.

# 4 Discussion

In general our work demonstrated that the JuraShooter StGB app is extensible and can be reused at a much lower level of costs. Nevertheless there are some restrictions and particularities which apply to this approach. They are discussed in the following section.

## 4.1 Restrictions and Limitations

**Complexity of Knowledge.** As mentioned already the game can primarily present knowledge of lower cognitive levels. Although other question types may be imaginable (e.g. questions which require ordering the answers) and would increase the supported level of complexity a little this app never will support mainly higher cognitive levels. This restriction is connected to the base game mechanic of answering questions.

**Limited Usage.** Despite of the game's transferability to many domains the possible use is limited. The first limitation could arise when the game is applied on too many subjects of a curriculum: students may get bored. Another problem may occur according to different gamer types: play tests have shown that some players like the game, others do not[11]. Another restriction could be the fact of different domain contexts. The original app was designed for iOS mobile devices as a relevant fraction of law students owns such a device. In contrast the online survey has shown that only for 12% of engineering students an iOS device is available. Such differences may also apply to the occurrence of gamer types – as some comments of play testers let assume. An efficacy study of the created app is necessary.

**Transferable Game Structure.** In general the chance to reuse a game depends on supported knowledge structures. JuraShooter StGB works with questions. This game mechanic is applicable to the most technical domains. Therefore the JuraShooter game engine can be reused easily. For many other games this may not be possible.

---

[11]  Admittedly this phenomenon is typical for all games.

**Maintenance.** Necessary maintenance work in the app framework in the future may have effects on existing apps. This could lead to unwanted dependencies and additional costs.

**Copyright Laws.** The reuse of JuraShooter StGB was possible as the author of the game is in favour of such an approach and supports it strongly[12]. For many other games this is not the case, e.g. the publisher of SimCity 5 is far more restrictive [12].

### 4.2    Other Results

**Yielding Play Tests.** Play tests have been performed with both experts and students. Their results revealed non expected difficulties and were highly useful for the design of questions. Also we can confirm the necessity of senior domain experts for the creation of question. As it is already mentioned in [8] this has a positive impact on quality and comprehensibility of questions.

**Design Problems of the App Framework.** The first usage of JuraShooter engine in another domain disclosed some design problems and teething troubles. For example every resolution change of a supported mobile device requires additional graphics. This could be cured by an appropriate design using relative coordinates. Also the CMS showed handling issues. Another design issue is utilization of the iOS platform: an HTML5 based single source strategy could open the app to a 4 times larger target group (12 % iOS users compared to 60 % iOS and Android users).

## 5    Conclusions and Outlook

Reuse of proven components is common also to other types of media, e.g. when it comes to designing the plot of a (movie) story there are references of working master plots [13]. So the reuse of established game mechanics and – if possible – underlying software is a promising approach when the game supports the knowledge structure of educational goals. Admittedly many games do not provide this opportunity. However in this case study we demonstrated the feasibility of such a strategy at 30% of the original costs. Further results of our work are heuristics for the procedures of content generation and story creation. Thus the process of app extension to other domains has been strengthened. Unstructured play tests have shown the usefulness and efficacy of the resulting *Sewer Rats* app. This application can support undergraduate education, it strengths are accessibility and short play durations (*casual gaming*) which may avoid procrastination. This hypothesis and the efficacy of the game have to be measured by a future experiment.

**Acknowledgement.** The authors thank the anonymous reviewers of this paper for their valuable comments.

---

[12] Based on the experiences of the Sewer Rats prototype the author of this app works on a license fee oriented business model to open the JuraShooter engine to other domains.

# References

1. Yourdon, E.: Death March. Prentice Hall (2003)
2. Fullerton, T.: Game Design Workshop: A Playcentric Approach to Creating Innovative Games. Morgan Kaufmann (2008)
3. Habgood, M.P.J., Ainsworth, S.E.: Motivating Children to Learn Effectively: Exploring the Value of Intrinsic Integration in Educational Games. J. Learn. Sci. 20, 169–206 (2011)
4. Egenfeldt-Nielsen, S.: Educational Potential of Computer Games (Continuum Studies in Education). Continuum (2007)
5. Papert, S.: Does Easy Do It? Children, Games, and Learning. Game Dev. 5 (1998)
6. Bruckman, A.: Can educational be fun? In: Game Developer's Conference, San Jose, California, pp. 75–79 (1999)
7. Söbke, H., Bröker, T., Kornadt, O.: Using the Master Copy - Adding Educational Content to Commercial Video Games. In: de Carvalho, C.V., Escudeiro, P. (eds.) Proceedings of the 7th European Conference on Games-Based Learning, vol. 2, pp. 521–530. Academic Conferences and Publishing International Limited, Reading (2013)
8. von Buttlar, R., Kurkowski, S., Schmidt, F.A., Pannicke, D.: Die Jagd nach dem Katzenkönig. In: Kaminski, W., Lorber, M. (eds.) Gamebased Learning: Clash of Realities, p. 384, Kopäd (2012)
9. von Buttlar, R., Söbke, H., Große-Wortmann, J., Pannicke, D.: JuraShooter StGB: On the Hunt for the cat King Mobile Drill & Exercise With fun Appeal. In: Escudeiro, P., Vaz de Carvalho, C. (eds.) Abstracts and Conference Materials for the 7th European Conference on Games-Based Learning, Porto, pp. 198–203. Academic Conferences and Publishing International Limited (2013)
10. Anderson, L.W., Krathwohl, D.R., Airasian, P.W., Cruikshank, K.A., Mayer, R.E., Pintrich, P.R., Raths, J., Wittrock, M.C.: A Taxonomy for Learning, Teaching, and Assessing: A Revision of Bloom's Taxonomy of Educational Objectives, Abridged Edition. Allyn & Bacon (2000)
11. Chan, E.: Methodische Wissensvermittlung mit Hilfe eines Drill-&-Exercise-Spiels am Beispiel der Siedlungswasserwirtschaft, Bachelor thesis, Bauhaus-Universität Weimar (2013)
12. Gaberdan, E.: Konzeption und prototypische Implementierung von Simulationsszenarien des Regenwassermanagements zur Entscheidungsunterstützung mit Hilfe von SimCity, Master thesis, Bauhaus-Universität Weimar (2013)
13. Tobias, R.B.: 20 Master Plots: And How to Build Them. Writer's Digest Books (2012)
14. Iz, H.B., Fok, H.S.: Use of Bloom's taxonomic complexity in online multiple choice tests in Geomatics education. Surv. Rev. 39, 226–237 (2007)
15. Bloom, B.S.: Taxonomy of Educational Objectives. Longman, London (1956)
16. Haladyna, T.M., Downing, S.M., Rodriguez, M.C.: A Review of Multiple-Choice Item-Writing Guidelines for Classroom Assessment. Appl. Meas. Educ. 15, 309–333 (2002)
17. Moreno-Ger, P., Torrente, J., Bustamante, J., Fernández-Galaz, C., Fernández-Manjón, B., Comas-Rengifo, M.D.: Application of a low-cost web-based simulation to improve students' practical skills in medical education. Int. J. Med. Inform. 79, 459–467 (2010)

# Narrative Serious Game Mechanics (NSGM) – Insights into the Narrative-Pedagogical Mechanism

Theodore Lim[1], Sandy Louchart[1], Neil Suttie[1], Jannicke Baalsrud Hauge[2],
Ioana A. Stanescu[3], Ivan M. Ortiz[4], Pablo Moreno-Ger[4], Francesco Bellotti[5],
Maira B. Carvalho[5], Jeffrey Earp[6],
Michela Ott[6], Sylvester Arnab[7], and Riccardo Berta[5]

[1] Heriot-Watt University, Riccarton, Edinburgh EH14 4AS, Scotland, UK
[2] Bremer Institut für Produktion und Logistik (BIBA), Germany
[3] National Defence University "Carol I", Bucharest, 50662, Romania
[4] Complutense University, Madrid 28040, Spain
[5] University of Genoa, 16145 Genova, Italy
[6] Consiglio Nazionale delle Ricerche (CNR), 16149 Genova, Italy
[7] Serious Games Institute, Coventry University, Coventry CV1 2TL, UK
{t.lim,s.louchart,n.suttie}@hw.ac.uk, baa@biba.uni-bremen.de,
ioana.stanescu@adlnet.ro, {imartinez,pablom}@fdi.ucm.es,
{franz,maira.carvalho,berta}@elios.unige.it,
{jeff,ott}@itd.cnr.it, s.arnab@coventry.ac.uk

**Abstract.** Narratives are used to construct and deconstruct the time and space of events. In games, as in real life, narratives add layers of meaning and engage players by enhancing or clarifying content. From an educational perspective, narratives are a semiotic conduit for evoking critical thinking skills and promoting knowledge discovery/acquisition. While narrative is central to Serious Games (SG), the relationships between gameplay, narrative and pedagogy in SG design remain unclear, and narrative's elemental influence on learning outcomes is not fully understood yet. This paper presents a purpose-processing methodology that aims to support the mapping of SG design patterns and pedagogical practices, allowing designers to create more meaningful SGs. In the case of narrative, the intention is to establish whether Narrative Serious Game Mechanics (NSGM) can provide players with opportunities for reasoning and reflective analysis that may even transcend the game-based learning environment.

## 1 Introduction

Discourse, the narration aspect of storytelling, plays an important role in defining a narrative environment through careful descriptions of both context and roles, ultimately motivating a player (in the case of Digital Games) to intervene and act. An often inherent part of the narrative discourse is the protagonists' exposition to a sequence of events that motivate them to act, essentially embarking on a narrative journey. Such exposition sections have been extensively documented by Propp [1],

Campbell [2] and many others [3-6]. They are extensively relied upon in Serious Game Design, where the learner is exposed to a narrative in order to evoke a player (as opposed to learner)'s desire to achieve the goals and discover what happens next. Three important techniques - immersion, reward, and identification [8] - are then exploited in order to keep the learner playing and thus learning.

At the most basic level, Chatman [7] differentiated between story and discourse, story representing the actual elements present in a story (content) and discourse the narration of a story and how it is presented to an audience (form). This distinction is relevant to the study of narrative mechanics in the context of Serious Games (SG) studies because story elements are tangible entities that can be analysed at a structural level, while discourse helps to shape an SG experience. For instance, if the purpose of an SG is to induce an affective response towards the negative aspects of a certain behaviour, the form and tone/aesthetics of the discourse (genre, filmography, graphic presentation, realism) are (or should be) in keeping with the main purpose of the SG, independent of the actual narrative content conveyed.

Research has revealed two key challenges in this area, namely a) the transition between an SG's underlying instructional design and its actual design implementation [9-11], and b) the insolvency in mapping game design patterns onto relevant pedagogical patterns [12]. A game mechanics workshop organised during the 2$^{nd}$ Alignment School of the EU co-funded Game and Learning Alliance Network of Excellence (GALA NoE) [13] concluded that the aforementioned transition lacks methodology. Consequently customers commissioning SGs are forced to make a leap of faith when gauging an SG developer's capacity to deliver a game that will achieve the desired learning outcomes. This echoes Wexler's [14] evidence on how the growing complexity of SGs impacts the way educators use SGs in teaching.

This paper presents a purpose-processing methodology to probe narrative discourse in SG and is ultimately intended as a means for investigating how SG design patterns map with pedagogical practices. To redress the dependence on SG developers in the creation/adaptation of SG content, a game-writing process based on narrative metaphors is also explored.

The proposed methodology has also been empirically elaborated [15] on eight SGs covering various genres and application domains of SGs: HotShot Business, Playing History: The Plague, SBCE (Set Based Concurrent Engineering process), ICURA, Go Venture Any Business, Prepare, Shortfall, Re-Mission.

## 2    Serious Games Design and Narrative Meaning Making

SGs are increasingly being seen as new ways of learning, and the subjective meanings given to elements of game architecture can result in players having a very different view about the game space. This is a key concern for SG designers, as the interrelationships between the motivational aspects of narrative game mechanics and gameplay style may not be fully appreciated.

Games with narrative elements are inherently a multidimensional comprising both a narrative genre and a gameplay genre. The fact that two games could share the same narrative genre but with vastly different gameplay (first person shooter vs. adventure game) increases the complexity of the issues involved when addressing game narratives.

Narrative is an area where definitions are still being formulated. Lack of clear examples of great game narratives remains, especially since SG is a young medium compared to narrative compositions in the best novels, films, and plays often leaves games seeming slightly deficient. There are a lot of key problems in game design that need to be solved, and this limits the kinds of stories that can be told [16]. Great history stories can be told and learners may enjoy them, but the essential tension between the freedom of the player and the constraints of narratives places severe limits on what can be achieved at the present time. There is a conceptual gap between the conventions of digital games and those of non-theatrical drama that needs to be addressed.

Crucially, the narrative cannot be fully appreciated if learners cannot grasp the gestalt of semiotic communication. Lastly, players may play in a style that the game was not designed for. Ideally, the SG learner should develop and take forward the epistemic values posed by a game's narrative mechanics. Tochon's [17] position on educational narrative being tied to the philosophy of Signs and Meanings has deep implications for the way the narrative contributes to educating the individual. People acquire identity from and through discourse, not from life itself but from the stories they collectively construct from events. This aligns with constructivism, the dominant learning theory over the last decade. Herein lays the challenge for the SG developer: to pragmatically translate the many levels of abstractions for knowledge construction such that the epistemological underpinnings are a process of instruction [18]. While Lindley's [19] and Harrell's [20] work on narratives in computer games motivates this work, so does the hypothesis that narratives offer a gateway for learners to combine reflective analysis and explore connotative meanings with other learning tools. Through the study of narrative in SG context, one could potentially assess whether game design patterns can be mapped (at least at a high-level of abstraction) with pedagogical practices.

## 3    Defining Narrative Serious Game Mechanics (NSGM)

Through narrative discourse, the objective is to discern the possible relations between the elements of the narrative/pedagogy/game design triad, essentially the narrative-pedagogy implications. These relations operate within four analytical categories: *narrative purpose, narrative process and instance, narrative structure* and *pedagogical implication*. These categories are described in detail in the next sections in relation to NSGM.

To establish the cause and effect of designed narration in SGs, the concept of Narrative Serious Game Mechanics (NSGM) is proposed. An NSGM is identified in a game design when aspects of narrative/storytelling such as dialogue, plot events or character actions/behaviours are used to elicit specific pedagogical outcomes. An NSGM is represented by a narrative element which directly contributes to or indirectly supports identified learning outcomes as part of a successful SG gaming experience. The definition is purposely broad as it needs to encompass the innovative ways in which narrative plays a role in SG design

The authors are currently investigating NSGM as part of their SG research in GALA NoE. The general aim is to map prevailing characteristics (patterns) of narrative mechanisms and shed light on the potential benefits of associated pedagogic goals and practices. This is being pursued through both top-down (theoretical) and bottom-up (analytical) investigation, an approach which should limit possible blurring of the boundaries between SGMs and allow the identification of a wide range of creative approaches adopted by SG designers.

## 4     A Purpose, Process and Structure Schemata

To establish an NSGM trace, it is important not only to investigate the purpose for narrative elements, but also their pedagogical context. A multi-layered approach that includes the individual, smaller story elements within the various interactive activities of an SG narrative is taken into account towards identifying NSGM. To extract a narrative-pedagogy association, there is a need to identify recurrent aspects such as the relationships between both protagonists and the narrative environment and the necessity for conflict, be it openly towards another person (person to person), environmental (person to context) or internal (person to self) [4].

**Table 1.** Establishing the purpose of an NSGM

| Type of NSGM | Description | Game purpose | SG purpose |
|---|---|---|---|
| *Exposition:* the purpose of the NSGM | What is the overall function of the NSGM? | What function articulates or progresses the game? From the player's perspective, what function does this NSGM play? | Pedagogically, what learning outcomes or processes are related to this NSGM? |
| *Discourse:* the form of the NSGM | What form does it take and how is it represented? | How are these functions concretely represented in the game? | How does the form (style, pace etc.) of this NSGM contribute to learning? |

Table 1 and Table 2 are used to establish and trace the modus operandi of SG narratives. In this manner, the relationship between tangible narrative components and tangible activities or information within an SG game sequence can be documented, as can the events that directly impact player activity (from a pedagogical perspective) and those that do not, but still play a supporting role. This also allows the epistemic/semiotic mechanism and value to be established.

**Table 2.** Establishing Process and Structure within an NSGM

| NSGM Experience | NSGM Process | Narrative Element | Description | Impact |
|---|---|---|---|---|
| *Pre, during and post*: event directly involving player interaction with the SG, or sequence where the player is not engaged in active game-like interaction with the SG, i.e., sequence of tasks / activities related to the NSGM occurrence. | *Process Step*: Chronology of activities /tasks related to the NSGM. Describes what comprises this step and its various elements. | *Structure*: Describes the mechanics of activity or information communicated to the player (information element, invitation to act, feedback, information communication, etc.) | Describes the actions of the player or the game in this phase of the process. | Describes the impact of the step on both the SG experience and the learning outcome both directly and indirectly |

Taken together, an NSGM forms a conceptual/structural layer and typically comprises a combination of several GMs. This is exemplified in Fig. 1, which illustrates a mapping of the *GoVenture AnyBusiness* (GVAB) SG [21]. The Learning Mechanic and Game Mechanic (LM-GM) levels are drawn from earlier work produced by some members of the present authoring team [22-25]. This mapping shows where NSGMs do reside in GVAB, and how they bridge ludic mechanisms and learning contents.

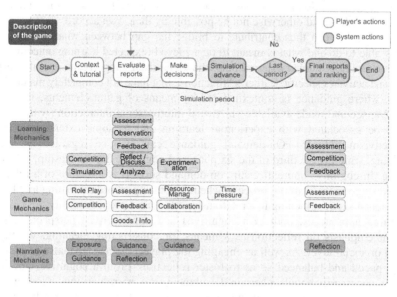

**Fig. 1.** NSGM mapping of Go Venture AnyBusiness

These mechanics layers can also be thought of as fibrous, mechanics-studded strands that are interlaced in different manners to form the fabric of SG design. The single mechanics on the different strands may overlap at some points in the weave to form a single node jointly serving learning, gameplay and narrative purposes. In other cases, the strands themselves may be tightly braided and bound so that the individual mechanics they bear are interlocked in a sequence or pattern. These are intuitive views of NSGMs.

## 5    NSGM Association with Pedagogy

At the most basic level, from a game design and pedagogic perspective, narrative exposition (NE), together with narrative discourse (ND), sets the scenario of the SG and enables the establishment of a ludo-pedagogic framework for learning. From the pedagogical perspective it introduces the domain area and the learning contents that the player will interact with as part of the SG-based learning experience. Critically, NE is central to how the SG simulates a context/situation. It is also the gateway to an immersive experience; it draws the player into an enticing, non-threatening game world that (amongst other things) offers the promise of a fruitful learning experience.

Any learner-centred approach must include suitable and timely support for the learner. SGs must provide (or at least allow for) guidance whenever the player perceives the need for further information, specific input, clarification, decision-making advice, etc. [26]. Pedagogically speaking, when the perceived need concerns a gap in domain-related knowledge, such support falls within the sphere of the Zone of Proximal Development [27, 28], namely in the area between what a learner can do (or achieve) by themselves and what they can do with external help. Through the scaffolding /help provided by the game, the learner can reach some of the educational objectives which would otherwise not be possible by their own accord.

Game elements can thus contribute to bridge the gap between what the learner is currently able to do and what is meant to be achieved (expected learning outcomes) and this is done without human external help; the game itself supports the overall learning process and activates specific learner's "functions" that have not completely matured yet.

Thus, where guidance is contextualized by means of game elements, within the narrative space and made available via virtual interpersonal interaction (with a NPC), it could be associated with experiential learning and to some extent with Social Constructivism [23, 25]. On-demand guidance can also be regarded as learner scaffolding, which is the third of the six phases of cognitive apprenticeship, following coaching. In cognitive apprenticeship, on-demand support is a feature of a relatively advanced stage in the learning process, when direct support is diminishing and learner independence is strengthening in a relationship of inverse proportionality.

Learning approaches, both in a cognitivist and constructivist perspective, place particular emphasis on reflection as a means for constructing meaning, whether at personal or social level. As well as engaging the player, the narrative also needs to be suitably paced and balanced so as to foster reflection. From a cognitive viewpoint, reflection necessarily entails a certain detachment from narrative flow, a loosening of the narrative reins as it were. This mechanic is critical for balancing the ludic-learning dichotomy of SG and hence of SGs' efficacy as learning environments. This balance should be easier to attain and maintain, when the reflection mechanic is implemented in a way that resonates with the narrative flow.

**Table 3.** Analysis of narrative-pedagogical implications in the GVAB game and the potential benefits of associated pedagogic practices

| NSGM - Type | Description of practice | Pedagogical implications |
|---|---|---|
| *Exposition*: To introduce and frame the world to engage the audience. | Text-based information push that presents game scenario / narrative: overall game mission, player role, objectives, environment features. | Introduces the learning contents and establishes gameplay motivation, which should be aligned and entwined with learning objectives and task/s. Only embodies experiential learning to the degree where information push is appropriately contextualized in the narrative and involves some interactivity/simulated experience, e.g. through interaction with NPC. |
| *Guidance*: Narrative elements to drive the player into exploring the world or interacting with Non-Player Characters (NPC) or fellow players. | On-demand consultation of an information source to facilitate navigation and gameplay, support decision making, provide clarification, help unroll the narrative, etc. Guidance may be generic or personalized (related to performance). <br><br> Consultation is often contextualized to fit the game/narrative scenario, e.g. via NPC or simulated messaging. This is a key to game environment authenticity and represents essential scaffolding of the gaming/learning experience. | To be effective, **any learner-centred approach** must include suitable and timely support for the learner. As effective agents of learner-centred experiences, SGs should provide such support whenever the player perceives the need for further information, specific input, clarification, decision-making advice, etc. In a wider sense, when the perceived need regards a gap in domain-related knowledge, the support falls within the Zone of Proximal Development; so if implemented as part of interaction with NPC, such support could be associated with **Social Constructivism** to some extent and also to **experiential learning.** More typically, on-demand guidance also represents (weak) learner **scaffolding**. This is the third of the six phases of **cognitive apprenticeship**, following **coaching**. In **cognitive apprenticeship**, on-demand support is a feature of a relatively advanced stage in the learning process, when direct support is diminishing and learner independence is strengthening (relationship of inverse proportionality). |
| *Reflection*: Key to learning and knowing where mistakes have been made. | Performance summary in preceding game phase delivered to player via NPC in a format befitting the game scenario. Strengthens sense of narrative sequence and provides opportunity for self-assessment and reflection on adopted game strategy. | Reflection plays an important part in most learning paradigms, especially those that tend more towards to **cognitivist** and **constructivist** learning theory than to **behaviourism**. It is a pillar of **experiential learning.** |

## 6    NSGM Association with Pedagogical Practice

The picture of narrative components in SGs that emerges from the authors' case studies is similar to that in entertainment games. This poses a problem, as it hinders identification of the narratives' relationship with pedagogy and educational purposes (as reflected by Harrell [20]). However, the adopted purpose-processing method revealed that there is a distinct lack of consideration for drama in the eight SGs studied. This is interesting, since it shows that narrative and storytelling were intended as framing devices for capturing and maintaining player interest/motivation rather than real engines of the experience.

Table 3 presents an analysis of narrative-pedagogy in the GVAB game. The table highlights the features of the NSGM and the implications it has for pedagogic practice. It also highlights the challenge posed when seeking to apply constructivism in the process of instructional design. The narrative elements encountered mainly tie the player's interactions to a specific theme and motivate the player to keep playing.

## 7    Practical Considerations: Narrative-driven Game Authoring

The authors' current case studies as well as the works of Lindley [19], Tochon [17] and Harrell [20] all suggest that is important to put educators in the driving seat, in order to achieve proper instructional game design. This requires creating appropriate instructor-oriented game-authoring tools so they can create/adapt contents in SGs [29].

However, most game-authoring tools and game engines (even those focused on narrative-centric genres) do not focus explicitly on designing narratives. Remarkably, most game-authoring metaphors focus solely on defining events and conditions, and the actual narrative of the game emerges by how those events and conditions happen at runtime (e.g., [30]). In consequence, the narrative of the game is typically represented in external documents, and the design and the actual implementation try to follow those documents and create a behaviour that matches that narrative.

This represents an important challenge when trying to create NSGMs, as the mechanic itself is never authored, but implied through other constructs. A deeper application of NSGMs would require game design and implementation processes that explicitly incorporate specific functions and capabilities for managing the narrative dimension of the authored game. This would ensure that the narrative have a central role in the SG design and explicitly contributes towards the learning and engagement goals.

However, this should not result in a process that can only edit narratives, as other game mechanics may typically be present even in strongly narrative games. As a potential approach, we could highlight the hybrid approach proposed by WEEV [24]. This is a methodology for authoring narrative-based point-and-click educational games tool and is embodied in an authoring tool of the same name. WEEV adopts a narrative metaphor to represent game stories as interaction elements of narrative significance (i.e. story, world and actors). An explicit visual representation of the story is used to describe the flow of the game (Fig. 2). This approach foregrounds the flow of the interactive story, making it easier to co-locate the mixing of sociological ideas with semiotic epistemology.

Interestingly, this authoring approach focuses solely on creating the narrative and on defining NSGMs. Other game elements necessary for SG design (such as graphics, variables, event triggers and logic conditions) are not explicitly contemplated in this stage, with the aim of facilitating the narrative authoring process. Instead, after the narrative development has been completely designed and refined, WEEV can generate all the internal logic required to support the narrative and offer the possibility of further editing the game to add other, non-narrative, game elements.

This explicit distinction of processes favours an increase in focus on NSGMs but also introduces a sort of separation that could prevent a real harmonious integration of narrative and game mechanics.

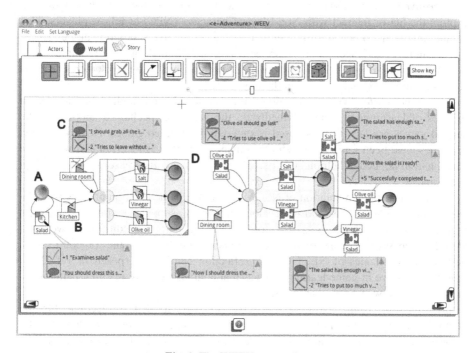

**Fig. 2.** The WEEV story editor

# 8    Conclusions

The Purpose/Process/Structure methodological approach has demonstrated its usefulness for identifying generic Narrative Serious Game Mechanics (NSGM) patterns. From a narrative perspective, this short study suggests that narrative in Serious Game design is so far limited to the application of narrative elements rather than to the development of a real drama. Drama structures narrative elements into a sequential manner so as to form a compelling user experience. The games that the authors have studied thus far show little evidence of dramatic structuring taking place. Instead, they incorporate narrative elements to tie the player's interactions with a specific theme and motivate the player to keep playing [25]. This in itself does not constitute a problem but it calls for further investigation as it could indicate potential gaps between practices in SG design and practices in design of related entertainment forms.

It is also important to note that the focus here is to provide insights into the narrative-pedagogical mechanism. Preliminary findings indicate that *Narrative Exposition* (NE) is an important storytelling element as it is the first contact between an author and the audience. The main objectives are to introduce and represent a starting point for a drama to unfold. For this reason, NE is often used as a framing device.

*Narrative Guidance* (NG) uses narrative elements to drive the player/protagonist to explore the SG or interact with Non-Player Characters (NPC) or fellow players. This stimulation needs to be carefully handled so that it effectively supports and enhances the learning experience, rather than eclipsing it. Similar care is required when integrating NG with the WEEV methodology because not all game elements (e.g. art resources) are easily defined within the methodology.

*Reflection* and *feedback* are important aspects of SGs and fundamental to current theories of learning. In terms of feedback, the narrative mechanics adopted in the studied games are largely those used in entertainment video games. However, some examples have been found in which performance feedback is incorporated within the game narrative, better helping the player to understand the reasons of poor/good performance.

The practical implementation of NSGM during the game creation process is also a significant challenge, as most development tools support narrative constructs implicitly. Among those tools that foreground the narrative constructs, we have identified the WEEV methodology as a promising approach: On the forecourt of SG design, the mechanics of NE, NG and Reflection can be repurposed in WEEV as reusable narrative in-game learning objects that contain narrative learning patterns for creating a game world and characters.

Investigations using narrative discourse are still needed to account for the contingent events that employ verbs of speech, motion, and action. The fundamental complexity in any conceptual framework/method of any postulated semiotics requires abstracting a closed system of signification to directly comprehend all its individual entities. The present study indicates a direction, but there is still much work to do in order to support authors in the design of learning effective SGs based on compelling and relevant narratives.

**Acknowledgments.** The work reported in this paper is co-funded under the European Community Seventh Framework Programme (FP7/2007 2013), Grant Agreement nr. 258169 and EPSRC/IMRC grant 113946. This work was also supported in part by the Erasmus Mundus Joint Doctorate in Interactive and Cognitive Environments, which is funded by the EACEA Agency of the European Commission under EMJD ICE FPA n 2010-0012.

# References

1. Propp, V.: Morphology of the Folktale. University of Texas Press (1998) (1st English translation published 1958)
2. Campbell, J.: The hero with a thousand faces. Fontana Press (1949)
3. Egri, L.: The Art of Dramatic Writing: It's Basis in the Creative Interpretation of Human Motives. Simon and Schuster, New York (1942)
4. McKee, R.: Story. Methuen Publishing Ltd. (1997)
5. Vogler, C.: The Writer's Journey: Mythic Structure for Storytellers and Screenwriters. Michael Wiese Productions, 3rd edn. (2007)
6. Sheldon, L.: Character Development and Storytelling for Games (2004)
7. Chatman, S.: Story and Discourse, narrative structure in fiction and film. Cornell University Press (1978)
8. Dansky, R.: Introduction into Game Narrative. In: Game Writing Narrative Skills for Videogames. Charles River Media, Massachusetts (2007)
9. Karagiorgi, Y., Symeou, L.: Translating Constructivism into Instructional Design: Potential and Limitations. Educational Tech. & Soc. 8(1), 17–27 (2005)
10. Bellotti, F., Berta, R., De Gloria, A.: Designing Effective Serious Games: Opportunities and Challenges for Research. Special Issue: Creative Learning with Serious Games, IJET 5, 22–35 (2010)
11. Bellotti, F., Berta, R., De Gloria, A., D'Ursi, A., Fiore, V.: A serious game model for cultural heritage. ACM J. Comput. Cult. Herit. 5(4) (2012)
12. Kelle, S., Klemke, R., Specht, M.: Design patterns for learning games. IJTEL 3(6), 555–569 (2011)
13. Bellotti, F., Berta, R., De Gloria, A.: Games and Learning Alliance (GaLA) Supporting education and training through hi-tech gaming. In: Proc. of ICALT 2012, pp. 740–741 (2012) (6268245 )
14. Wexler, S., Corti, K., Derryberry, A., Quinn, C., Barneveld, A.V.: The eLearning Guild: 360 report on immersive learning simulations (2008)
15. Serious Games Society, http://www.seriousgamessociety.org/index.php/83-content-popup/116-repository
16. Bateman, C.: Game Writing: Narrative Skills for Videogames. Cengage Learning (2006)
17. Tochon, F.V.: Presence Beyond the Narrative: semiotic tools for deconstructing the personal story. Curriculum Studies 2(2), 221–247 (1994)
18. Karagiorgi, Y., Symeou, L.: Translating Constructivism into Instructional Design: Potential and Limitations. Edu. Tech. & Soc. 8(1), 17–27 (2005)
19. Lindley, C.A.: Story and Narrative Structures in Computer Games. Developing Interactive Narrative Content (2005)
20. Harrell, D.A.: Theory and Technology for Computational Narrative: An Approach to Generative and Interactive Narrative with Bases in Algebraic Semiotics and Cognitive Linguistics (2007)
21. Baalsrud Hauge, J., Bellotti, F., Berta, R., Carvalho, M.B., De Gloria, A., Lavagnino, E., Nadolski, R., Ott, M.: Field assessment of Serious Games for Entrepreneurship in Higher Education. J. of Convergence Info. Tech. 8(13), 1–12 (2013)
22. Lim, T., Louchart, S., Suttie, N., Ritchie, J.M., Aylett, R.S., Stănescu, I.A., Roceanu, I., Martinez-Ortiz, I., Moreno-Ger, P.: Strategies for Effective Digital Games Development and Implementation. In: Baek, Y., Whitton, N. (eds.) Cases on Digital Game-Based Learning: Methods, Models, and Strategies, pp. 168–198. IGI Global (2012)

23. Arnab, S., Lim, T., Carvalho, M.B., Bellotti, F., de Freitas, S., Louchart, S., Suttie, N., Berta, R., De Gloria, A.: Mapping learning and game mechanics for serious games analysis. British Journal of Educational Technology (2014), doi:10.1111/bjet.12113

24. Marchiori, E.J., Torrente, J., del Blanco, Á., Moreno-Ger, P., Sancho, P., Fernández-Manjón, B.: A narrative metaphor to facilitate educational game authoring. Comp. & Edu. 58(1), 590–599 (2012)

25. Ott, M., Tavella, M.: A contribution to the understanding of what makes young students genuinely engaged in computer-based learning tasks. Procedia-Social and Behavioral Sciences 1(1), 184–188 (2009)

26. Kirschner, P.A., Sweller, J., Clark, R.E.: Why minimal guidance during instruction does not work: an analysis of the failure of constructivist, discovery, problem-based, experiential, and inquiry-based teaching. Edu. Psych. 41(2), 75–86 (2006)

27. Vygotsky, L.S.: Mind and society: The development of higher psychological processes. Harvard University Press, Cambridge (1978)

28. Chaiklin, S.: The Zone of Proximal Development in Vygotsky's analysis of learning and instruction. In: Kozulin, A., Gindis, B., Ageyev, V., Miller, S. (eds.) Vygotsky's Educational Theory and Practice in Cultural Context, pp. 39–64 (2003)

29. Bellotti, F., Berta, R., De Gloria, A., Primavera, L.: Supporting authors in the development of Task-Based Learning in Serious Virtual Worlds. BJET 41(1), 86–107 (2010)

30. Bellotti, F., Berta, R., De Gloria, A., Primavera, L.: Adaptive Experience Engine for Serious Games. IEEE Trans. on Comp. Intel. and AI in Games 1(4), 264–280 (2009)

# Video Game Personalization
# via Social Media Participation

Johannes Konert, Stefan Göbel, and Ralf Steinmetz

Technische Universität Darmstadt, Multimedia Communications Lab – KOM,
Rundeturmstraße 10, 64283 Darmstadt, Germany
{johannes.konert,stefan.goebel,
ralf.steinmetz}@kom.tu-darmstadt.de

**Abstract.** Social Media and user-generated content can be used as a 'call for action' to let users contribute content to other users' multimedia experience. If combined with Serious Games and used for knowledge exchange among peers, Social Media content can be used to influence and enrich one's gameplay experience as well as raise attention of connected persons in an Online Social Network (OSN) environment. In this paper we will describe the technical setup of a serious game connected to an OSN (here: facebook) via a social communication middleware. Befriended persons that are currently online can contribute content to specific calls from the game via a dynamically generated web interface that is linked to published notifications in the OSN. Results of a first study show that both, game player and connected people of the OSN, appreciate the personalization and participation via user-generated content that is integrated into the game play.

**Keywords:** Social Serious Games, Middleware, Adaptation, Personalization, Social Media, Influencing.

## 1 Motivation and Target

Social Media is not only used for social interaction, exchange of opinions and self-expression, but is as well strongly used for documentation, knowledge transfer (peer tutoring) and rating of creative solutions of others (peer assessment) [KaHa10]. Thus, learning with social media is practiced in a mostly informal way. The content of user-generated items and the interactions among the users have become a research focus due to the impact this content-based knowledge exchange can have. The factors and technological solutions that determine successful and effective use of Social Media have to be found.

Learning of domain specific issues by game-based training, collaborative problem solving and immersive 3D simulations is a rapidly growing field of Serious Games. More generally, computer games keep the player immersed into the game play by adapting the difficulty of challenges to the player's abilities dynamically. Besides keeping a player in this channel of game flow, personalization of the game content

S. Göbel and J. Wiemeyer (Eds.): GameDays 2014, LNCS 8395, pp. 35–46, 2014.

itself can increase immersion and acceptance of the Serious Game - and thus the acceptance of learning content integrated into the game [GWRS10].

Both, Social Media content and participation of other users in Online Social Networks are promising sources for personalization and individualization of game play experience for the player. Moreover, inviting befriended users to influence the game play, contribute own creative content and participate in the game play of the player is expected to increase awareness of players' activities and achievements outside of the game, raise curiosity for the game among users not playing yet and not at least entertain the players' social environment by the possibility to contribute in a creative way to their friends game play experience.

## 2    Related Work

The benefits of Serious Games for learning have been investigated for several application areas. Even though collaborative gaming for training and simulation is as well one of the manifold areas of Serious Games, the focus of this work is on educational games, which are mostly single-player and focus on adaptation of difficulty, speed and game content to the players' gaming and learning profiles [GWRS10]. These types of games are used as an addition in school class lessons as well as to spark interest in covered learning topics for users playing in their leisure time.

Beside this, Social Media has proven its benefits for learning in specific contexts as well. Web-based platforms like SocialLearn[1] from The Open University for learning content exchange among students use the creation of Social Media content as a way to activate their learners and improve the content quality for every participant. Thus, leaners take as well the role of teachers and learn by consuming, creating, changing, and assessing content and tutoring each other [BrGo03].

From a pedagogical point of view, the benefits of Peer Education (tutoring and assessment) have been investigated and described by Damon [Damo84]. More recent studies focusing on virtual environments emphasize the interest into peers' tasks solutions for assessment and the positive aspects of peer tutoring [LDUC11].

First steps towards the interconnection of (Serious) Computer Games and Social Media are the manifold Social (Casual) Games available free to play online. These are games that are casually played or with easy to use interfaces which are connected to OSNs [LoGo04]. Ines de Loreto and Abdelkader Gouaïch identify Asynchronous Play as one important characteristic of such games. Players interact by e.g. exchanging items or favors, but do not have to be online or in the game at the same time. As Nick O'Neill states in his criteria list about Social Games, these games are mostly turn-based and casual games connected to OSNs, but still Multiplayer in a sense that there is an awareness of others' actions in games [Onei08]. We summarize his four criteria as Casual Multiplayer, which means a single-player game play, but multiplayer atmosphere due to asynchronous play and awareness – and thus interplay - of the activities of others. Aki Järvinen describes in the design framework for social network

---

[1] http://sociallearn.open.ac.uk/, last accessed 11/14/2013

games how the structure of an OSN can be integrated into game play and how a beneficial interdependency with (and impact to) the OSN can be achieved (what he describes as four interacting parts) [Järv10]. We summarize his criteria as Beneficial Social Media Interaction. Finally, we add the concept of Coopetition to describe such games. It results in game design using mostly cooperative actions and choices for players and bears competition indirectly (e.g. by leaderboards). Consequently, game activities cannot be used disadvantageous and targeted on specific users.

In summary, a Social (Casual) Game can be defined as a video game satisfying the criteria of Asynchronous Play, Casual Multiplayer, Beneficial Social Media Interaction and Coopetition.

Architectural frameworks providing support to create Social Serious Games do not exist yet (to the best of our knowledge). Still, major game studios like Blizzard, Electronic Arts or Sony have their own OSNs to interconnect players and foster their creation and exchange of game related content[2]. Their computer games update player profiles via proprietary API, but do not allow participation or influencing of game play from the OSNs to the games. Other middleware solutions exist to maintain players online profiles independently of specific game studios and their OSNs [HBRS09].

## 3 Research Questions and Approach

As we focused in earlier publications on the benefits of Social Media content for learning and knowledge exchange in Serious Games the focus is here on the personalization and participation aspects [KRMG12]. From the motivation the following research questions have been derived:

— **RQ1:** Will befriended users of a (serious) game player react to OSN-placed posts and have a positive perception of it? (Viral marketing aspect)
— **RQ2:** Will they accept the concept of contributing content to a friend's game play? (Activation of environment)
— **RQ3:** How well will participants value the technical implementation of the concept? (Functionality aspect)
— **RQ4:** Will players appreciate such participation from outside within their game play? (In-game perception)

To investigate the research questions we created a social middleware (SoCom) connecting the prototype of a commercial Serious Game that is currently under development on one side with the OSN facebook on the other side. The SoCom middleware works as an abstraction layer to allow game developers to easily connect to several OSNs and start participations via calls to an Application Programming Interface (API). The extensions added to the serious game and the resulting possible participations used by befriended users in the OSN are described. Finally, we show the setup for the first study, questionnaire results and relate them to the research questions.

---

[2] See e.g. Blizzard's http://www.battle.net/, last accessed 11/14/2013.

## 4    The SoCom Architecture and Functionality

To enhance (existing) educational games with Social Game functionality the SoCom architecture provides three major modules for game developers: Content Integration (CI), Peer Group Formation (PG), and Game Adaptation (GA).

The Content Integration (CI) is for storage and retrieval of user-generated content for knowledge exchange among players. Beside major content types (text, image, audio) it supports any proprietary content identifier and binary data. Metadata adds semantic information concerning the type (question, hint, solution) and the related game context [KRMG12].

The second module, Peer Group Formation (PG), allows a sophisticated grouping of players to form learning groups based on multi-dimensional criteria [KBGS13].

The third module, Game Adaptation (GA), enables game developers to adapt the game play experience to the player's individual social network environment. Therefore developers can access the profile data and social network metrics or open new participations by using and parameterizing pre-configured influence patterns (for details see following section 4.1).

As the functionality of the first two modules is described in other publications, the following sections focus on Game Adaptation (GA).

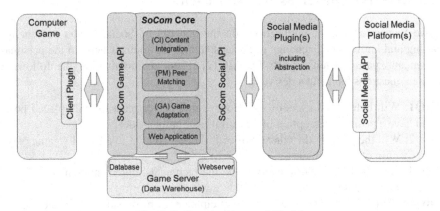

**Fig. 1.** SoCom Architectural Model

### 4.1    Game Adaptation Module

To personalize the game for the player a developer can access two different types of content via the GA module: OSN profile data of the player and uploaded content or voting results of participations. The OSN profile data is provided in a normalized form. Thus game developers can process data from different OSNs simultaneously without respecting naming or formatting differences e.g. of friend lists or hobbies. Moreover, accessing uploaded content to personalize the game play offers diverse and new chances to enrich the game as game developers can themselves decide which participation offers they provide and ask users connected with the player to contribute. For this purpose the GA module offers a three-step procedure for participations.

First, the game developer creates a new participation via the API. The only mandatory parameters are the headline question and the type of provided content (text, audio, video or proprietary). Other parameters allow setting pre-defined answers (choices), a timeout, the minimum and maximum number of selectable items and whether or not newly added answers (if enabled) are visible to others. These parameters allow a variety of different participations: from single-choice or multiple-choice to picture uploads and voting as well as selecting n of m items.

Second, the SoCom middleware collects the content provided by OSN users (if upload is enabled) and stores voting results. Therefore, SoCom publishes messages in the supported OSNs (see Fig. 2). The OSNs used are determined and configured by the users in their settings. Depending on the characteristics of each OSN, SoCom publishes a wall post, a feed message or group message(s) containing a description and offers a hyperlink to follow the call for action.

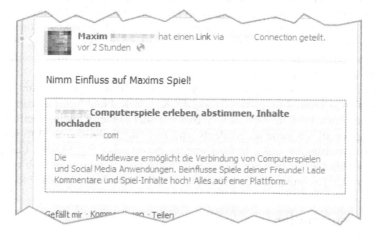

**Fig. 2.** Call for Participation as published on facebook

**Fig. 3.** Participation of type text with free answers. All texts are in German (due to study scenario).

The hyperlink will direct the interested participants to a dynamically created webfrontend. It generates a voting and/or upload page respecting the settings mentioned before (for result, see Fig. 3). Users can add new options (if allowed) and can vote for existing answers as well.

Third, the game instance can pull the results of the participation from the SoCom middleware and use such information in the game (depending on the desired effects and game characteristics). For example, several provided pictures uploaded by users can decorate the wall of an office in a 3D first person game and signs attached to them can name the contributors.

## 5    Social Serious Game Prototype

For a first study and investigation of the research questions we needed an existing Serious Game suitable to add the extensions and connect it to SoCom in order to let users enrich the game play of a friend from the OSN. We decided to use and extend an existing game (despite developing a new one) due to following reasons: (a) The target use case for *SoCom* is the extension of existing educational games, (b) An existing game, created by a professional game studio, is expected to better fulfill the user experience expectations of the players.

Thus, we used the prototype of a freshly developed 3D third-person point and click adventure that is created by game studio DECK13 from Frankfurt, Germany. As the game is not released yet, the title may be BizConsulter in the following sections.

Target group of the game are students who are potentially interested to start a career in the consulting business. In the game the player takes the role of a trainee who stands in for his mentor in a client project. The player is confronted with real world problems related to communication issues typical for consulting business (see Fig. 4).

## 6    Implementation

**Game Client Side.** For better usability client side stubs are provided for game developers. These stubs allow local method calls and hide the communication channel implementation between client and SoCom middleware server. Still, the server-side API is completely documented and condensed in public interface definitions (one for each module CI, PG and GA) which are implemented by the client stubs. Currently clients are available for C++, C#, the game engine Unity 3D[3] (via C#) and PHP5. The server side APIs expect HTTP GET or HTTP POST requests with the parameters as documented. All methods return JavaScript Object Notations (JSON) for results, that may contain error codes and messages (e.g. for missing or invalid parameters) or the result.

**Server Middleware Core.** The SoCom middleware and its modules are implemented using Java 1.6 SE Servlets running on a Jetty v8.0.3[4] servlet container and web server.

---

[3]  Unity 3D game engine, Unity Technologies, see http://unity3d.com/, last accessed 11/14/2013

[4]  Apache License 2.0 and Eclipse Public License 1.0-based Jetty webserver, see http://www.eclipse.org/jetty/, last accessed 11/14/2013

**Fig. 4.** Scene 'Mission-Takeover' of BizConsulter game

For persistency an abstraction layer interface has been designed to store and re-trieve the objects. It is currently implemented for the relational database HyperSQL[5].

For the extensibility the existing modules (currently CI, PG and GA) register their namespace for the Uniform Resource Locator (URL) scheme. All sub-paths of the registered patterns (and HTTP parameters) are managed by the modules themselves.

**OSN Side.** For each OSN a plugin implements the necessary SoCom interface to allow calls routed through by SoCom core. The plugins provide a list of supported methods (posting, voting, etc.) to allow game developers to disable game functionali-ty depending on the support.

**User Frontend.** The user frontend is implemented as a Google Web Toolkit v2.5 (GWT) application running on the same Jetty instance as the Server Middleware Core. If the user opens a URL pointing to a SoCom participation, the GWT client-side code extracts the participation ID from the URL and fetches the participation data in JSON format from the server-side methods and renders the elements in the user's browser. Currently the user frontend can display all combinations of selectable pre-defined options and upload components. For user-provided options the name and time of upload is displayed and a link is set to the SoCom player profile (see Fig. 3).

# 7     First Study

## 7.1     Setup

The study was conducted on 22nd of November 2012 with students enrolled in the Master's degree studies for Computer Science at our university (N=5, 1f/4m, aged 21-27). Due to privacy protection each participant was given a new facebook test account. All these accounts have been made friends among each other before and profiles are left clean. So, each test person was instructed to first set the first name

---

[5] BSD-License based *HyperSQL*, see http://hsqldb.org/, last accessed 11/14/2013.

and an individual profile picture to allow some identification with the profile. Then they were divided randomly into two groups to allow an A-B-Test setup. Group A first played the game, group B was instructed to fill out the provided facebook profile with further information, upload pictures and be aware of the events in their surrounding social network as they would usually when using facebook. The study was then divided into four phases:

**Phase One (15min).** Members of group A played each a simplified subset of the game that can be finished within the provided time. Members of group B used their facebook profile, added more information and reacted to events they may be aware of.

During the game play of test persons from group A, the game instances created and published new participation possibilities via the SoCom GA module on facebook which could be seen and activated by members of group B. Additionally, the game published success messages of gathered achievements with screenshots from the game on the players' facebook wall. These messages could be as well liked and commented by the members of group B.

**Phase Two (10min).** Members of both groups filled out parts of the Influence Questionnaire (IQ) (see following Section 7.3) and members of group A filled as well the User Experience Questionnaire (UXQ) to assess their game play experience.

**Phase Three (15min).** Roles were switched. Now members of group B played the game and members of group A were advised to use the provided facebook profile, add information and react on events.

**Phase Four (10min).** The IQ was completed by both groups and members of group B filled the UEQ for their game play experience.

After the phases a discussion round with all test persons was conducted for additional 30 minutes to collect insight into their perception, opinions and suggestions for future version of the game and participation possibilities.

## 7.2    Evaluated Participations

The simplified game play of BizConsulter can be divided into 8 scenes the player plays in a more or less sequential order: Mission-Takeover, Retrieval-of-Presentation-File, Call-for-Action-Accountant, Assistant-Convincing, Progress-Report, Retrieval-of-Archive-File, Delivery-of-Files, Mission-Success. As it is not essential to know the scene details, we only describe here the creation of participations and the retrieval of results as well as the retrieval and usage of OSN profile information.

For Mission-Takeover the game instance requests the players name, gender and city of residence and replaces all naming of the players avatar in dialogues by the real name. Additionally the location of the 'customer's headquarter' in BizConsulter is set to the hometown of the player. Depending on the gender of the player different participations are created and send via SoCom to facebook. If the player is male, the OSN friends are offered to contribute a name suggestion for the female assistant of the male senior accountant (mainly used for scene Assistant-Convincing). If the player is female, the OSN friends are asked to name the male senior accountant (mainly used for scene Call-for-Action-Accountant). When the user selects the dialog option "Yes, let's do it" to take over the job, the game publishes as well an achievement message on the wall with a screenshot. In the following scenes the provided names are used within dialogs to name the NPCs accordingly.

In brief, OSN users can create name suggestions or vote for answers submitted by others before. The name with the most votes is used in all NPC dialogs (if there is a tie, it is chosen randomly). The screenshots and messages can be 'liked' and commented. This influences the cooperativeness of the assistant (dialogue difficulty).

## 7.3     Questionnaire(s)

The UXQ is partly based on the user Experience Questionnaire of Lennard Nacke [Nack09]. The reliability of the UXQ has been shown before by evaluations in cognitive psychology with other game prototypes [GöGH13]. In summary, the UXQ measures 17 aspects with 3 items each to calculate from overall 51 items scores for the User Experience with the game and an overall User Experience score. All items are encoded on a 10 point Likert scale with 0 as lowest value (disagreement) and 10 as highest value (agreement).

The IQ is a new questionnaire and targets four aspects to measure: A1: Viral marketing perception of game activity, A2: Activation of environment, A3: technical functionality and A4: in-game perception of contributed content and personalization.

Similarly to the UXQ each aspect is measured with at least 3 items which are as well encoded on a 10-point Likert scale. The aspects focused by the IQ are attributed to the research questions (A1 for RQ1, A2 for RQ2, A3 for RQ3, and A4 for RQ4).

## 7.4     Results

All four IQ-aspects have been rated by participants above 6.5 (mean=7.13, $\sigma^2$=1.95). The mean sum score for User Experience is 3.62 ($\sigma^2$=1.8) and is in no case above 4.76. All participants reached the game end within 10 to 18 minutes (mean=13.6min, $\sigma^2$=8.8). None of the person-related values like age, gender, hours of computer game playing, time to game end or group membership (A/B) correlates significantly with the measured IQ-aspects A1-A4 or the UXQ sum measure. A diagram plot of the results split into both groups A (first playing game, then facebook) and B (first facebook, then game) is drawn in Fig. 5.

Based on these first indications the research questions can be answered as followed:

**RQ1:** *Will befriended users of a (serious) game player react to OSN-placed posts and have a positive perception of it (IQ measure A1=IQ4+IQ5+IQ6)?* **Yes**, with a mean value of 6.87 for A1 the users rate it clearly as positive and recognize the posts made by the game within the OSN. Their interest in games with such participation functionality has been raised (IQ6 mean=6.6) and they agree to have read the messages more active due to participation possibilities (IQ4 mean=8.75). In conclusion, the participants do want to recognize when a 'call for participation' is offered.

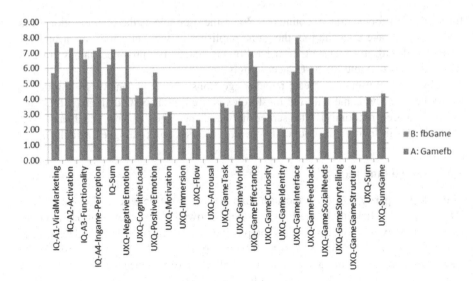

**Fig. 5.** Results of Questionnaires IQ and UXQ

**RQ2:** *Will they accept the concept of contributing content to a friend's game play (IQ measure A2=IQ12-IQ9-IQ10)?* **Yes,** with a mean value of 6.43 users like the idea of contributing content to a friend's gameplay. Still, as seen with reversely encoded question IQ9 (mean=6.8) the users felt they need more information about the game context which they will contribute content to. Thus it is targeted for next versions of *SoCom* to display context data next to the vote and upload form of the website to assist participating users in their content contribution (or voting) decision.

**RQ3:** *How well will participants value the technical implementation of the concept (IQ measure A3=IQ11+ IQ13+IQ14)?* **Positively,** with mean value of 7.01 users appreciate the technical usability. Orientation and usage was rated good in IQ13 (mean=7.0) and they had all functionality expected for the tasks at hand as rated with IQ14 (mean=7.8). As the main visible GUI users interact with is the website generated for taking part in participations, it can be assumed that the GWT-based realization with the AJAX-based dynamic interface was an adequate choice to allow quick and intuitive participation by votes and/or uploads.

**RQ4:** *Will players appreciate the participation from outside within their game play (IQ measure A4=IQ1+IQ2+IQ3-IQ7-IQ8)?* **Yes,** with mean value of 7.24 this value is the highest of the IQ measures (A1-A4). The users value the positive impact of contributions from their friends as well as the personalization aspect. Negative associations have not been reported in IQ7 and IQ8 (mean$_{IQ7}$=2.4, mean$_{IQ8}$=3.4).

Thus the main aim of the study that is reflected in the title of the paper is: Personalization of a video game via social media participation appears to be possible. For the scenario of our study participants reported positively as well from the aspect of being asked for participation while outside of the game (as OSN member) as well as the aspect of perceiving the participations within the game.

## 7.5   Interpretation

In addition to answering the main research questions, the collected data provides insight into differences among the user groups (A/B), leaving room for interpretation.

Even though the differences in values for the IQ measures and UXQ measures between the group A (first playing the game) and B (first using facebook) are not significant, some tendencies can be seen in the data.

First, members of group B have been on average 2.67 minutes faster in finishing the game. Beside other unmeasured effects, this can be interpreted to be an effect of their participations before. Thus, users which know from their facebook usage which types of questions and possible participation they recognized before, may try to reach the corresponding game scenes faster to see which content others contribute for them. Curiosity might thus be a factor increasing game play speed.

Second, as shown in Fig. 5, there is a strong difference between the low UXQ-Sum value (mean of all UXQ values) and the IQ values. Due to the short game play and linearity of the game story the users seem to be bored from the game even though it was graphically designed with one of the newest game engines. It can be assumed that a longer, more complex, and adaptive game play may as well increase the effects of participation possibilities as more variety is possible in 'calls for participation'.

Third, Fig. 5 shows the highest percental difference between the user groups A and B within the IQ measures for the aspects *A1 Viral Marketing* and *A2 Activation*. As the participants of group A knew from the game play experience how well they enjoyed the contributed items from the other users (of group B), it seems to be valid to assume that they had an increased motivation to pay attention to messages published in the name of the playing users of group B (higher value for A1).

# 8   Conclusion and Future Work

With the described middleware architecture SoCom we offer a solution to enable game designers to add social participation possibilities to their computer games. Such functionality can support the personalization and enrichment of game play with profile data and metrics from a player's Online Social Network (OSN) as well as user-generated content that is contributed by the player's friends. After pointing out the current state of the art in Social Media for personalization, participation and learning, the field of Serious Games has been introduced. With the focus on improving a players experience by personalization with data from Social Media, the criteria necessary for a Social (Casual) Game have been derived. Afterwards, the identified research questions have been addressed: First, by the introduction of the architectural solution SoCom. Second, the key facts concerning its implementation were named. Third, the study setup and results are described and interpreted. In the study we focused on the connection of the Serious Game BizConsulter with the OSN facebook. Here, tendencies could be found that answer the stated research questions positively. We found indication that participation of users from OSNs has beneficial effects on the users awareness of participations, the contribution of content and on the receiving players.

Even though the described study corroborates our opinion of the benefits achievable by using Social Media and active participation of OSN users to personalize and enrich the game play experience of Serious Game players, a follow up study could benefit from a much greater scope with more participants as well as a longitudinal study to prevent the positive bias of users for new functionality. As participants suggested during discussions after the study, more types of participation possibilities as well as more contextual information are expected to increase the positive effects.

**Acknowledgments.** This project (HA project no. 258/11-04) is funded in the framework of Hessen ModellProjekte, financed with funds of LOEWE – Landes-Offensive zur Entwicklung Wissenschaftlich-ökonomischer Exzellenz, Förderlinie 3: KMU-Verbundvorhaben (State Offensive for the Development of Scientific and Economic Excellence).

# References

[BrGo03] Brazelton, J., Gorry, G.A.: Creating a Knowledge-Sharing Community. Communications of the ACM 46(2), 23 (2003)

[Damo84] Damon, W.: Peer Education: The Untapped Potential. Journal of Applied Developmental Psychology 5(4), 331–343 (1984)

[GöGH13] Göbel, S., et al.: Evaluation of Serious Games. In: Bredl, K., Bösche, W. (eds.) Serious Games and Virtual Worlds in Education, Professional Development, and Healthcare, 1st edn. Hershey, pp. 105–115. IGI Global, Hershey (2013) ISBN: 9781466636736

[GWRS10] Göbel, S., Wendel, V., Ritter, C., Steinmetz, R.: Personalized, Adaptive Digital Educational Games Using Narrative Game-Based Learning Objects. In: Zhang, X., Zhong, S., Pan, Z., Wong, K., Yun, R. (eds.) Edutainment 2010. LNCS, vol. 6249, pp. 438–445. Springer, Heidelberg (2010)

[HBRS09] Hildebrandt, T., et al.: Capturing and Storing Profile Information for Gamers Playing Multiplayer Online Games. In: Abdallah, M. (ed.) 8th Annual Workshop on Network and Systems Support for Games, NetGames 2009, pp. 1–2 (2009) ISBN 9781424456048

[Järv10] Järvinen, A.: Social Game Design for Social Networks. PlayGen, http://playgen.com/game-design-for-social-networks (accessed on January 22, 2011)

[KaHa10] Kaplan, A.M., Haenlein, M.: Users of the World, Unite! Business Horizons 53(1), 59–68 (2010)

[KBGS13] Konert, J., et al.: GroupAL: ein Algorithmus zur Formation und Qualitätsbewertung von Lerngruppen in E-Learning-Szenarien. In: Breitner, A., Rensing, C. (eds.) Proceedings of the DeLFI 2013, pp. 71–82. Köllen, Bremen (2013) ISBN 9783885796121

[KRMG12] Konert, J., et al.: PEDALE - A Peer Education Diagnostic and Learning Environment. Journal of Educational Technology & Society 15(4), 27–38 (2012)

[LDUC11] Li, C., et al.: PeerSpace-An Online Collaborative Learning Environment for Computer Science Students. In: 2011 11th IEEE International Conference on Advanced Learning Technologies (ICALT), pp. 409–411. IEEE (2011)

[LoGo04] Di Loreto, I., Gouaïch, A.: Social Casual Games Success is not so Casual. Word Journal of the International Linguistic Association (2004)

[Nack09] Nacke, L.E.: Affective Ludology. Blekinge Institute of Technology (2009)

[Onei08] O'Neill, N.: What exactly are social games? Social Times, http://www.socialtimes.com/2008/07/social-games (accessed on January 18, 2011)

# A Case Study of a Learning Game about the Internet

Fares Kayali[1], Günter Wallner[2], Simone Kriglstein[3],
Gerhild Bauer[4], Daniel Martinek[5], Helmut Hlavacs[5],
Peter Purgathofer[1], and Rebbeca Wölfle[5]

[1] Vienna University of Technology,
Institute of Design and Assessment of Technology, Austria
{fares,purg}@igw.tuwien.ac.at
[2] University of Applied Arts Vienna, Institute of Art and Technology, Austria
guenter.wallner@uni-ak.ac.at
[3] SBA Research, Vienna, Austria
skriglstein@sba-research.at
[4] The Vienna University Children's Office, Austria
gerhild.bauer@univie.ac.at
[5] University of Vienna, Faculty of Computer Science, Austria
{daniel.martinek,helmut.hlavacs}@univie.ac.at, rwoelfle@gmail.com

**Abstract.** This paper describes the design of the learning game *Internet Hero*, in which the player is transported into a fictional world representing the Internet. The game shall convey learning contents about the technical and social basics of using the Internet. We connect game design to learning principles and evaluate the game through gameplay metrics and interviews with children. We show that we were able to build an engaging game while at the same time building on a strong theoretical foundation on digital game-based learning.

**Keywords:** game based learning, learning principles, case study.

## 1 Introduction

This paper is concerned with the design of a digital game-based learning experience about the Internet for children. 98% of children in Germany aged 6 to 13 use the Internet at home, 21% do so on their own computers or devices without being supervised by their parents. At the same time it is known that children often use the Internet carelessly without enough reflection and conscious awareness of the consequences of their decisions (cf. [1]). Brown and Vaughan [2] say that *Play is exploration, which means that you will be going places where you haven't been before.* What they refer to is a view of games as possibility spaces which allow to explore activities without fearing the consequences. A safe-to-fail game environment can enable children to learn about the Internet and consequences of their actions in this space in a playful and explorative way.

S. Göbel and J. Wiemeyer (Eds.): GameDays 2014, LNCS 8395, pp. 47–58, 2014.

The context for this paper is formed by the project *Play the Net*. The project's goal is to develop a game for children aged 9 to 12, which enables them to playfully experience how the Internet works, how they can surf the net safely and the dangers they might face online. The project was run as a one year long cooperation between the University of Vienna and the Vienna University Children's Office from 2012 to 2013. The result of the project is the game *Internet Hero* (for details see [3]), in which the player has to solve different mini-games correlating to four aspects of Internet use: emails, malicious programs, social networks, and connection types. In order to complete the mini-games players need to understand the basic technical or social aspects of these topics. This paper primarily discusses the the e-mail and malicious programs mini-games which were evaluated through gameplay metrics and interviews. To bridge gameplay and learning our design decisions were guided by the 36 learning principles established by J.P. Gee [4]. We used these principles as inspiration and starting points for the game design process. The core question answered in this paper is, if a game designed following the theory on digital game-based learning also appeals to its players as a game. We further discuss which game-based learning principles are suitable for a learning game around the Internet targeted at children aged 9 to 12. To answer these questions we will first present theory on games and learning, discuss the game design with respect to learning principles [4] and later reflect on the efficiency of these design decisions through an analysis of gameplay metrics and interviews.

## 2    Related Work

Games can be understood as rule-based systems [5]. Rules in games both act as constraints and affordances. Balancing player freedom with constraints is one of the core challenges in game design. Also abstraction [6] and arbitrary (sometimes even unrealistic) constraints [7] are necessary to make games playable in the first place. Frasca [8] says rules further experimentation more than they limit a player's freedom. Freedom and constraints are not antagonists but together lead to ideal spaces for explorative play. To empower players to explore possible interactions with the game world, the game has to act as a safety net where negative repercussions are removed. Squire and Jenkins [9] state that in an ideal case *the constraints of the game make flaws in the students' thinking visible to both teachers and students, enabling students to learn from the consequences of their actions*. The structure of the game not only defines the conditions of success, but also the nature of the choices that need to be taken to succeed.

Systems thinking has been identified as a core learning concept [10], which sees games as representations of systems formed by dynamic and interactive parts. Systems remain stable through a feedback loop between their parts and variables. Interacting with the game thus means taking part in the feedback loop and thereby triggers meaningful learning. The Internet can be understood as a complex structure of interacting social and technical systems. Therefore a learning game with its rule based representation is suitable to let children explore this space.

Kurt Squire [11] characterized three areas of learning where games play an important role: collaborative learning, learning through failure, personalized learning. Following the initial comments on games as safe-to-fail spaces learning through failure is of particular importance to our project. In Gee [12] three specific areas of learning through games have been defined. These are empowered learners, problem solving and understanding.

In their systematization of serious games Michael and Chen [13] also talk about combining fun and learning. They describe that in learning games the serious (learning) content may be like a Trojan horse, hidden in context with fun gameplay. According to Ito et al. [14] three additional important contexts are given: peer-supported learning, which describes everyday exchanges with peers and friends; interest-powered learning, which establishes personal interest; and relevance of learning contents and academically oriented learning, which means that learning benefits from the ability to align learning contents with individual goals. *Internet Hero* primarily tries to raise personal interest through the identification with in-game characters and establishes a social context through play in class and shared leaderboards.

Several studies with respect to unsafe Internet use have been conducted over the years. Among them we would like to mention the recent work of Valcke et al. [15] which also contains many references to other studies on this topic.

With respect to work on games on Internet safety, Nagarajan et al. [16] are discussing the possibilities of game design for cybersecurity training and provide an overview of important training topics, including protection from malware and handling of e-mails from unknown senders or spam. Juhari and Zin [17] developed *Cyberworld Adventure* for children 9-12 years old which uses a similar structure as our game (different levels relating to different Internet safety topics). Also targeting a similar age group as our work, *Net-Detectives* (cf. [18]) is a supervised online role play activity where children take on the role of a detective and receive help from human experts. *Anti-Phishing Phil* [19] is an online game to teach people how to protect themselves against phishing attacks. In all three cases, the authors reported a positive impact of the game on children's knowledge of Internet safety. *SimSafety* is an online virtual game environment to foster understanding of Internet safety risks. Its design and technical considerations have been described in Kalaitzis et al. [20]. Results of an evaluation of an early version of the system to assess game usability can be found in Xenos et al. [21].

## 3  Internet Hero

The story of *Internet Hero* revolves around a young child (the player) who accidentally gets transported into a fictional world representing the Internet and who finds himself in a quest to save this world from evil forces. As the story develops, the player meets the mail-sorting android *Ping* who becomes the players' companion in the game. *Ping* acts as a tutor for the player who provides explanations of aspects of the Internet and of the mini-games. These mini-games are embedded in the game's narrative meta structure. In the following, two mini-games – which were the subject of our evaluation – are described in more detail.

**Fig. 1.** *E-Mail* (left) and *Malicious Software* (right) mini-games

## 3.1  E-Mail Mini-Game

*Ping* works in a mail server and is currently overwhelmed by a wave of spam mails. He needs help separating legitimate emails from spam mails and asks the player to assist him by sorting 20 different mails. Spam mails need to be thrown away while legitimate e-mails need to be forwarded to their recipients. The player's task is to read the incoming e-mails and decide whether they contain any unsolicited advertising or suspicious URLs, senders, or attachments. After the player has read the e-mail and decided if it is a spam mail or a legitimate mail, they can send it forward or destroy it by dragging the e-mail either to the right side of the screen or onto the trash bin on the left side (cf. Figure 1, left). In case players manage to correctly categorize two or more e-mails in a row they get a chain bonus as an extra reward.

## 3.2  Malicious Software Mini-Game

After the spam-wave is over *Ping* expresses his gratitude to the player, but soon starts feeling sick because he got infected by a virus. The player accompanies him to the hospital, where an USB-doctor explains a few of the different kinds of malware and how to stop them from weakening *Ping*. The player has to stop the disease from destroying *Ping*'s CPU by playing a tower-defense-like mini-game (cf. Figure 1, right). The player can build different types of defense towers on predefined building lots. There are three types of towers to choose from: shooter, scanner, and firewall. The firewall stops various malicious programs (viruses, Trojans, and worms) from getting to the CPU, the scanner identifies Trojans as malware, making them vulnerable to shooters. In order to win the mini-game the player has to survive ten waves of attacks. Each wave enters from one of two sides of the game field. Each time a malicious program is killed it drops *Ping-Points*, the mini-game's virtual currency, which can be reinvested into new towers or upgrades. If an enemy reaches the CPU, *Ping*'s health-bar loses life. Once the CPU is destroyed the mini-game is lost.

**Fig. 2.** Children played and tested the game during the *Children's University* event

## 4   Methods

The approach of the project can be characterized as explorative. In explorative design [22] knowledge is constructed through interacting with the matter to be explored. In our case we explore learning games and their workings through making them and reflecting back on the process. This approach can also be called design as research [23]. The process of generating research results through game design in particular has also been outlined in Stapleton [24].

The evaluation used a mixed methods approach, including different on-screen questionnaires consisting of open and closed questions and data logging for which purpose the game was instrumented to automatically record different aspects of the player activity. With regard to the former, one questionnaire assessed general demographic characteristics (e.g., age, gender), a questionnaire after each mini-game collected feedback about the mini-game itself, and a last questionnaire at the end of the evaluation collected opinions on the game in general. This way we were able to collect detailed data on the player-game interaction (e.g., for balancing purposes) on the one hand and to obtain subjective opinions on the game on the other hand.

## 5   Sample

The evaluation was conducted at two workshops during the *Children's University* event which took place at the University of Vienna (cf. Figure 2). During the workshops children were able to play the first two mini-games of *Internet Hero* for approximately 60 minutes. 36 children (50% male, 50% female) between 9 and 13 years ($M = 10.7, SD = 1.1$) have participated in the evaluation with the vast majority of them stating to play computer games regularly, ranging from once per month ($n = 10$), to one to four times per week ($n = 20$) or even daily ($n = 4$). Only two of the children reported to never play computer games at all.

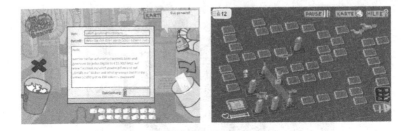

**Fig. 3.** *E-Mail* (left) and *Malicious Software* (right) mini-games after improvements

## 6   Results

In general the game was well received by the children. On a four point scale with categories *very good*, *good*, *so-so*, and *bad*, 56% of the children rated the game as *very good* and 40% as *good*. The graphics were rated as *very cool* by 40% of the children and as *well done* by another 56% on a similar four point scale. However, the sound received mixed feedback. While 32% and 28% of the children rated the sound as *very cool* and *well done* respectively, 32% judged the sound as *so-so* and 8% as *bad*. Children indicated, for instance, that they had problems to understand the computerized voice of *Ping* – the player's sidekick.

### 6.1   E-Mail Mini-Game

One-fifth of the children (21.2%) considered the mini-game to be *very good*, the majority (57.6%) as *good*, 18.2% as *so-so*, and the remaining 3% as *bad*. The responses to the question *What did you not like about the mini-game?* of the post-game questionnaire showed that children most disliked that the phrasing of the emails was sometimes ambiguous (stated by 8 children). Two children also stated that they missed feedback if the mail was categorized correctly or not. However, analysis of the logged data showed that children were able to recognize spam e-mails quite well, getting it right 79.3% (78.3% males, 80.1% females) of the time.

**Improvements.** Based on these results we made the following changes to the *E-Mail* mini-game (cf. Figure 3, left):

- Rephrased the text of the e-mails where children made the most mistakes.
- Added an indicator to the user interface if and how many of the e-mails were categorized correctly. We suspect that the concerns of some children regarding ambiguous phrasing can be partly attributed to the circumstance that children did not get feedback on the correctness from the game which may have therefore caused them to feel uncertain whether they interpreted the text correctly or not.

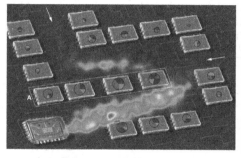

**Fig. 4.** Heat map where coins have been collected overlaid with pie-charts showing which types of towers (red = shooter, green = scanner, blue = firewall) have been built at the different locations

**Fig. 5.** Heat map depicting locations where *Trojans* have taken damage

## 6.2 Malicious Software Mini-Game

Compared to the *E-Mail* mini-game, the *Malicious Software* mini-game was better received by the children, with more than half of them (55.2%) rating the game as *very good*. 31% rated the mini-game as *good*, 10.3% as *so-so*, and 3.5% as *bad*. On average, children played 4.1 rounds (4.2 males, 3.9 females) of *Malicious Software*. However, some of the log files of these rounds were erroneous due to technical problems during the evaluation and were therefore excluded from the following analysis, leaving log-data from 118 rounds.

Figure 4 shows which types of towers have been built at the different locations. The size of a pie chart is proportional to the number of towers built at the certain locations and the colored sections represent the type of the towers (red = shooter, green = scanner, blue = firewall). In general, shooters were built more frequently ($M = 3.43$, $SD = 3.13$) than firewalls ($M = 2.12$, $SD = 1.26$) and scanners ($M = 1.41, SD = 0.85$) across all 118 rounds. This suggests that children were able to successfully defend against *Trojans* without using scanners to expose them. As the heat map in Figure 5 shows, children were rather waiting to attack them until the *Trojans* eventually dropped their disguise in the attempt to assault the CPU.

As evident from Figure 4, towers were preferably built along the horizontally arranged building lots in the center of the map (labeled *A*). At these locations towers were able to reach viruses in the corridor above and below. In general, defense concentrated on the corridor toward the CPU, since regardless if the viruses entered the map on the top left or right side, enemies eventually have to pass through this corridor. This is also reflected by the heatmap overlaid in Figure 4 which shows where coins have been collected (and therefore indirectly also reflects where enemies have been killed).

To assess if there are differences in behavior between male and female players as well as between players of different age and in order to observe trends in

**Table 1.** Mean values and standard deviations (in brackets) for game-related variables of the *Malicious Software* mini-game. Statistically significant differences ($p < .05$) between males and females are marked with a gray background.

| | Round 1 | | | Round 3 | | |
|---|---|---|---|---|---|---|
| | male ($N = 17$) | | female ($N = 18$) | male ($N = 12$) | | female ($N = 15$) |
| score | 478 (386) | | 296 (323) | 1068 (555) | ↔ | 487 (477) |
| coins | 11.8 (14.4) | | 6.7 (8.7) | 30.6 (21.2) | ↔ | 13.4 (14.1) |
| waves | 9.8 (0.7) | ↔ | 8.8 (1.4) | 9.9 (0.3) | | 9.5 (1.1) |
| shooters | 3.2 (2.0) | ↔ | 1.3 (1.3) | 6.3 (4.4) | ↔ | 2.7 (2.4) |
| scanner | 1.8 (0.75) | ↔ | 1.2 (1.2) | 1.5 (0.5) | | 1.2 (0.7) |
| firewalls | 2.4 (0.8) | | 2.3 (1.4) | 2.0 (1.7) | | 2.5 (1.1) |

the behavior over multiple rounds we looked at the data of the first and third round. Table 1 lists the mean values and standard deviations of different game-related variables for these two rounds. The effect of gender with respect to these variables was analyzed using Mann-Whitney U tests. The statistical analysis shows that males and females significantly differed with respect to the number of survived waves in the first round ($U = 97$, $p = .02$), with males surviving on average one wave more than females. However, the difference is not significant in the third round anymore, with both males and females surviving almost all 10 waves on average. In general, the mini-game was easily won by the children with males already surviving on average 9.8 waves out of 10 in the first attempt.

Focusing on the type of towers which have been built by males compared to females, females built less scanners than males in the first round ($U = 93.5$, $p = .038$). More interestingly, females also constructed significantly less shooters than males, both in the first ($U = 61$, $p = .002$) as well as in the third ($U = 43$, $p = .02$) round even though shooters are necessary to kill the viruses and to receive coins and score points in turn. A closer inspection of the collected metrics of all 118 rounds revealed that girls sometimes only used firewalls to hold back the enemies until the last wave entered the level and the game counted as won. This strategy was only used by one boy in a single round, whereas six of the girls have pursued it at least once. Females therefore scored on average lower than males as evident from Table 1. This difference is statistically significant in the third round with males achieving more than twice the score ($U = 41, p = .015$) and collecting more than twice as many coins ($U = 45.5, p = .03$) as females. Comparing the scores from the first with the third round, males seem to have been much more concerned to improve their score than females.

No significant differences between the age groups – neither for round one nor for round three – for any of the variables in Table 1 could be observed.

**Improvements.** In view of these findings we implemented the following major changes (see Figure 3, right):

– To increase the value of scanners, *Trojans* are now immediately disabling firewalls if not exposed by a scanner before. This makes *Trojans* at the same time more dangerous and should counteract that children wait to attack them until they reach the CPU. As an alternative *Trojans* could, for example, cause more damage to the CPU or could be made more resistant against shooters. However, we think this solution makes more sense in the educational context of the mini-game, that is, teaching children about the dangers of viruses.

- Instead of earning points for killings, points are now awarded for the survived time and for the remaining CPU health. This should make the scoring scheme better suited for different styles of play (whereas the previous one favored offensive play – more frequently employed by males as the above analysis showed). Secondly, this should circumvent that children restrict their defenses to the immediate proximity of the CPU.
- The map itself had been made larger and now includes two corridors leading to the CPU. This should make the game a bit more challenging and varied.

## 7    Discussion: Connecting *Internet Hero* to Learning Principles

The discussion is structured by several of Gee's [4] learning principles relevant to our game. In the following we first cite a principle and then discuss the gameplay elements relevant to it:

> *Active, Critical Learning Principle: All aspects of the learning environment (including ways in which the semiotic domain is designed and presented) are setup to encourage active and critical, not passive, learning.* [4]

The whole game was set up following this principle as the player acts as part of the game world. The world itself is made out of learning contents, sometimes directly and often in metaphorical sense. Interviews confirmed this decision as players appreciated the game and its visual design.

> *Semiotic Principle: Learning about and coming to appreciate interrelations within and across multiple sign systems (images, words, actions, symbols, artifacts, etc.) as a complex system is core to the learning experience.* [4]

The *Malicious Software* mini-game was built to represent the differences in malicious software and to help players understand possible strategies against it. Players had to understand the abstracted game representation as well as introductory text and cutscenes to interact with it. Only the combination of gameplay and instructions establishes enough context to enable a transfer to a real setting.

> *'Psychosocial Moratorium' Principle: Learners can take risks in a space where real-world consequences are lowered.* [4]

The evaluation of the *Malicious Software* mini-game showed that players also explored less successful strategies in fighting back the various pieces of malicious software. Overall real-world consequences are not an issue in *Internet Hero*.

*Committed Learning Principle: Learners participate in an extended engagement (lots of effort and practice) as an extension of their real-world identities in relation to a virtual identity to which they feel some commitment and a virtual world that they find compelling.* [4]

To enforce this aspect players are given responsibility within the game world. Not only do they have to follow the story and overcome technical and social issues but players also must save their in-game companion to further attachment to the game world.

*Self-Knowledge Principle: The virtual world is constructed in such a way that learners learn not only about the domain but about themselves and their current and potential capacities.* [4]

While the game world strongly abstracts the technical basics and includes many metaphors it still includes many likenesses to further ease transfer back to the real world. For example the ability to identify simpler types of spam in the game is very related to the ability to identify real email spam.

*'Regime of Competence' Principle: The learner gets ample opportunity to operate within, but at the outer edge of, his or her resources, so that at those points things are felt as challenging but not 'undoable'.* [4]

The evaluation and metrics of the *Malicious Software* mini-game showed that many difficulty adjustments are necessary to uphold game flow. This principle fully correlates with good game design practice in balancing difficulty in a game so that players are neither overwhelmed nor bored.

*Multimodal Principle: Meaning and knowledge are built up through various modalities (images, texts, symbols, interactions, abstract design, sound, etc.) not just words.* [4]

The learning contents of the game are conveyed through several channels. The most important always is the gameplay of a particular mini-game itself. Interaction with the matter always forms the core of the learning experience in *Internet Hero*. Additional information is conveyed though the companion *Ping*, instruction texts and cut scenes.

*Explicit Information On-Demand and Just-in-Time Principle: The learner is given explicit information both on demand and just in time, when the learner needs it or just at the point where the information can be best understood and used in practice.* [4]

The companion was designed to fulfill this particular role. *Ping* plays a role in all of *Internet Hero*'s mini-games and gives timely information. In a game for children this aspect is of particular importance because they should not be overwhelmed with information.

*Discovery Principle: Overt telling is kept to a well-thought-out minimum, allowing ample opportunity for the learner to experiment and make discoveries.* [4]

From the feedback we noticed that it is still necessary and good to tell some things more overtly than initially planned. At the same time we tried not to spoil experimentation as could be witnessed in the *Malicious Software* mini-game.

## 8    Conclusions

With *Internet Hero* we created a game built upon learning principles. The analysis of gameplay and the discussion of individual learning principles primarily illustrated the importance of a game world which is both engaging and at the same time acts as a representation of the learning contents. The evaluation showed that the game was interesting to its target audience. The biggest challenge lies in the right level of abstraction where learning contents are maintained while at the same time designing interesting gameplay. Learning games face the risk to be either fun and worthless, or boring and worthwhile. This can at least partly be attributed to the fact that the notion of *playing a game* is a difficult one in the context of learning. Also, it has proven really hard for a game to be both fun and valuable as a learning tool. This in a way has become the central challenge for learning games: be a game that really is *played*, i.e., used voluntarily, and for fun or recreation. While we have not yet evaluated the transfer of learning contents from *Internet Hero* to the real world, our evaluation so far can confirm that building upon learning principles did still result in an appealing game experience. A future study will address the relation of entertainment to measured learning outcomes.

**Acknowledgments.** The Project was funded by net.idee (`www.netidee.at`, project number 326). We would like to thank all additional project team members, namely Karoline Iber, Leopold Maurer, Kornelius Pesut, Patrik Hummelbrunner and Benjamin Kitzinger as well as the children at the *Children's University Vienna* and the *A1 Internet für Alle Campus* who participated in the evaluation.

## References

1. Medienpädagogischer Forschungsverbund Südwest: Jim-Studie 2012. Jugend, Information (Multi-) Media. Technical report (2012)
2. Brown, S.L., Vaughan, C.C.: Play: How it shapes the brain, opens the imagination, and invigorates the soul. Avery Publishing Group (2009)
3. Bauer, G., Martinek, D., Kriglstein, S., Wallner, G., Wölfle, R.: Digital Game-Based Learning with 'Internet Hero' - A Game about the Internet for Children aged. In: Proc. FROG 7th Vienna Games Conference, pp. 9–12. New Academic Press (in press, 2014)

4. Gee, J.P.: What video games have to teach us about learning and literacy. Palgrave MacMillan, New York (2007)
5. Juul, J.: Half-Real: Video Games Between Real Rules and Fictional Worlds. MIT Press (2005)
6. Juul, J.: A Certain Level of Abstraction. In: Baba, A. (ed.) DiGRA 2007, pp. 510–515. DiGRA Japan (2007)
7. Grünvogel, S.M.: Formal models and game design. Game Studies 5(1), 1–9 (2005)
8. Frasca, G.: Simulation 101: Simulation versus Representation (2001), http://www.ludology.org/articles/sim1/simulation101.html (accessed: January 2014)
9. Squire, K., Jenkins, H.: Harnessing the power of games in education. Insight 3(1), 5–33 (2003)
10. Torres, R., Wolozin, L.: Quest to learn: Developing the school for digital kids. MIT Press (2011)
11. Squire, K.: From content to context: Videogames as designed experience. Educational Researcher 35(8), 19–29 (2006)
12. Gee, J.P.: Learning by design: Games as learning machines. Interactive Educational Multimedia (8), 15–23 (2004)
13. Michael, D.R., Chen, S.L.: Serious games: Games that educate, train, and inform. Muska & Lipman/Premier-Trade (2005)
14. Ito, M., Gutiérrez, K., Livingstone, S., Penuel, B., Rhodes, J., Salen, K., Schor, J., Sefton-Green, J., Watkins, S.C.: Connected learning: an agenda for research and design. Digital Media and Learning Research Hub (2013)
15. Valcke, M., Wever, B.D., Keer, H.V., Schellens, T.: Long-term study of safe internet use of young children. Computers & Education 57(1), 1292–1305 (2011)
16. Nagarajan, A., Allbeck, J., Sood, A., Janssen, T.: Exploring game design for cybersecurity training. In: IEEE Int. Conference on Cyber Technology in Automation, Control, and Intelligent Systems (CYBER), pp. 256–262 (2012)
17. Juhari, S.F., Zin, N.A.M.: Educating Children about Internet Safety through Digital Game Based Learning. Int. Journal of Interactive Digital Media 1(1), 65–70 (2013)
18. Wishart, J., Oades, C., Morris, M.: Using online role play to teach internet safety awareness. Computers & Education 48(3), 460–473 (2007)
19. Sheng, S., Magnien, B., Kumaraguru, P., Acquisti, A., Cranor, L.F., Hong, J., Nunge, E.: Anti-phishing phil: the design and evaluation of a game that teaches people not to fall for phish. In: Proc. 3rd Symposium on Usable Privacy and Security, pp. 88–99. ACM (2007)
20. Kalaitzis, D., Valeontis, E., Delis, V., Fountana, M.: Experiences from developing online VR environments: The SimSafety case study. Social Applications for Life Long Learning (2010)
21. Xenos, M., Papaloukas, S., Kostaras, N.: The evaluation of an online virtual game environment (SimSafety) using HOU's software quality laboratory. Social Applications for Life Long Learning (2010)
22. Ehn, P., Löwgren, J.: Design [x] research: Essays on interaction design as knowledge, Malmö University, School of Arts and Communication (2004)
23. Burdick, A.: Design (as) Research. In: Laurel, B. (ed.) Design Research: Methods and Perspectives. MIT Press (2003)
24. Stapleton, A.J.: Research as Design-Design as Research. In: Proc. DiGRA 2005 Conference - Changing Views: Worlds in Play (2005)

# Word Domination

## Bringing Together Fun and Education in an Authoring-Based 3D Shooter Game

Philip Mildner, Christopher Campbell, and Wolfgang Effelsberg

Univ. of Mannheim,
Dept. of Computer Science IV, Germany
{mildner,effelsberg}@informatik.uni-mannheim.de,
ccampbell@pi4.informatik.uni-mannheim.de

**Abstract.** In this paper, the multiplayer serious game *Word Domination* is presented. The key aspects of this project are to create one fixed game scenario with strong emphasis on motivational aspects and to combine this with a variable learning content. Therefore, a web-based authoring tool has been created that allows for the integration of arbitrary quizzes into the game. This frees teachers from hassling with game design details. At the same time, it offers players the same level of engaging gameplay throughout different learning scenarios by making use of the popularity of 3D shooter games. Apart from the beneficial aspects of in-game learning, the game also offers rankings and statistics, which might serve as a motivational aspect on the one hand, and as an evaluation tool for instructors on the other hand. In addition to a description of game mechanisms and the technical background of the game, this paper will present suggestions for application scenarios and further development possibilities. Some player impressions and reactions were gathered in a study at the University of Mannheim and at the Darmstadt *GameDays* 2013 exhibition, during which the game was played by a broad audience.

## 1 Introduction

The industry of digital games has been rapidly growing for many years, and the stereotypical image of the gamer as a socially-defunct male teenager has long faded. Playing video games has become an activity that attracts people of both genders, all ages and various backgrounds. Computers and consoles have since long entered private spaces, such as living rooms or children's bedrooms and are integrated in the daily lives of almost all children and many adults [1–3]. By combining approved elements of game design with a serious content, serious games aim to add a beneficial value to the large amount of time and effort that players put into playing digital games. The concepts of learning and playing are no longer treated as disjunct or opposing activities but as intertwined and interdependent practices [4–6].

Serious games have entered many areas of application, such as the health sector, the military, governments and businesses [7]. The largest field of serious games applications, however, is the academic education sector, which comprises

S. Göbel and J. Wiemeyer (Eds.): GameDays 2014, LNCS 8395, pp. 59–70, 2014.

schools and universities. Proponents of serious games for schools argue that traditional teaching methods are no longer suitable for a generation of "digital natives" that grew up in an environment full of technology and games [8, 4, 6]. Traditional teaching-methods follow an instruction-based, content-centered approach, in which students follow passively [8, 4]. Digital games, on the other hand, revolve around players and their actions, and encourage active exploration by allowing free movement and experimentation in a trial-and-error fashion [9]. Additionally, they provide adaptive challenges, constant feedback and appropriate rewards for all preferences [8–10].

While in theory using learning games seems to be a good way to reach the current generation of students, the implementation of such games bears several obstacles. First, there is a huge gap between entertainment games and educational games in terms of graphics, gameplay mechanics and, most importantly, fun and motivational aspects. This is not surprising at all when comparing budgets and development effort. Modern entertainment games compete with Hollywood movies in terms of costs and big game companies are involved. Educational games, on the other hand, mostly are developed by small teams for a much smaller audience. This includes commercial learning games that, among others, can be used for the acquisition of foreign languages or learning maths as well as games that were developed in an academic setting [11, 12]. This results in the fact that many available educational games focus on the correct integration of the learning content, leaving the fun part of the game behind. While this is reasonable for some applications, players that are accustomed to entertainment games will get bored soon this way.

A possibility to utilize the motivating characteristics of entertainment games is to use "commercial-of-the-shelf" games in an educational setting. Studies have shown that games such as *SimCity*, *Civilization* or *Age of Empires* indeed can be used for delivering learning content [8, 13, 14]. However, teachers are restricted to the exact setting the game provides. To mitigate the problem, authoring tools have been created. These tools allow non-professional game designers to easily create custom-made games with an arbitrary learning content [15]. Similar storytelling frameworks are also used in education to let students create their own stories or games [16]. Again, a problem with such tools can be to correctly combine learning and fun parts, so analyses have to be carried out to find the right balance between entertainment game and learning application [17].

*Word Domination* has been designed with the aforementioned shortcomings in mind. *Unity3D*[1] was used as game engine to provide a modern 3D environment that is able to reassemble the look of commercial entertainment games. With a multiplayer first-person shooter game one of the most popular genres of commercial games was chosen. To allow users to integrate their own learning content an authoring tool has been created along with the game. However, the game world and its mechanics are fixed so that the authoring interface is purely meant to integrate learning content in form of question catalogues. This guarantees the same engaging gameplay for all different kinds of learning contents

---

[1] http://unity3d.com/

that is presented in Section 2. During development strong emphasis was laid on motivational factors of the game as further explained in Section 3. Section 4 then describes a study that has been carried out at the University of Mannheim and presents feedback gathered at a public presentation of the game. The paper concludes with a conclusion and an outlook on the further development of entertaining learning games.

## 2    The Game

*Word Domination* is a round-based online 3D shooter. It has been designed to incorporate the engaging game elements of multiplayer action games as well as the knowledge transfer of a generic quiz. By design, the resulting game had to be a tradeoff: As the game should support any learning content that can be modeled as a quiz, it could not be tailored to one specific scenario like, e. g., teaching maths skills or learning foreign languages. Instead, the learning content has been integrated in a way that allows to use the same gaming scenario for different learning topics.

### 2.1    Rules

Based on the game mode "domination" that can be found in popular multiplayer games, two opposing teams must conquer the map by controlling the majority of platforms that are spread throughout the map. In difference to common entertainment games, however, players do not shoot at each other with weapons. Instead, players can hinder their opponents by throwing spheres at them that "contain" easy, medium or hard questions. Players that get hit will have to answer a question before they can continue to conquer platforms.

Upon entering a game room, players choose a character and are subsequently assigned either to the red or the blue team. Thereupon, players are released into a realistic 3D environment which they experience from a first-person-perspective (see Fig. 1). As in traditional first-person shooters, players can control their avatar by moving in all horizontal directions, as well as jumping and running.

Players can choose between different levels of difficulty that are modeled as different kinds of bullet types: If a player chooses to throw easy questions, there will be 5 bullets for each shot, making it easier to hit the opponent, while medium questions will result in 3 bullets, and for a hard question only 1 bullet will be released. If a player's avatar gets hit by a question it will be captured in a sphere for a certain time period unless the player manages to answer the question correctly within that time frame. If they do not know the answer, players have the opportunity to ask a nearby fellow team member to answer the question for them. For orientation, a mini-map displays all player positions on the map and will switch part of the map to red or blue if a player conquers a platform. In addition to six platforms that can be conquered, the map includes some strategical elements, such as a lake in the middle that divides the north from the south, a destructible wall in the middle of the map and "boosters" that will

**Fig. 1.** Screenshot of the game showing the different game and control elements. At this time the red team has conquered one platform and is in the lead over the blue team.

shoot the player's avatar over the map, making the game play highly dynamic and unpredictable. A scale that ranges from blue to red indicates which team is in favor of winning the round. If one team has conquered more platforms than the other team, the pointer will move along the scale towards the team that has currently conquered more platforms. As soon as it reaches the end the respective teams wins this game round.

### 2.2 Web Interface

In order to offer variable learning content, a web application has been developed that enables registered users to create question catalogues. Within a question catalogue, users can create questions and answers related to a certain topic. On completion, the question catalogue can be chosen in the room creation process of the game and its questions will be displayed if players are hit. A question that only contains one answer will be displayed as a text field in the game, whereas many answers, at least one of which must be correct, will result in multiple choice check boxes within the game.

The web application offers further functionality in that it displays user rankings and detailed user statistics, as well as game logs. The highscore displays the ranking of all active players. The scores are calculated by summarizing all values that are collected from the game sessions. These include how often a player hit other players, how he or she answered questions, how often a player conquered a platform and whether a player won a game (see Fig. 2). These values can be viewed in detail for each player including an overview how the player performed for each covered question catalogue. In addition to this, the web application offers detailed games statistics that show every hit and the associated question as

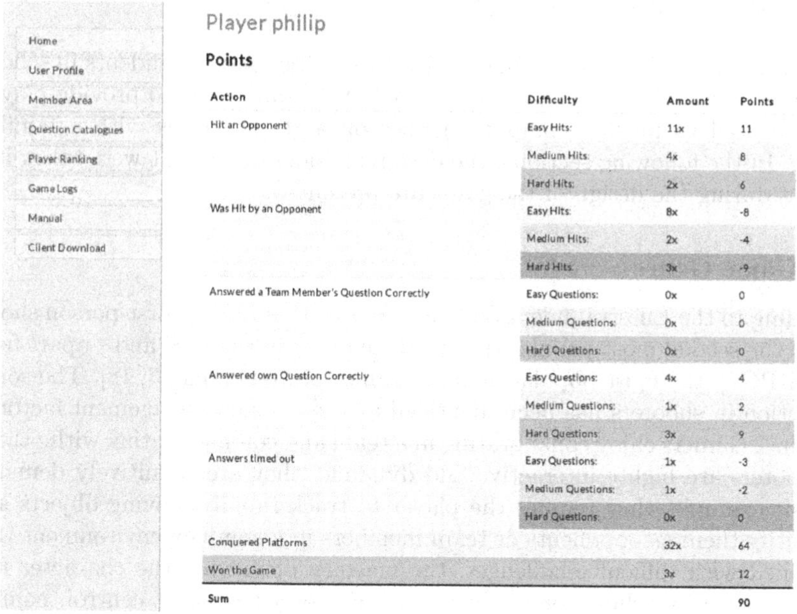

Player philip

**Points**

| Action | Difficulty | Amount | Points |
|---|---|---|---|
| Home | | | |
| User Profile | | | |
| Member Area | | | |
| Question Catalogues | | | |
| Player Ranking | | | |
| Game Logs | | | |
| Manual | | | |
| Client Download | | | |

| Action | Difficulty | Amount | Points |
|---|---|---|---|
| Hit an Opponent | Easy Hits: | 11x | 11 |
| | Medium Hits: | 4x | 8 |
| | Hard Hits: | 2x | 6 |
| Was Hit by an Opponent | Easy Hits: | 8x | -8 |
| | Medium Hits: | 2x | -4 |
| | Hard Hits: | 3x | -9 |
| Answered a Team Member's Question Correctly | Easy Questions: | 0x | 0 |
| | Medium Questions: | 0x | 0 |
| | Hard Questions: | 0x | 0 |
| Answered own Question Correctly | Easy Questions: | 4x | 4 |
| | Medium Questions: | 1x | 2 |
| | Hard Questions: | 3x | 9 |
| Answers timed out | Easy Questions: | 1x | -3 |
| | Medium Questions: | 1x | -2 |
| | Hard Questions: | 0x | 0 |
| Conquered Platforms | | 32x | 64 |
| Won the Game | | 3x | 12 |
| Sum | | | 90 |

**Fig. 2.** Screenshot of the web interface showing parts of the detailed statistics for one player. Other pages like the editable question catalogue and detailed game logs are accessible through the menu on the left side.

well the history of the conquered platforms. The web interface along with the downloadable game client is publicly available.[2]

## 2.3   Technical Background

The game client is implemented with Unity3D. For the server side *Smartfox*[3] was chosen, because it offers easy-to-use game server functionality that can be extended with own extensions. The game server is connected to a MySQL database that stores the question catalogues as well as the game and player statistics. The web site connects to the same database, so question catalogues are consistent between game clients and server at all times.

Obviously the creation of game sessions is trivial as it only requires running the game client and—if intended—adding new questions to the catalogue through the web interface. The implementation of further game levels would just affect changes to the game client, so the game could be extended easily without touching the core game mechanics. To integrate different learning content other than quizzes, however, client, server and web site would have to be changed resulting in a substantial implementation effort.

---

[2] http://ls.wim.uni-mannheim.de/de/pi4/research/projects/word-domination/
[3] http://www.smartfoxserver.com/

## 3   Design Considerations

*Word Domination* has been primarily designed to be used by students in schools and universities. Consequently, a main goal of the game was to provide players that are used to playing computer games on a regular basis with a familiar setting. In the following sections, the design considerations that were taken into account during the design of the game are presented.

### 3.1   Game Genre

According to the Entertainment Software Association (2012), first-person shooters are the second most popular digital game genre in the U.S. and—apart from MMORPGs—the most popular genre of games played online [3, 18]. The social interaction in shooters has been identified as the primary engagement factor of the genre. Gamers enjoy collaborating in a team and communicating with others. As shooters are highly interactive and dynamic, they are cognitively demanding. For example, they require the player to track rapidly moving objects and to identify them as opponents or team members in a complex environment [19]. Combined with difficult challenges, the mastery of moving the character and simultaneously watching for opponents generates a feeling of control, competency and efficacy. This, in turn, contributes to the flow state that creates a deep immersion and a feeling of pleasure for players of shooter games [20, 19]. Additionally, the game genre has a strong emotional appeal in that it provides a space for acting out behaviors and experimenting with identities [21].

By focusing on the highly motivational aspects of shooter games and combining them with a variable learning content, *Word Domination* aims to create an intrinsically motivating experience that serves a purpose beyond entertainment. The scenario suggests that the game is mainly targeted towards typical "hardcore" gamers that are used to playing complex games on their computers or gaming consoles. However, the game is suited for a broader audience, too, by providing different ways how the game can be played (see Section 3.3).

### 3.2   Motivational Elements

*Word Domination* includes a series of elements that were integrated to make the game more interesting and appealing to players. This includes a reward system, support for different player types and challenges players have to solve.

**Rewards.** In many situations, players are rewarded or punished with points. These points are entered into a database and are used to create rankings and player-specific statistics in a web application. Additionally, the question record for each player is stored, which can be used in an evaluation to display the question catalogues on which players performed best or worst. On the one hand, this is an important evaluation tool for instructors, who are enabled to identify strengths and weaknesses for each player. On the other hand, the score system was developed to be an effective reward mechanism that motivates players.

**Player Types.** As *Word Domination* is a competitive 3D shooter, it offers the most attraction for the "killer" and "achiever" player types formulated by Bartle [22]. However, there are some additional elements that might appeal to other player types as well and the game could easily be enhanced in many regards. Explorers, for instance, might enjoy the game more if maps are dynamically created and platforms have to be discovered before they can be conquered. Socializers might find the game more appealing if there is a in-game chat that can be used by players to discuss the gaming session.

**Challenges.** As the game is a team-based multiplayer game, the challenge for each player somewhat depends on the own team's and the opposing team's skills. However, the fact that players can choose different shot modes, which results in the respective question difficulty, makes the game somewhat adaptable to different skill levels. Novice players should choose to shoot easy questions, which will result in five bullets, and therefore making it easier for them to hit an opponent. At the same time, players can choose what goal they want to follow. Players experienced in 3D action games might try to capture as many players of the opposing team with hard questions. Other players might try to excel in the supporter role by answering questions for their teammates. In this way, the game offers challenges to different kinds of player types.

## 3.3  Application Areas

Being a multiplayer game, *Word Domination* enables social interaction. As learning from a computer game has been identified to not only affect players but also onlookers, a possible application scenario would involve pairs of learners, who share responsibilities. While one of them actively plays the game, the other might try to answer the questions if the active player gets hit. This would enable animate discussions and the separation of competencies, as the active players might be chosen according to their skills in video games and the onlookers according to their knowledge in the topic of the question catalogue. Such a distribution would be assumable in a child-parent combination, for example. Furthermore, *Word Domination* enables collaborative learning, as players that have to answer a question can ask their team members for help.

The fact that the game is a quiz makes it applicable for many subject fields and different teaching methods. In a school environment, for instance, teachers might create a set of questions on a certain subject in order to have students review the lesson's content or to prepare students for an upcoming exam. In a different approach, students might benefit from thinking of questions and answers on their own or in group work. Additionally, students might be intrinsically motivated to play the game in their leisure time with their peers, which would lead to them dealing with their learning content more than by playing other video games. By examining the online statistics, players and teachers can identify each player's strong and weak subjects and devise strategies in order to improve on these subjects.

Further steps could be to integrate the game into existing learning management systems or to link the game mechanics with a grading system like proposed in [23]. However, the quiz-style approach somewhat limits the game's teaching capabilities, as it rules out a deeper involvement in topics. Players will not deal with the content in an exploratory manner but rather control their existing knowledge, while playing *Word Domination*. While players can create their own question catalogues to learn new knowledge apart from only training existing content, the whole process is still limited to a quiz. Thus, *Word Domination* cannot be seen as an alternative to teaching or training but rather as a supplementary activity that, in the best case, is intrinsically motivating for its players.

## 4    Discussion

While the combination of engaging gameplay and a variable learning content into *Word Domination* promised good results in theory, the actual implementation needed to be testified by studies and qualitative feedback. Results were gathered in a university study as well as in a public demonstration of the game.

### 4.1    Experimental Results

To get insights on how the game is suited for use in universities, a question catalogue for the "Advanced Computer Networks" course was created. In a small study, six master students—all male—in the business informatics degree played the game with questions related to the course. After playing, they were asked to share their experience in self-evaluation by filling out a questionnaire. The first part of the questionnaire focused on game mechanics, such as challenge difficulty, game speed and character control. The second part aimed to identify which elements of the game were perceived as motivating by the players. Questions focused on the flow experience (concentration and immersion), the social aspect (multiplayer-based), rewards (online rankings and statistics), challenges, goals and graphics. The final part of the survey included questions related to whether the game was seen as a suitable learning tool. The answer possibilities to each question were weighted.

In terms of game mechanics, participants were only intermediately satisfied with the game. This is confirmed in additional remarks by players who stated that they missed the opportunity to adjust mouse sensitivity; that they found it hard to hit other players and to identify them as opponents; that the answer time for questions was too short; that they missed a tutorial which introduced them to the controls; and the relatively weak score of game graphics (see Fig. 3). If *Word Domination* is compared to contemporary games this is somewhat understandable, as modern 3D shooters offer high definition graphics, a range of customization possibilities, and elaborate character controls. However, this indicates that video game players' level of expectation is very high, which puts developers of serious games under pressure. A deduction of these findings might be that in order to be interesting for experienced players, serious games in 3D

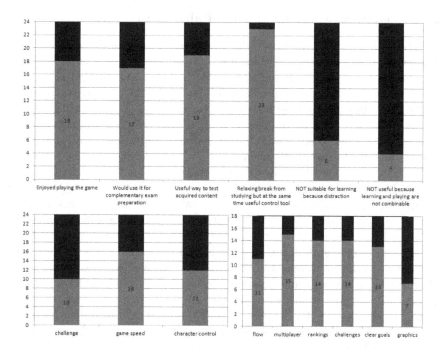

**Fig. 3.** Results of the university study. Numbers in red bars show the weighted score of approval for a question whereas black bars show the amount of disapproving answers.

environments need to move on the same high level of standards as commercially available games. However, this hypothesis is somewhat negated by the fact that although game controls and graphics were perceived as intermediate, players' responses on the motivational aspects were mostly positive.

Concentration and immersion (which are indicators for the flow state), the game's social component (the multiplayer-mode), rewards (online rankings and statistics), challenges and goals were seen as encouraging elements in regard to motivation by the majority of participants. This leads to the assumption that games might not necessarily need to incorporate the best graphics in order to be fun to players. This assumption is reinforced by the fact that all players enjoyed playing the game and that the majority would use it for complementary exam preparation. Most of participants also agreed that the game would be beneficial as an exam preparation tool, especially if played in relaxing breaks of studying. The vast majority disagreed that the game would be an unnecessary distraction during exam preparation, and that playing and learning are not combinable. These results were promising and set the directions for potential further development of *Word Domination*. However, evaluations with a bigger sample size will be necessary to get more representative results.

## 4.2   Presentation at the GameDays Rallye 2013

In addition to the study, the game was presented at the GameDays 2013 Rallye in Darmstadt, Germany, during which insights and opinions were gathered. *Word Domination* was played by around 60 players of all ages and diverse backgrounds with questions about the city of Darmstadt. In general, the game received positive feedback and most of the players stated that they had fun while playing. However, as presented in the following, some of the player's comments and further observations led to additional lessons learned, which might prove as useful considerations for future developments.

Firstly, the classic way of controlling a character in a 3D environment with the keyboard and mouse can by no means be presupposed. The vast majority of participants, regardless of age, did not know about this way of controlling the character and especially had problems with the coordination of moving and simultaneously looking in the right direction. However, children were much faster than adults at understanding the controls and at learning how to effectively move around in the environment. This is an expected confirmation to the theory that individuals that grow up surrounded by technology will be quicker at grasping new concepts and at easily adapting to their usage. So in order to provide common starting points for all players, a 3D game should introduce gameplay mechanisms with preliminary tutorials and support struggling players with ingame help mechanisms.

Apart from problems related to controls, several participants, especially older women, saw the act of shooting an opponent as hostile and refused to do so. It should be noted that *Word Domination* does not include any display of violence or death, and guns are represented in a non-realistic manner, which makes the game comparable to paint ball rather than to a war simulation. Nevertheless, the mere activity of aiming and shooting at somebody had a repelling effect on a few players, while others did not show any related concerns. For developers of serious games, this implies that the 3D shooter genre should be handled with great care and always in consideration of the target audience.

Thirdly, some players remarked that the flow of the game sometimes was disturbed for them because of speed changes. While players move around in order to conquer platforms, hit opponents and avoid being hit, the game speed is very high. While trapped in a question, however, the speed suddenly becomes very low and a great deal of concentration and patience is required. Several players experienced the fundamental difference of the two tasks as obstructive to the experience of game flow.

In general, the insight were valuable and decisive for further development considerations, which emphasizes the need for testing a serious game with a limited group of players, ideally during the development phase and before the final game is released.

# 5   Conclusion

The development and evaluation of *Word Domination* has shown that serious games do not have to be on the same technical level as commercial entertainment games, as long as they manage to create a fun experience. This can be achieved by including certain game design elements, such as rewards, feedback, adaptive challenges and by considering player preferences. Affordable and effective tools are available for the technical development, which can support programmers and game designers to create immersive environments and to establish multiplayer functionality. By strictly separating between the game and the learning scenario, an application could be implemented that is advantageous to all involved parties: Game designers can focus on creating a game that is highly motivating and fun to play. Teachers, on the other side, can concentrate on integrating just the exact learning content they intend to submit. In *Word Domination* this has been implemented by providing a web-based authoring tool that can be used to create arbitrary question catalogues but does not change the overall game scenario. Players obviously benefit from this by playing a learning game that has been optimized both for fun and for learning.

The evaluation of *Word Domination* showed that indeed it is possible to combine learning content with engaging gameplay. In its current state, the game mainly attracts players that are already accustomed to similar entertainment games. This can be seen as positive, because learning games are able to compete with entertainment games in terms of player attractiveness. However, to improve the range of the target audience, the game should support more player types by integrating other game mechanics. Other current studies on the benefits of serious games have produced promising results, but future research must focus on which games are most effective in which context and how to implement them within a framework of corresponding activities [24, 5]. If used appropriately, serious games are capable of facilitating and simultaneously improving traditional methods in many regards, leading to a shift towards the digital age and the "digital natives" generation.

# References

1. Lenhart, A., Kahne, J., Middaugh, E., Macgill, A.R., Evans, C., Vitak, J.: Teens, video games, and civics: Teens' gaming experiences are diverse and include significant social interaction and civic engagement (2008)
2. Rideout, V., Foehr, U., Roberts, D.: Generation M²: Media in the Lives of 8-to 18-Year-Olds (2010)
3. Entertainment Software Association: 2012 Sales, Demographic and Usage Data: Essential Facts about the Computer and Video Game Industry (2012)
4. Stapleton, A.J.: Serious games: Serious opportunities. In: Australian Game Developers Conference, Academic Summit, Melbourne (2004)
5. Eck, R.V.: Digital game-based learning: It's not just the digital natives who are restless. EDUCAUSE Review 41(2) (2006)
6. Breuer, J., Bente, G.: Why so serious? On the Relation of Serious Games and Learning. Eludamos. Journal for Computer Game Culture 4(1), 7–24 (2010)

7. Susi, T., Johannesson, M., Backlund, P.: Serious games: An Overview (2007)
8. Prensky, M.: Digital Game-Based Learning. Paragon House (2007)
9. Charsky, D.: From Edutainment to Serious Games: A Change in the Use of Game Characteristics. Games and Culture 5(2), 177–198 (2010)
10. Klopfer, E., Osterweil, S., Salen, K.: Moving learning games forward (2009)
11. Munz, U., Schumm, P., Wiesebrock, A., Allgower, F.: Motivation and Learning Progress Through Educational Games. IEEE Transactions on Industrial Electronics 54(6), 3141–3144 (2007)
12. Mildner, P., Campbell, C., Himmelsbach, M., Malassa, C., Miczka, M., Effelsberg, W.: A serious game for architectural knowledge in the classroom. In: Göbel, S., Müller, W., Urban, B., Wiemeyer, J. (eds.) Edutainment 2012/GameDays 2012. LNCS, vol. 7516, pp. 72–77. Springer, Heidelberg (2012)
13. Squire, K.: Changing the game: What happens when video games enter the classroom. Innovate: Journal of Online Education 1(6) (2005)
14. Charsky, D., Mims, C.: Integrating commercial off-the-shelf video games into school curriculums. TechTrends 52(5), 38–44 (2008)
15. Göbel, S., Salvatore, L., Konrad, R.: StoryTec: A Digital Storytelling Platform for the Authoring and Experiencing of Interactive and Non-Linear Stories. In: 2008 International Conference on Automated Solutions for Cross Media Content and Multi-Channel Distribution, pp. 103–110. IEEE (November 2008)
16. Kelleher, C., Pausch, R.: Using storytelling to motivate programming. Communications of the ACM 50(7), 58–64 (2007)
17. Maciuszek, D., Martens, A.: Integrating Cognitive Tasks in Game Acitivities. In: 2012 IEEE 12th International Conference on Advanced Learning Technologies, pp. 376–378. IEEE (July 2012)
18. Van Rooij, A.J., Schoenmakers, T.M., Vermulst, A.A., Van den Eijnden, R.J.J.M., Van de Mheen, D.: Online video game addiction: Identification of addicted adolescent gamers. Addiction 106(1), 205–212 (2011)
19. Colzato, L.S., van Leeuwen, P.J., van den Wildenberg, W.P., Hommel, B.: DOOM'd to Switch: Superior Cognitive Flexibility in Players of First Person Shooter Games. Frontiers in Psychology 1(8) (April 2010)
20. Frostling-Henningsson, M.: First-person shooter games as a way of connecting to people: "brothers in blood". Cyberpsychology & Behavior: The Impact of the Internet, Multimedia and Virtual Reality on Behavior and Society 12(5), 557–562 (2009)
21. Jansz, J.: The emotional appeal of violent video games for adolescent males. Communication Theory 15(3), 219–241 (2005)
22. Bartle, R.: Hearts, clubs, diamonds, spades: Players who suit MUDs. Journal of MUD Research 1(1), 19 (1996)
23. Moreno-Ger, P., Burgos, D., Martínez-Ortiz, I., Sierra, J.L., Fernández-Manjón, B.: Educational game design for online education. Computers in Human Behavior 24(6), 2530–2540 (2008)
24. Young, M.F., Slota, S., Cutter, A.B., Jalette, G., Mullin, G., Lai, B., Simeoni, Z., Tran, M., Yukhymenko, M.: Our Princess Is in Another Castle: A Review of Trends in Serious Gaming for Education. Review of Educational Research 82(1), 61–89 (2012)

# Dynamically Adaptive Educational Games: A New Perspective

Pejman Sajjadi*, Frederik Van Broeckhoven**, and Olga De Troyer

Vrije Universiteit Brussel, WISE Research Group, Pleinlaan 2, 1050 Brussels, Belgium
{ssajjadi,frederik.van.broeckhoven,Olga.DeTroyer}@vub.ac.be

**Abstract.** Dynamically adapting educational games seem to be useful for sustaining the engagement of the player to the game. Although there exist several examples of adaptive educational games, they mostly only base the adaptation on the performance of the player, and only adapt the difficulty level or the learning content of the game. In this paper, we propose a model for a richer dynamic adaptation, in which several aspects are taken into account for providing a more personalized gaming experience to sustain the engagement of the players to the game.

**Keywords:** Educational games, Adaptive games, Real-time adaptation.

## 1 Introduction

One of the challenges in designing educational games is to come up with a game that is appealing, fun to play, and most importantly engaging; but perhaps the greatest challenge is to sustain the engagement of the player. According to several authors, e.g., [1,2], a successful game is such that its players experience the "flow state", introduced by Csikszentmihalyi [3] and meaning the state of absolute and utter engagement to an activity. It is shown that the flow state has a positive impact on learning [4] and should therefore be considered when designing educational games. Moreover, in his "Experiential Gaming Model" [2], Kiili also uses the flow theory for facilitating a positive user experience of the player, but also stresses *the importance of designing and balancing challenges in order to generate an optimal learning experience for players* (page 2). Furthermore, motivation is also considered as a key factor for reaching the flow state [5]; the game must be motivating enough for its players to keep playing it. However, in the literature, no consensus about the source of motivation in games can be found. For some [6,7], the key source of motivation is the narrative context of the game, whereas for others [5,8] the system of rewards and goals is the true cause of motivation. In either case, motivation seems to plays an important role. Similarly, in educational games, it is also recommended that an effective design should consider the motivation of the learner, in particular both intrinsic and

---

\* Supported by the Vrije Universiteit Brussel, HOA26 project: Towards Cognitive Adaptive Edu-Games.
\*\* Supported by IWT (www.iwt.be), SBO-project: Friendly ATTAC.

S. Göbel and J. Wiemeyer (Eds.): GameDays 2014, LNCS 8395, pp. 71–76, 2014.

extrinsic motivation [5, 8–10]. The two mentioned terms have been differentiated as follow: *"Intrinsic motivation pushes us to act freely, on our own, for the sake of it; extrinsic motivation pulls us to act due to factors that are external to the activity itself, like reward or threat"* (page 1) [5]. Also stimulating intrinsic motivation (in addition to stimulating extrinsic motivation) could be important in sustaining the engagement of the learner (player), especially in the case of people with low motivation for learning, since the use of extrinsic motivation may not always work for these people. However, as it is evident from its definition, the source of intrinsic motivation can be quite different from person to person. Thus, adaptation of the educational game to the individual learner could be a way to increase the intrinsic motivation. On the other hand, while at the start of the game the learner's intrinsic motivation can be good, it may (quickly) decrease during the game for all kind of reasons. Dynamically adapting the game, i.e. while the learner is playing the game rather than only adapting the game when starting the game or at a new level, could be a way to deal with varying motivation. However, achieving *effective* dynamic adaptation in games is quite challenging, and even more challenging in educational games. This is mostly due to the need of having a balance between learning and fun in these games [11, 12], and at the same time providing the correct level of challenge to the player (not under challenging but also not overburdening [2]).

In this paper, we propose a new model for dynamically adaptive educational games. The model allows for adapting an educational game based on different aspects and at different moments, in order to provide a rich personalized experience, to sustain the engagement of the learner, and thus providing a more suitable frame for experiencing the flow state. The rest of the paper is organized as follows: section 2 discusses adaptive games, section 3 introduces the proposed model, and section 4 provides conclusions and future work.

## 2   Adaptive Games

In the context of educational games, different researches on adaptation have been performed, for example, in the *ELEKTRA* project [13] the notion of micro-adaptivity is introduced to guide and support learners in acquiring knowledge by informing them, providing hints, or intervening when a misconception occurs. There are methods for predicting the actions that the player might take while playing the game and then adapting certain aspects of the game accordingly [14]. There are also methods for generating adaptive game worlds based on the players and their experience model [14].

In educational games, the adaptation of games is mostly in the form of difficulty adjustments or content adaptations, ranging from its simplest form of adjusting the difficulty level of exercises or content on each new start based on the previous performance, to dynamic adjustments based on the real-time performance. There are models that use both parameters, performance and content, for creating adaptive educational games. For example, "The Competence-based Knowledge Space Theory" [15] is a prime example of a model providing different learning paths for the same learning topic to the players based on their competencies. We agree that these type of adaptive games do indeed provide a personalized experience, but we wonder whether they also meet one of the requirements for successful learning, i.e. take into consideration that *"people learn in different ways and at different paces"*? [1] The current adaptation techniques can deal with the aspect "people learn at different paces", but not with the aspect "people learn in different ways". We argue that performance and content, although being undoubtedly important factors for adapting games, are merely two factors out of a group of factors that can be used for creating an effective learning experience in educational games.

## 3   Proposed Model

We propose a new model for dynamically adapting educational games. The overview of our model is given in Figure 1. Our model is roughly built on top of the experiential gaming model proposed by Kiili [2], which in turn is based on the flow theory [3] and the Kolb's learning style theory [16]. Based on Kiili's work, the goal of his model is to provide a link between gameplay and experiential learning. At the heart of his model lie *challenges* that should be based on educational objectives. These challenges should be appropriate for the player to sustain motivation and engagement.

In our model, similar to Kiili's, challenge is of considerable importance. As a structuring framework for defining the challenges, we opt for the *learning style model of Kolb*, which advises to go from concrete experience to reflective observation, abstract conceptualization and then active experimentation. The challenges in the game should be determined based on the educational objective of the game and Kolb's learning style theory. As an example, for a game with the educational objective of learning mathematical concepts, the first few challenges of the game would be defined based on concrete experience, then a reflective observation on the challenges should be provided to the player, then challenges on abstract conceptualization, and finally on active experimentation. Furthermore, the challenges must be tightly coupled with the game.

As the personality of the player may have an impact on how he can be motivated to play, learn, and stay engaged, our model also takes into consideration the personal traits of the learner. To model *the personality of the player*, we currently use the big five personality trait theory [17], one of the most researched and accepted theories in describing human personality. In this theory, five dimensions are used to characterize the personality of a person (Neuroticism, Extraversion, Openness to experience, Agreeableness, and Conscientiousness). The values of the big five personality traits of the learner will be used as the starting point for personalization; for instance if the player is generally an anxious (Neuroticism) person, lesser or even no temporal constraints could be considered in the game.

As we also want to give due consideration to the fact that "people learn in different ways", we also consider the *learning style* of the player. For this, we use the VARK learning style theory [18], where learners are categorized into four groups based on their learning preferences (Visual, Aural, Read/Write, or

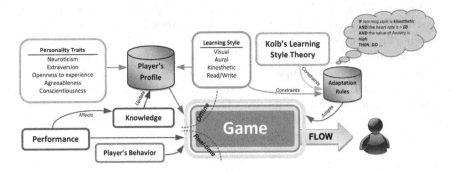

**Fig. 1.** Dynamic Adaptive Educational Game Model

Kinesthetic). The VARK learning style theory is actually an instructional theory indicating what method of instruction is going to be more appropriate for a person. For example, a person might learn better, if the learning material is presented to him/her in a more visual way (visual learning style) or if the person could kinesthetically interact with the learning objectives perhaps through gestures using for example Microsoft Kinect (kinesthetic learning style).

Furthermore, and well-accepted, the knowledge level of the player also plays an important role in the adaptation, as the learning challenges should not be too easy but also not too difficult. The knowledge level of the player can be assessed from the records of the previous performances of the player.

All three previously mentioned dimensions: knowledge, personal traits, and learning style, will be determined before the player commences playing the game, e.g., through questionnaires, or they may be predefined if the educational game targets a specific group of people (e.g., kinesthetic learners). This information will be saved in *the profile of the player* and used in each play session. Personal traits and learning style are considered to be rather stable during a given period of time (although they may change during the lifetime of a person), and therefore we consider them to be fixed during the playtime. Knowledge, on the other hand, may increase during playtime and thus, updates the profile of the player after each session. Since the mentioned three factors are used for adaptation before the player actually starts playing the game, we called this *offline adaptation*.

On the other hand, *performance* and *player's behavior* can be used in real time to dynamically adapt the game, therefore we call this *real time adaptation*. There are several elements that can be measured for determining the performance of the learner (e.g., success rate, number of errors, task completion time); similarly, there are also different elements that can be taken into account to determine the player's behavior or state (e.g., facial expression, eye gazing, speech analysis, heat rate, and attention level). Nowadays, a variety of (non-intrusive) devices exists to determine the variations in the value of these elements in real-time (e.g., high definition cameras for detecting heart rate, cameras with thermal lens for detecting anxiety, cameras with facial expression recognition). Also some devices promise to assess more than one element at the same time, e.g., Microsoft Kinect 2.0 would measure heart rate, eye gazing, and facial expressions. Based on these values, the game can be adapted in real-time to sustain the engagement of the player by trying to keep the flow state. To perform the adaptation, the adaptation engine (abstracted as part of the game component in the figure) uses a set of *adaptation rules*. Based on the inputs (offline and real-time) relevant adaptation rules will be triggered. The adaptation rules are in the form of CONDITION-ACTION rules. An example adaptation rule could be:

```
IF(learning_style=='kinesthetic' && heart_rate >60 && anxiety=='High')
THEN{ difficulty_level-=1;
      ENVIRONMENT_TEXTURE(Relaxing);
      GAME_MUSIC(Relaxing);
      IF(EXISTS(Temporal_Constraint))
      THEN{ remove(Temporal_Constraint);   } }
```

There are many aspects of a game that can be adapted, (e.g., textures of game objects, the environment, the sounds, NPC interactions). What should be adapted at a specific moment is specified by the adaptation rules. In order to determine the conditions (IF-part) and the consequences (THEN-part) of these adaptation rules, experiments and research in close collaboration with experts in psychology and pedagogy is required. Note that the adaptation of the educational material of the game should be done with respect to the Kolb's theory; Kolb's Learning style theory in fact constraints the possible adaptation rules.

## 4   Conclusion and Future Work

We started by giving the motivation for having adaptive educational games. We noticed that for most educational games the adaptation is limited to the level of difficulty. However, this does not guarantee that the player stays engaged. Personality aspects, such as the personal traits and the learning style of the player, should also be taken into consideration. Therefore, a new model for more effective adaptation of educational games is proposed. The model is based on different existing and well-accepted theories from different domains: the flow theory of Csikszentmihalyi, the learning style model of Kolb, the big five personality trait theory, and the VARK learning style theory. In addition, we propose a distinction between two types of adaptation, offline adaptation and real-time adaptation. For offline adaptation, we not only consider the current knowledge level of the player but also his personality and learning style. For the real-time adaptation, we propose to monitor not only the performance of the learner, but also the behavior (or state) of the learner. This latter becomes more and more feasible thanks to new non-intrusive technologies. Using this information, the game can be dynamically adapted so that the players not only experience the flow state, but this experience sustain for longer periods. In future work, we will examine how we can do the adaptation in order to achieve this goal and keep the perfect balance between playing and learning. This is not straight forward; there is always the chance that by performing a certain change, the experience of the user is distorted. Furthermore, it is also necessary to evaluate the suitability and effectiveness of the different theories used (flow model, VARK, Big Five, and Kolb's theory).

# References

1. Harteveld, C.: Triadic game design. Springer (2010)
2. Kiili, K.: Digital game-based learning: Towards an experiential gaming model. The Internet and Higher Education 8(1), 13–24 (2005)
3. Csikszentmihalyi, I.S.: Optimal experience: Psychological studies of flow in consciousness. Cambridge University Press (1992)
4. Webster, J., Trevino, L.K., Ryan, L.: The dimensionality and correlates of flow in human-computer interactions. Computers in Human Behavior 9(4), 411–426 (1994)
5. Denis, G., Jouvelot, P.: Motivation-driven educational game design: applying best practices to music education. In: Proceedings of the 2005 ACM SIGCHI International Conference on Advances in Computer Entertainment Technology, pp. 462–465. ACM (2005)
6. Dickey, M.D.: Three-dimensional virtual worlds and distance learning: two case studies of active worlds as a medium for distance education. British Journal of Educational Technology 36(3), 439–451 (2005)
7. Fisch, S.M.: Making educational computer games educational. In: Proceedings of the 2005 Conference on Interaction Design and Children, pp. 56–61. ACM (2005)
8. Amory, A., Naicker, K., Vincent, J., Adams, C.: The use of computer games as an educational tool: identification of appropriate game types and game elements. British Journal of Educational Technology 30(4), 311–321 (1999)
9. Jennings, M.: Best practices in corporate training and the role of aesthetics: Interviews with eight experts. In: Proceedings of the 2001 ACM SIGCPR Conference on Computer Personnel Research, pp. 215–219. ACM (2001)
10. Dondlinger, M.J.: Educational video game design: A review of the literature. Journal of Applied Educational Technology 4(1), 21–31 (2007)
11. Prensky, M.: Digital game-based learning. Computers in Entertainment (CIE) 1(1), 21 (2003)
12. Klopfer, E., Osterweil, S., Salen, K., et al.: Moving learning games forward. Education Arcade, Cambridge (2009)
13. Kickmeier-Rust, M.D., Albert, D.: Micro-adaptivity: protecting immersion in didactically adaptive digital educational games. Journal of Computer Assisted Learning 26(2), 95–105 (2010)
14. Erev, I., Roth, A.E.: Predicting how people play games: Reinforcement learning in experimental games with unique, mixed strategy equilibria. American Economic Review, 848–881 (1998)
15. Kickmeier-Rust, M.D., Peirce, N., Conlan, O., Schwarz, D., Verpoorten, D., Albert, D.: Immersive digital games: The interfaces for next-generation E-learning? In: Stephanidis, C. (ed.) Universal Access in HCI, part III, HCI 2007. LNCS, vol. 4556, pp. 647–656. Springer, Heidelberg (2007)
16. Kolb, D.A.: Learning style inventory. McBer and Company (1999)
17. Judge, T.A., Higgins, C.A., Thoresen, C.J., Barrick, M.R.: The big five personality traits, general mental ability, and career success across the life span. Personnel Psychology 52(3), 621–652 (1999)
18. Fleming, N., Baume, D.: Learning styles again: Varking up the right tree! Educational Developments 7(4) (2006)

# A Serious Game for Public Engagement in Synthetic Biology

Markus Schmidt, Olga Radchuk, and Camillo Meinhart

Biofaction, Vienna, Austria
{schmidt,radchuk,meinhart}@biofaction.com

**Abstract.** Science gamification is an alternative way of science communication aimed to enhance public engagement in the dialog between scientists and broad audiences. This approach conveys information through an informal environment where individuals are more likely to engage in new knowledge areas. One of such new areas is synthetic biology, which aims to apply engineering principles to biology and create new biological parts or systems, or re-design existing biological systems for useful purposes. Biofaction developed the educational game SYNMOD, aimed to communicate basic scientific principles of synthetic biology, in an entertaining and engaging way. The game is based on the SYNMOD project, which aimes to design and produce novel antibiotic molecules. The aim of the game is to help memorize the names and 1-letter codes of 20 standard amino acids, provide additional information about amino acids, explain the modularity of lantibiotic synthesis, and stimulate further interest to synthetic biology among players.

**Keywords.** Science gamification, synthetic biology, SYNMOD, lantibiotics, amino acids.

## 1    From Science to Science Gamification

Nowadays science is progressively getting more complicated and specific, which consistently moves it away from lay people. While the most accurate way to present the results of a scientific study is to present the study itself, it requires a considerable scientific background in both the audience and presenters, which is very often not the case. In order to overcome this problem, popularization of science needs to be applied, presenting a scientific topic in a manner that can be easily understood without pre-existing knowledge. Science communication and public engagement employ numerous approaches, including science gamification. Games can be seen as an alternative way of science communication that acts through an informal environment where individuals would be more open to engage in new knowledge areas (Torrente, Moreno-Ger, Martínez-Ortiz, & Fernandez-Manjon, 2009). Information is represented in familiar forms that individuals can relate to and enjoy, while the message is integrated naturally in a context, and communicated in a language that the target audience better understands (Whitton, 2007; Wideman, Owston, Brown, Kushniruk, Ho, & Pitts, 2007; Sharples, 2006; Sandu, & Christensen, 2011).

S. Göbel and J. Wiemeyer (Eds.): GameDays 2014, LNCS 8395, pp. 77–85, 2014.
© Springer International Publishing Switzerland 2014

The notion of gamification refers to the use of game design, mechanics and techniques to promote and enhance non-game activities, such as education, sales, or health. Its goal is to encourage people to perform tasks considered to be boring (learning, memorizing data, developing automatic technical skills, performing routine tasks etc.) by means of making these tasks more engaging, enjoyable, and motivating (Deterding, Khaled, Nacke, & Dixon, 2011).

Communication of science through a game helps players to develop a new set of mental and physical capabilities due to such characteristics of a game environment as freedom to fail, to experiment, to exert an effort, and, finally, to interpret the results of one's own activities (Gunter, Kenny, & Vick, 2008; Klopfer, Osterweil, & Salen, 2009). Further activities support a learning process: defining a goal and moving towards its accomplishment, collaborating or competing with other players, and overcoming obstacles.

Science and game design are mutually dependent on each other. A scientific approach can make games more appealing to the audience by providing a meaningful goal and a nearly real life experience. Also, games enable experimenting with the game environment to figure out the best way to achieve the goal. In a good game that players enjoy, the experiments should be rewarded in a way that stimulates further experimenting. The player should also understand what experiment is being conducted at any given time, how well it succeeds or fails, and what variables it depends on. Using this approach can bring a lot of detail to a computer game world.

According to Henson and Blake, games can educate, engage, and create space for experimentation and research (Henson, & Blake, 2011). As such, gaming has very large potential for science engagement, and the games industry needs to establish collaborations with scientists in order to creatively and technically design and represent scientific information (Facer, Joiner, Stanton, Reid, Hull, & Kirk, 2004; Murphy, 2011).

However, it is very important to maintain the balance between playability and the addition of any extra information in order to create a truly "scientific" game. Another important issue for a meaningful communication is the relevance of game design to the information being communicated. The majority of simple scientific games run into two extremes: either they represent modifications of entertaining games, which provides only superficial knowledge about the topic, or they represent interactive real scientific problems that provide almost no entertainment (Wideman et al., 2007). Very often settings of such games do not correspond to their storyline, or the activities a player is required to undertake do not have anything in common with the outcome of the game.

## 2    A Synthetic Biology Mobile Game

Synthetic biology (SB) is a new and emerging field of science and engineering. Its aim is to apply engineering principles to biology. Although SB was already mentioned 100 years ago by the French scientist Stéphane Leduc, the term was "re-invented" about a decade ago by MIT engineers who wanted to make biology easier to engineer (Campos, 2009; Campos, 2012). The most commonly used definition describes SB as the design and construction of new biological parts, devices, and systems, and the re-design of existing, natural biological systems for useful purposes. SB as an interdisciplinary field brings together experts – and their scientific cultures - from a number of different areas, most notably biology, biotechnology, genetic engineering, chemistry, nanotechnology, engineering, and informatics (IT). Applying the toolbox of engineering disciplines to biology, SB engineers attempt to realize a whole set of potential applications such as novel chemicals, pharmaceuticals, and biofuels (Schmidt, 2012).

Previous communication studies have shown that the core principles of SB are frequently omitted in traditional communication processes, such as newspapers (Kronberger et al., 2012).

The SYNMOD game is an effort of Biofaction to design an educational game that communicates some of the key scientific principles of SB but that is also entertaining, engaging, and motivating at the same time (Annex). The game was developed for mobile devices because of their constantly growing popularity and the usage not only for communication purposes. Along with entertainment applications, there is also an opportunity to promote educational experiences via mobile devices. Given that the success and popularity of a mobile application is directly related to the number of devices it can run on, we have chosen the most popular operating systems – iOS and Android.

Our approach is further supported by numerous studies devoted to the concept of mobile game-based learning (Roschelle, 2003; Collins, 2005; Sánchez, Salinas, & Sáenz, 2007; Suki, & Suki, 2007; Sharples, Arnedillo-Sánchez, Milrad, & Vavoula, 2009). According to Robertson (2011), small simple games for mobile devices are the most likely arena for future science communication. Advantages of mobile interface for the Synmod game include:

- Mobility allows users to access the contents exactly at the moment they need it without restrictions related to place or time.
- Mobile devices are perceived by the majority of people as "cool gadgets", which can motivate in particular young people to use mobile-based learning applications.
- Technology-enhanced learning stimulates motivation of players, promotes creativity, provides short and effective feedback cycles, and facilitates the development of analytic and problem-solving skills.
- Small mobile games are not too expensive to produce, can be made freely available to users and have broad reach.
- They allow a combination of gaming and scientific content.

## 2.1    Game Context

The project SYNMOD, funded by the European Science Foundation,[1] applies a comprehensive SB approach to the design and production of novel antibiotic molecules. More and more pathogenic microorganisms have become multi-drug resistant and few antibiotics remain available to combat these bugs. SYNMOD aims

---

[1] See: http://www.esf.org/coordinating-research/eurocores/
running-programmes/eurosynbio/projects-crps/synmod.html

to produce novel antibiotics through modular shuffling of existing peptide modules, thus providing an antibiotic design and production system of unusual robustness and predictability. The scientific project consisted of several steps:

- Peptide modules, obtained from peptide antibiotics (lantibiotics), were defined and re-combined in order to detect novel antibiotic activities stemming from these new combinations.
- Post-translational machinery of reduced complexity was assembled using thoroughly characterized expression elements. It was created in a way that makes it context-insensitive, i.e. suitable to be incorporated in any microorganism.
- The machinery was implemented in the bacteria *Staphylococcus carnosus*, which served as a chassis to produce preparative quantities of a variety of novel lantibiotics.
- Based on this project, Biofaction developed a computer game aimed to demonstrate how the active antibiotic assembly line works.

## 2.2 Game Objectives

The game serves as an educational tool for a target audience of high school students and others interested in synthetic biology, medicine and biology in general. Specifically, the game is designed to:

- help players memorize the names and 1-letter codes of 20 standard amino-acids;
- provide additional information on the structure, functions, interactions, and the biological role of the amino acids (accessible via the PubChem web site);
- explain the modularity of lantibiotics synthesis;
- provide a "first-hand" experience in the synthesis of biologically active molecules with real-life outcomes;
- stimulate interest to synthetic biology and motivate players to learn more about it.

## 2.3 Game Design

The game was designed by Camillo Meinhart and Markus Schmidt from Biofaction. The colaboration of a filmmaker (Camillo Meinhart) with a scientist (Markus Schmidt) enabled a gamedesign that combines entertaining qualities with scientific accuracy. The grafic design followed a previously produced animation film "The Synmod Team" (https://vimeo.com/27490490) and was also created by Camillo Meinhart.

Sound design was done by Moritz Walmueller in collaboration with Camillo Meinhart.

| | |
|---|---|
| Genre: | Puzzle |
| Game elements: | Drag-and-drop |
| Game content: | Science and humor |
| Theme: | Synthetic biology |
| Style: | Cartoon |
| Game sequence: | Simulation |
| Game taxonomy: | Non-fiction Simulation/Game |

| Player immersion: | Strategic |
| Technical form: | 2D graphic |
| Control: | Haptic |
| Number of players: | 1 player at a time |
| Distribution: | Available for free download at AppStore and Google Play |

**Key Features.** The game has two major environments: the peptide slot machine environment and the amino acid environment.

*Peptide Slot Machine Environment*

The game features 5 levels that correspond to 5 pathogenic bacteria a player has to eliminate. Bacteria are represented as cartoon "nasty bugs" that change their facial expression and sound depending on the level of efficiency of an antibiotic. The degree of efficiency of the novel antibiotics that has to be assembled in the slot machine can be 0%, 20%, 40%, 60%, 80%, and 100%, which correspond to the neutral expression in the beginning of the game, laughing at 0% efficiency, being serious at 20%, unsatisfied at 40%, angry at 60%, about-to-die at 80%, and dead at 100%.

Each new combination of peptide modules may bring additional percentage to the efficiency, but may also decrease it. A player is free to choose the mode of play – s/he can assemble all modules at first and then combine them one-by-one, or assemble them one-by-one whilst testing for efficiency.

A slot machine presented at start contains 5 wheels, 3 of them have 5 slots for peptide modules, and 2 of them – 4 slots for peptide modules and 1 empty slot each (to indicate that several antibiotics can be build up of 4 modules instead of 5). The total number of peptide modules that are used is 23, and they are the same throughout the game.

Players' controls include a "Test" button to test a newly assembled antibiotic, a "Reset" button to reset the progress in the game (both are available from the main screen), and a "Return" button to return to the main screen, available at the module-assembling screen (Fig. 1).

TEST button to apply peptide combinations

One of five different bacteria

Slot machine containing completed and uncompleted peptide modules

**Fig. 1.** Screenshot of the slot machine environment

*Amino Acid Environment*

The peptide modules for the slot machine have to be assembled in the amino acid environment. Amino acids are depicted as cartoon creatures, whose shapes remind on their function or source of origin (e.g. Lysine, which is contained in such foods as meat, eggs, milk, is depicted as a bone; Serine, which takes part in transmission of brain signals, - as a brain etc.) The game features 20 standard amino acids, 3 uncommon ones, and sulfur bonds between 2 molecules of Cysteine (called Lanthionine). Connection of two amino acids results in release of a water molecule (Fig. 2).

**Fig. 2.** Screenshot of the amino acid environment: peptide chain assembling

**Game Play.** The final goal of the game is to destroy all 5 bacteria by means of synthesizing a novel antibiotic remedy that has 100% efficiency against the given bacteria.

The start screen depicts the slot machine, a bacterium, and a pipeline that transports a synthesized antibiotic to it. Operating buttons, visible for user at this stage, include a "Test" button (upper left corner of the screen), and a "Reset" button (lower right corner of the screen). An arrow on the left side of the slot machine indicates the row, which contains peptide modules forming an antibiotic. From the beginning of the game, 5 synthesized peptide blocks are provided (1 on the second wheel and 4 on the fifth wheel). Other slots are marked with a question mark to indicate a peptide module to be assembled, or an "X" mark to indicate an empty slot.

In order to create a missing peptide module, a player is required to press any question mark, which forwards him/her to the amino acid environment where a set of amino acids is provided. The scheme of the module (represented by the shapes of amino acids) is situated in the center of the screen, with one amino acid being permanently anchored in the first position, and the rest distributed randomly over the screen. The amount of the amino acids provided corresponds to the number of empty positions in a peptide module. The only one button available for the player is "Return", situated in the lower left corner of the screen. The player is required to drag each amino acid on the place specifically assigned for it using a fingertip. Every time the player touches an amino acid, its name can be heard.

Two hints on how to place the amino acids correctly are available for the player: some of the shapes contain a 1-letter code commonly used in biology (that do not, however, correspond to the first letter of their full names); shapes of the amino acids correspond to their shapes provided in the empty positions.

Some of the peptide modules are linear, but some of them contain loops, made by sulfur bonds between 2 amino acids. Loops are being formed immediately during the game.

Upon the completion of the level (by having eliminated one type of bacteria) the slot machine re-shuffles the peptide modules and new bacterium appears immediately. In the end of the game the player receives a message: "Victory! You have successfully found a solution against all bacteria!". S/he needs to press the "OK" button, which forwards him/her to the screen with the completed slot machine and the first bacterium. In order to start the game again, the player needs to press the "Reset" button.

Time of game play required to complete one level is approximately 15-20 min; the time to complete the whole game is approximately 60 min. Upon the completion of the game, a player can reset the progress and start playing again.

# 3    Conclusion

The first version of the game is available for download at AppStore and Google Play (http://www.biofaction.com/project/synmod-mobile-game/). Further work will include the usability and playability testing of the current version of the game. The data obtained from this evaluation will be used to introduce a number of improvements in the second release of the game. Further evaluation will be conducted to determine the effectiveness of knowledge acquisition while playing the game.

# References

1. Campos, L.: That Was the Synthetic Biology That Was. In: Schmidt, M., Kelle, A., Ganguli-Mitra, A., de Vriend, H. (eds.) Synthetic Biology: The Technoscience and its Societal Consequences, pp. 5–21. Springer, Netherlands (2010)
2. Campos, L.: The BioBrick™ road. BioSocieties 7, 115–139 (2012)
3. Collins, T.G.: English Class on the Air: Mobile Language Learning With Cell Phones. In: Fifth IEEE International Conference on Advanced Learning Technologies, pp. 402–403. IEEE Press, New York (2005)
4. Deterding, S., Khaled, R., Nacke, L., Dixon, D.: Gamification: Toward a Definition. In: Proceedings of the 2011 Annual Conference Extended Abstracts on Human Factors in Computing Systems. ACM, New York (2011)
5. Facer, K., Joiner, R., Stanton, D., Reid, J., Hull, R., Kirk, D.: Savannah: Mobile Gaming and Learning? Journal of Computer Assisted Learning 20(6), 399–409 (2004)
6. Gunter, G.A., Kenny, R.F., Vick, E.H.: Taking Educational Games Seriously: Using the RETAIN Model to Design Endogenous Fantasy Into Standalone Educational Games. Educational Technology Research and Development 56(5-6), 511–537 (2008)

7. Klopfer, E., Osterweil, S., Salen, K.: Moving Learning Games Forward: Obstacles, Opportunities, and Openness. The Education Arcade, Massachusetts Institute of Technology (2009)
8. Kronberger, N., Holtz, P., Wagner, W.: Consequences of Media Information Uptake and Deliberation: Focus Groups' Symbolic Coping With Synthetic Biology. Public Understanding of Science 21(2), 174–187 (2012)
9. Murphy, C.: Why Games Work and the Science of Learning. In: Interservice, Interagency Training, Simulations, and Education Conference (2011)
10. Robertson, D.: Playing Science: Science and Video Games,
   http://refractiveindex.wordpress.com/2011/06/07/playing-science-science-and-video-games/
11. Roschelle, J.: Keynote Paper: Unlocking the Learning Value of Wireless Mobile Devices. Journal of Computer Assisted Learning 19(3), 260–272 (2003)
12. Sánchez, J., Salinas, A., Sáenz, M.: Mobile Game-Based Methodology for Science Learning. In: Jacko, J.A. (ed.) Human-Computer Interaction, Part IV, HCII 2007. LNCS, vol. 4553, pp. 322–331. Springer, Heidelberg (2007)
13. Sandu, O., Christensen, L.L.: Outrageous Outreach – Unconventional Ways of Communicating Science. Communicating Astronomy with the Public Journal 11, 22–30 (2011)
14. Schmidt, M.: Synthetic Biology: Industrial and Environmental Applications. Weinheim, Germany (2012)
15. Sharples, M.: Big Issues in Mobile Learning. Kaleidoscope, University of Nottingham (2006)
16. Sharples, M., Arnedillo-Sánchez, I., Milrad, M., Vavoula, G.: Mobile Learning. In: Balacheff, N. (ed.) Technology-Enhanced Learning: Principles and Products, pp. 233–249. Springer, Dordrecht (2009)
17. Suki, N.M., Suki, N.M.: Mobile Phone Usage for m-Learning: Comparing Heavy and Light Mobile Phone Users. Campus-Wide Information Systems 24(5), 355–365 (2007)
18. Torrente, J., Moreno-Ger, P., Martínez-Ortiz, I., Fernandez-Manjon, B.: Integration and Deployment of Educational Games in e-Learning Environments: The Learning Object Model Meets Educational Gaming. Educational Technology & Society 12(4), 359–371 (2009)
19. Whitton, N.: Motivation and Computer Game Based Learning. In: Proceedings of the Australian Society for Computers in Learning in Tertiary Education, Singapore (2007)
20. Wideman, H.H., Owston, R.D., Brown, C., Kushniruk, A., Ho, F., Pitts, K.C.: Unpacking the Potential of Educational Gaming: A New Tool for Gaming Research. Simulation & Gaming 38(1), 10–30 (2007)

# Appendix: Our Way to Translate Science to Lay People

| Real Science | Our game |
|---|---|

Real Science column — amino acid chemical structures:

gly g Glycine · ala a Alanine

arg r Arginine · asn n Asparagine · asp d Aspartic Acid

cys c Cysteine · gln q Glutamine · glu e Glutamic Acid

his h Histidine · ile i Isoleucine · leu l Leucine

lys k Lysine · met m Methionine · phe f Phenylalanine

pro p Proline · ser s Serine · thr t Threonine

trp w Tryptophan · tyr y Tyrosine · val v Valine

Our game column — character figures:

Alanine · Arginine · Asparagine · Aspartic acid

Cysteine · Glutamine · Glutamic acid · Glycine

Histidine · Isoleucine · Leucine · Lysine

Methionine · Phenylalanine · Proline · Serine

Threonine · Tryptophan · Tyrosine · Valine

*Only in connection with Sulfur-bridges:* · 2-Aminobutyric acid · Dehydro-butyrine · Dehydro-alanine

**Nisin**

| Modul | A | B | C | hinge | D-E/tail |
|---|---|---|---|---|---|
| Gal | IASKFLC | TPGCARTG | * | * | SFNSTCC |
| Nis | ITSISLC | TPGCK | TGALMGC | NMK | TATCNCSIHVSK |
| Mut | FKSWSFC | SLGTGVKNP | | NMKK | SFNSTCC |
| Subl | | TIGCGGG | | NMKV | |
| Pep5 | RASVKQC | | | PMK | TVACKGKNGCK |
| Epic | KATRQVC | | | NVK | |
| Epil | KVSKKYC | | | NMS | |
| LcnA2 | YISTNTC | PTTKCT | | NK | |
| Plnw/B | AASIAVC | | | K | |
| Acta | | SSGNVC | | G | |
| LacS | | | | FKY | SAKHHC |

TEST ICE

# Story Maker

Diomar Rockenbach[1], João B. Mossmann[1,2,3], Eliseo Reategui[2], Marta Bez[1],
Marsal Branco[3], and Luciana Meyrer[3]

[1] Feevale University, Computer Science, Novo Hamburgo, Brasil
{diomar,mossmann,martabez}@feevale.br
[2] Federal University of Rio Grande do Sul (UFRGS), PGIE, Porto Alegre, Brasil
{eliseoreategui,mossmann}@gmail.com
[3] Feevale University, Digital Games, Novo Hamburgo, Brasil
{mossmann,marsal,lucianasmeyrer}@feevale.br

**Abstract.** This paper presents a system that supports digital storytelling, in an attempt to assist teachers in literacy development with a tool that is distinct from traditional teaching methods. Game elements were introduced in the system as a way to engage students in writing tasks. A script based on the Hero's Journey was employed as a main guideline to structure the students' stories. An experiment with four students was carried out to evaluate the system's usability and the users' subjective satisfaction. A Think-Aloud protocol was used to collect data with participants. Results showed that in most of the users' answers (86%) a positive feedback was given, both for the game's ease of use as well as for its application to support the storytelling process.

**Keywords:** Serious Games, Storytelling, Literacy.

## 1    Introduction

Among technologies able to promote collaboration and contribute with learning processes, digital games stand out. Such artifacts have become part of everyday life [1], with an increasingly important role in Education [2]. As McGonigal [3] points out, nowadays children are accustomed to the digital world and experience it in a very different way from previous generations. Because of the ease of access to sophisticated games and virtual worlds, they consider natural the high involvement that games provide, as well as the active participation required in such type of activity. This project proposes a game to support literacy by incorporating ludic and collaborative practices which may engage students in writing activities. This article presents the game developed as part of this research, as well as experiments to evaluate its interface. The game proposes the usage of the Hero's Journey [4] as a basic structure for the development of narratives by students.

## 2    Related Work

One of the main arguments for the use of games in education is that they can influence the user's motivation, creating learning conditions in which motivation, interest, and affection are key elements [5].

S. Göbel and J. Wiemeyer (Eds.): GameDays 2014, LNCS 8395, pp. 86–91, 2014.

In the project described here, we propose a game to support literacy, a concept associated to the individual's ability to make competent use of reading and writing [6]. In the late 1990s Ferreiro and Teberosky [7] advocated that literacy could not take place through mechanical and repetitive practices without taking into account the student's background and context. Proficiency in literacy nowadays calls for higher standards of reading comprehension and analysis [8].

One of the pedagogical strategies to address literacy development in the classroom is storytelling, an approach that contributes to the improvement of oral language, reading comprehension, and writing [9]. And as storytelling connects both the listener and the teller it also promotes social interaction, which is seen by researchers as an important aspect in literacy instruction, being based on people's desire to talk to others.

Different research efforts have been made towards the development of digital tools and strategies for storytelling. Robin [10] discusses how digital storytelling has been used in Education and propose a theoretical framework explaining how it can engage teachers and students in writing practices. Sylvester et al [11] have shown how digital storytelling can assist students with learning difficulties in writing. Garcia and Rossiter [12] showed how digital storytelling could be exploited as a pedagogical strategy. Although these are relevant initiatives towards the development of literacy practices, none of these projects has focused on the association of gaming components to a tool to support storytelling.

The field of Education has also seen the introduction of different game platforms that allow teachers and students to develop their own games. e-Adventure [13] is an example of this kind of platform, which allows the development of 2D digital games and simulations that can be executed in web-based environments. StoryTec [14] is another example, being more tailored to the development of non-linear stories. Teatrix [15] is yet another example of learning environment which enables students to develop their stories, but this time in a collaborative way in a 3D platform. In our project, we have been more concerned with the use of a story structure based on the Hero's Journey. We have also focused on the possibility of allowing teachers to define a central theme to the stories, which has been implemented with the use of a text mining software that extracts relevant concepts from texts provided by the teachers in the setting up of a storytelling activity. The next section presents our game proposal in more detail.

# 3    Story Maker

The proposal of Story Maker is to be an educational game focused on storytelling as a way to support literacy. The building mode of these narratives is organized around the Hero's Journey, a narrative structure created by Joseph Campbell in 1949 [4], in which the hero passes through twelve distinct events. Although many current success sagas have used the Hero's Journey, not all stories fit perfectly on the model proposed by Campbell. Still, in general they end up following the steps suggested by the author, omitting one or another event from the list.

Inside Story Maker, the structure of a narrative is composed by chapters. Among the chapters that compose it, some were set to have a bigger importance: Common world, Call to Adventure, Tests, Allies and Enemies, Maximum Probation and Reward. In addition, it was also established that the story should have a hero and a villain.

For the structuring of these chapters, the teacher initially defines a guiding theme about which students will write their stories. Based on this theme and on a text provided by the teacher, a text mining tool is used to find a list of relevant terms [16]. From the extracted terms, a graph is generated linking them according to the way they appear in the text. These results are then used to find images from the internet in an automated way. These images, as shown in the example of Figure 1 (A) with the Mario character, can be used later by the student in the structuring of their stories. At this stage, the teacher has the possibility to select the most appropriate ones to be used in the students' stories. A database of images is then created to be used with the students when they work in the writing of their stories.

(A) Images taken from the teacher's use of the system          (B) Chapter of the Hero's definition

**Fig. 1.** Images taken from Story Maker

Each chapter can contain from one to all images in the selected image base. The main goal behind this is to guide the creation of the stories and even inspire the users in their writing. All chapters have the same structure, but besides the name of the chapter, the system displays an explanation, in the upper right corner, describing what needs to be developed. Figure 1 (B) shows the first stage of the game, in which the student selected two images of characters that will be part of his/her story. Following the Hero's Journey structure, this time the profile of each of the characters is described. Each narrative can be viewed and evaluated by the teacher or by other students, allowing them to collaborate with the development of each other's stories by posting comments and rating them.

## 4    Story Maker Evaluation

With the goal of evaluating the game, we conducted a review process, which had as main purpose to assess the following aspects:

- Usability: we sought to identify whether the developed interface presented usability problems;
- Subjective satisfaction: an evaluation of the overall satisfaction of users, seeking their views on the strengths and weaknesses of the proposed system.

A workshop was held for the participants to use and evaluate the system, in order to explain how the tests would be performed.

## 4.1  Methodology

A workshop was held with the purpose of explaining the project, how the tests would be performed as well as to collect the data needed to evaluate the system. Four undergraduate students in technology participated in the experiment. The tests were carried out with a computer with internet access, two filming cameras, one being positioned behind the user to capture the computer screen and the other positioned in front of the user, just behind the monitor in order to capture his/her face, recording facial expressions. A microphone was also used to capture verbal and non-verbal user utterances.

Then, a particular activity was given to participants so that they could use the system to create a story. In this phase, a Think-Aloud [17] protocol was used in order to collect data about users' perceptions about the use of the system.

In the experiment carried out, users were instructed to speak aloud about every action and decision they thought before and after performing a task. Concluding the assessment, each participant was given a form with questions about the ease of use of the software, as well as questions about the overall user satisfaction. Participants were also asked to signal strengths and weaknesses of the proposed system.

## 4.2  Results Evaluation

Initially, the data collected in the experiment was analyzed regarding the system's interface and its usability, based on tests performed with four participants. The questionnaire had yes/no questions regarding different aspects of the system, each of them detailed below.

### Interface and Usability
The questionnaire's first two questions dealt with, respectively, the ease use and learnability of the software. The results related to the tool ease of use were satisfactory, with positive comments from all participants. With regards to its learnability, some participants reported having some difficulty at first. However, after exploring the software a little more, they managed to better understand the way it operated.

The third question asked if the software could make the storytelling process more productive. All participants responded positively. These positive reviews can be confirmed through the Think-Aloud Protocol recorded videos and by the observations made during these tests, where it was observed that all participants started writing their stories fairly fast, using the Hero's Journey as an organization strategy.

The fourth issue concerned the structure of the narrative based on the Hero's Journey, inquiring if the participants encountered difficulties in understanding and using this structure. None of the participants reported any type of difficulty in using this structure. It was possible to verify from observations of the tests, and also from the stories generated, that all participants understood the structure and didn't have any difficulty in its use. Question number 5 asked participants about the use of images as a way of suggesting a topic. Three participants reported that "it is good because it serves as a source of inspiration". Two of them said "it is good because it helps guide the narrative." These statements can be confirmed by two factors: it is possible to note in the recorded videos that the participants relied completely on the images to start writing their stories, using them as an inspiration source and also as a way of guiding their writing. The elaborated stories explicitly involved elements from the images used. In general, the results obtained were satisfactory since in the total number of answers given by the four subjects (24 responses), 86% were considered positive.

**Subjective Satisfaction**
The first question inquired participants about the tool's strong points. Some highlighted responses were: *"the software guides the storytelling process using the Hero's Journey"*, *"the software helps you not to miss any detail and build a good narrative model"*, *"initial inspiration"* and *"the use of images serves as an inspiration factor"*.

The second issue was related to the software negative aspects, highlighting comments such as: "too few images to choose from", "inability to enlarge the pictures" and "best advice on how to use the application appear on the home screen." These comments are important even though most of them are already under study to be incorporated in the new versions of the tool.

The third question asked if the software could be used as an educational tool. All participants answered affirmatively. One of the responses was highlighted: "Yes, because with this software it is possible to keep the focus in the story being developed, which may be useful in tasks such as children's text and literacy development, relating images and writing.". The fourth question asked participants whether they would use the software if it were available. All of them said yes. The fifth and final question asked participants' to give their opinion about the software. Comments such as "the project is truly innovative," "I consider it a software with great potential," "interesting proposal" stood out.

## 5     Conclusion

This paper proposed a tool to guide students in digital storytelling by using a narrative structure that is known as the Hero's Journey. Regarding the use of games by children and adolescents, it is known that such tools involve challenges that lead users to interactive practices with which they are already familiar.

The tool proposed here has been developed based on the use of a text mining system to extract relevant terms from texts that serve as a starting point for the storytelling process. Among the main results, we understand that the tool provided users with relevant support in the storytelling process. The use of the Hero's Journey as a main narrative structure was also judged positively by the participants. As future work, the developed tool is being expanded to become a social network. This should allow more exchanges among its users.

# References

1. Zichermann, G., Cunningham, C.: Gamification by Design - Implementing Game Mechanics in Web and Mobile Apps. O'Reilly (2011)
2. Klopfer, E., Osterweil, S., Salen, K.: Moving Learning Games Forward: Obstacles, Opportunities and Openness. The Education Arcade/MIT (2009)
3. McGonigal, J.: Reality Is Broken: Why Games Make Us Better and How They Can Change the World. Penguin Books, New York (2011)
4. Campbell, J.: The Hero with a Thousand Faces, 3rd edn. Princeton University Press, Princeton (1973)
5. Aldrich, C.: The complete guide to simulations and serious games. Pfeiffer, San Francisco (2009)
6. Prensky, M.: Digital Game-Based Learning. Paragon House, St. Paul (2007)
7. Ferreíro, E., Teberosky, A.: Ana. Psicogênese da língua escrita, p. 300. Artmed, Porto Alegre (1999) (in Portuguese)
8. Neuman, S.B., Copple, C., Bredekamp, S.: Learning to read and write: Developmentally appropriate practices for young children. National Association for the Education of Young Children, Washington, DC (2000)
9. Miller, S., Pennycuff, L.: The Power of Story: Using Storytelling to Improve Literacy Learning. Journal of Cross-Disciplinary Perspectives in Education 1(1), 36–43 (2008)
10. Robin, B.R.: Digital Storytelling: A Powerful Technology Tool for the 21st Century Classroom. Theory Into Practice 47, 220–228 (2008)
11. Sylvester, R., Greenidge, W.: Digital Storytelling: Extending the Potential for Struggling Writers. The Reading Teacher 63(4), 284–295 (2009)
12. Garcia, P., Rossiter, M.: Digital Storytelling as Narrative Pedagogy. In: Gibson, D., Dodge, B. (eds.) Proceedings of Society for Information Technology & Teacher Education International Conference, pp. 1091–1097. AACE, Chesapeake (2010)
13. Blanco, A., Torrente, J., Fernández-Manjón, B.: Integrating educational video games in LAMS: The <e-Adventure> Experience. In: Proceedings of the 5th International LAMS Conference (2010), http://lamsfoundation.org/lams2010sydney/papers.htm (accessed in January 2014)
14. Göbel, S., Salvatore, L., Konrad, R.A., Mehm, F.: StoryTec: A Digital Storytelling Platform for the Authoring and Experiencing of Interactive and Non-linear Stories. In: Spierling, U., Szilas, N. (eds.) ICIDS 2008. LNCS, vol. 5334, pp. 325–328. Springer, Heidelberg (2008)
15. Prada, R., Machado, I., Paiva, A.: TEATRIX: Virtual Environment for Story Creation. In: Gauthier, G., VanLehn, K., Frasson, C. (eds.) ITS 2000. LNCS, vol. 1839, pp. 464–473. Springer, Heidelberg (2000)
16. Reategui, E., Klemann, E., Finco, M.: Using a Text Mining Tool to Support Text Summarization. In: IEEE International Conference on Advanced Learning Technologies, Roma, Itália (2012)
17. Ericsson, K., Simon, H.: Protocol Analysis: Verbal Reports as Data. The MIT Press, Cambridge (1993)

# Teaching the Achiever, Explorer, Socializer, and Killer – Gamification in University Education

Carsten Fuß, Tim Steuer, Kevin Noll, and André Miede*

htw saar – Hochschule für Technik und Wirtschaft des Saarlandes, Germany
andre.miede@htwsaar.de

**Abstract.** Modern students have ubiquitous access to mobile devices for communication, entertainment, and other purposes. In addition, most students are avid players of either (or both) digital and other kinds of games. Thus, university lecturers (and school teachers as well) regularly face the challenge of competing with games and other entertainment content about their students' attention, often even during class. In this paper, we propose a concept for the gamification of university education and demonstrate a prototype implementing this concept. Both the concept and the prototype serve as the first step for further research towards an integrated gamifaction approach and measuring its impact.

## 1  Introduction

*Gamification* can be described as the transfer of (video) game elements into daily life and situations outside the virtual playground – the underlying idea is to provide additional motivation for people to perform tasks, e. g., at work or at school [1]. In order to achieve this, gamification is based on general concepts found in (video) games such as gaining experience or sharing one's own knowledge and ideas with other people. This is the base for new visions, for communication with unknown people due to newly discovered similarities during play, and for the motivation to keep players performing tasks they consider not as interesting as playing a video game. For example, this approach uses rewards to keep people playing and uses the natural desire of humanity for games to their advantage. Therefore, gamification can have a serious impact on students and lecturers by integrating game elements into the university workday, thus, improving both learning and teaching. There are several successful examples for gamification already influencing our life such as Stack Overflow or Duolingo.[1] [2]

A common ground of all these ideas is the introduction of motivating, often funny elements into more or less boring, ordinary tasks that before were branded as musts, not as wants. Thereby, the players are given playful reasons for doing things, e. g., they are challenged as much as possible and offered small, reachable goals they really want to achieve on their own (and not based on the daily chore

---

* Corresponding author.

[1] http://www.stackoverflow.com and http://www.duolingo.com

S. Göbel and J. Wiemeyer (Eds.): GameDays 2014, LNCS 8395, pp. 92–99, 2014.

to learn, to work, or to earn money) [3]. Furthermore, learning is considered to be more effective when it is fun and an enjoyable experience.

The goal of this *demonstration paper* is to introduce a gamification prototype for university education and its underlying concepts. It does not aim at replacing traditional lectures and exames but encouraging students to be more involved in their fields of study and facilitating the creation of learning communities.

Because of the space constraints, additional material such as screenshots etc. of the prototype are provided via a companion website:

http://www.miede.de/gamedays2014/

The remainder of this paper is structured as follows: Section 2 gives an overview of important underlying gamification concepts. The key points of our general gamification approach and its prototypical implementation are described in Section 3. Section 4 compares our work with other, already existing projects and Section 5 concludes the paper with a summary and outlook.

## 2   Underlying Concepts

Our gamification approach is based on two basic concepts, Bartle's taxonomy and Fogg's Behavior Model, which are briefly outlined in the following.

According to *Bartle's taxonomy*, most players of video games belong to one of four main groups of player types: the achiever, the explorer, the socializer, and the killer. All four groups play the same game for totally different reasons. [4]

The first type of player, the so-called *achiever*, is looking for a challenge and wants to beat the game by not losing too much or by not winning too easily. This type of player wants a well-balanced game with the opportunity to experience positive results very often. In comparison, the *socializer* wants to make friends and to meet new people through shared interests besides winning the game. Therefore, the socializer wants to enjoy the game in groups and wants to be able to let other players be part of his world. The complete opposite is the *killer*, who is not satisfied with just winning the game. He wants to impress others with his skills, e. g., by letting other people lose. The last type of player is the *explorer*, who wants to explore an unknown world, discovering all of its secrets. He expects many collectibles and reasons to look left and right while playing and trying to reach the final (game) goal. [4,5]

The other basic concept used is *Fogg's Behavior Model* which describes the reasons to play a game. It is divided into the three core elements *trigger*, *motivation*, and *ability*. The trigger describes an effect, letting the player know that he has to do a specific action right now. The role of the motivation can be represented in the form of a reward or achievement, giving the player a reason to invest time into the game. The final component is the ability, making it possible for the player to perform the wanted action, i. e., not frustrating him with impossible tasks. According to Fogg, a game concept is successful if it combines these elements, creating a new high of motivation based on pairs of opposites such as pleasure/pain, hope/fear, and social acceptance/rejection. [6,7]

As we have seen, gamification is already successfully in use and also a promising approach to be introduced into the life of students. On the one hand, many in the last two generations grew up with video games being a big part of their lives, so probably most of them are already familiar with this concept. On the other hand, education is an even bigger part of our lives, however, often considered to be not as attractive as playing games. Of course, there is no way to exchange "pure" learning by an enjoyable alternative that teaches you the same, but it can be helpful to to have fun with your work. Thus, our gamification concept is based on the idea to combine these two big halves into a whole.

With the two concepts described above in mind, we decided to introduce gamification into the working day of university students. Therefore, we started the project to develop a gamification concept and an app-based prototype in order to provide students with an addition to the current learning approaches.

## 3    Gamification Concept and Prototype

### 3.1    Concept Outline

The core of the gamification concept is solving *tasks* that are linked to university topics. For now, the focus is on multiple choice tasks, offering either (four) written answers or image answers to be selected. We are also working on "full-text answers" which are requesting the player to insert a complete answer of his own.

Several tasks with similar topics and difficulty are grouped to *lessons*. By starting a lesson, the player has to complete all contained tasks in a row. By cancelling, he has to retry from the beginning next time. If all answers of the player were successful, he passed the lesson. A couple of lessons are combined to *skills*, solved by finishing all contained lessons. The skills are organized in a *skill tree* as known from, e. g., role playing games, that are divided into different levels depending on their difficulty to cover dependencies. The players have an overview about different skill trees to solve. Every skill tree represents a subject which is part of the players' studies. At the beginning of a skill tree, the player can only access the skills from the first level, but he is able to unlock new skills by solving the required linked skills.

In addition to advancing within the skill tree, the player receives *credits* for solving tasks. These are an in-game currency, needed to buy *items* like *experience multipliers* for boosting their effectiveness in the game. Also, players collect *experience points* determining the level of the player (these are scaled by the maximum of possible/reachable experience). When a new *experience level* is reached, the player's *avatar*, which can be selected at the beginning of the game and which represents the player, will change its appearance, i. e., based on the experience level and the already unlocked parts of the skill tree. So far, the avatars show several comic animals like a turtle, lobster, sloth, or alpaca.

Also, the player can choose a *group* to participate in, i. e., forming different teams that compete based on their members' performance. For example, the groups represent classic rivalries between operating system users such as Windows vs. Linux vs. Mac or between different fields of study such as business administration vs. computer science vs. architecture.

Furthermore, *achievements* can be obtained by completing *quests* not directly linked to tasks. Some examples to receive achievements are solving the first skill tree, collecting a special amount of credits, or reaching a special amount of experience points.

The *rankings* of both players and their different groups can be seen in high-score tables. A group's highscore collects the experience points from all users being a member of this group and ranks them by this amount, i. e., all players of the group against each other and different groups against each other. In addition, the user highscore not only displays the ranking of a single player, it also shows a hint for players with just a few more or less points in order to identify other students with similar progress.

The player profile stores and visualizes the collected credits, experience, the group memberships, and (optional) personal information. Furthermore, it displays the current state of the player's avatar. Inside the profile, a list of all achievements can be found together with the information whether they have already been unlocked or not.

Another import point is the creation and organisation of the tasks. All tasks, lessons, skills, and skill trees are created by a selection of lecturers and their teams. These persons are (hopefully constantly) adding new ones and updating the existing ones. Also, they take care of structuring the different elements and of determining their difficulty, i. e., their value for the students' progress in terms of credits, experience, and so on.

## 3.2   Implementing the Concept

The two key points during the implementation of the rough concept were on the one hand, realizing the gamification elements described above in order to keep the students enjoying the "game", and on the other hand, achieving an instructive character of the application in order to create a learning benefit for the players.

A first point was making the game attractive for the four types of players. Therefore, we created a major factor for everyone of them to support their interests. At first, for all types, there is an almost endless game due to the continuously growing and updating content. Especially for the *achiever*, it is interesting, that he can find tasks in all difficulties from easy to very hard. Additionally, he has further motivation from the fact, that he will lose neither credits nor experience points by making mistakes with a normal playthrough, so he can only win.

The *killer's* main point of interest will be the highscore, i. e., where he can monitor his success over the rest of the students. Additional elements are already envisioned, e. g., game concepts like a duel, where the killer will be directly able to reap points from his "victims". From a didactic point of view at an university, "killer" elements have to be introduced and evaluated very carefully, of course.

The motivation for the *socializer* results in two points: Firstly, he can already connect to others by checking their profiles, i. e., identifying students with similar

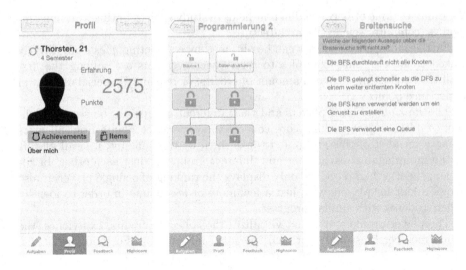

**Fig. 1.** Selected screenshots of the implemented prototype

skills and/or interests. Furthermore, he can cooperate and support teammates either inside the game or directly in real-life by assisting them in their daily study. Secondly, in the highscore, he can find out which other players are on the same level as he is. As a combination of these two features, he can easily find people he could effectively work with, who can support him or who he can be helpful for.

At last, the *explorer* should be interested in the different collectibles he can get, the mass of skills he can master, and the experience he can earn. An addition attraction for him could be secret lessons with totally different content and special achievements. These are planned for further expansions which are not triggered by a simple playthrough, but hidden behind a funny or unorthodox usage patterns.

Another key element was the integration of "Fogg's Behavior Model". The first part, the *ability* to perform a task is mainly implemented through two game mechanisms. First, there is a hierarchical skill tree that supports a step by step knowledge gain without confronting the player with too difficult tasks too early. Second, the player solves always a small group of tasks (a lesson) instead of a single one for a better memory of the learned facts.

The second part of Fogg's model, the *trigger*, is currently represented by showing the player the passed tasks in a row with the next challenges. So, as long as the player does not finish all of them, there is always the annoying view of an uncompleted skill tree or an uncompleted lesson list. Conceptual but not implemented yet is a notifcation system that reminds the player to do some lessons in order to maintain his position in the highscore table or to fulfil the learning workload of the semester.

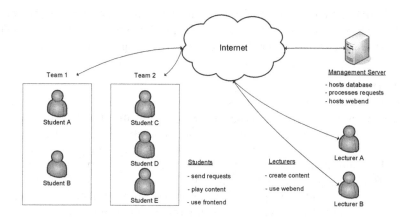

**Fig. 2.** Schematic overview of the participating entities

The *motivation* for the player is represented through the rewards he will earn in a short time, e. g., gaining experience and credits for finishing one single lesson or by having always the possibility to get a novel achievement never seen before. Also he will see his progress in unlocking new skills and the chance to compare this progress with the one of other students.

There are also some general elements improving the acceptance of the game, e. g., the fun factor based on special unlockable skills. These can be tasks with a sense of humor such as questions testing your "nerd wisdom" or your knowledge about famous quotations. Possible are also interactive tasks such as a walk-through of the university by searching for important room numbers or locating notable objects. Last but not least, QR-code-based challenges, riddles, or tasks inspired by geocaching could be included for variety purposes as well.

A last point is the straightforwardness of the app, because the user plays a kind of quiz game known to all of us. By simple controls using the touchpad of a mobile device, i. e., just clicking a button, there is not much to learn about the user interface (and, thus, not much to do wrong).

Figure 1 shows selected screenshots of the implemented prototype.

### 3.3   Technological Architecture

The application is designed as a classic client-server model, clients being apps for both iOS and Android smartphones and a server hosting the backend existing of a database, the Web frontend, and the public websites. A PostgreSQL database is used to store all content, including the users, their personal statistics, and all tasks, communicating with the backend that is realized in Grails, delivering the needed information to either the apps or the Web frontend via JSON. The internal part of the Web frontend is used for administrative work and for managing the tasks. The purpose of the other part of the Web frontend is providing general information about the app and offering downloadable versions. The app itself, the most important component for the player, is the way to complete tasks, checking the highscore, and to personalize the player's virtual presence (profile). Figure 2 gives a schematic overview of the participating entities.

## 4  Related Work

There are several projects focussing on gamification in an university context. These university-related projects have in common, that they usually try to encourage the students to do more for their field of study or that they try to support the building of different student communities for learning or social networking. However, comparing these projects shows that while they share the same intention they differ clearly in their target groups as well as to what extent they try to enhance the students' life with gamification concepts.

Comparing the work of *Fitz-Walter et al.* [8] with our work shows for example some common factors. Both projects are based on an mobile implementation for smart phones aiming for a as large as possible pervasiveness among the target group. Their game concept includes also an achievement system with easy to reach achievements in the first stages of the game and more difficult achievements in the later stages of the game. On the other hand, while their system is almost completely based on the achievement system, our project encompasses more game mechanics like skill trees, highscores, and group dynamics. In addition the target group of both systems differs also, while Fitz-Walter et al. aim for fresh students in their orientation phase, we aim for all students in our field of study.

Considering the work of *Iosup and Epema* [9], both their and our project are primary designed for enhancing the learning motivation of students with different game mechanics. In addition some of these game mechanics overlap, e.g., the point systems or unlocking content. Nevertheless, there are also large differences in the target group. While Iosup and Epema' work is fully integrated in just a single university level course about cloud computing, our work is an additional channel for learning and repeating content for a variety of courses.

In addition, the approach of *Preston* [10] also uses gamification, offering every student a mobile game application. While this application is also intended to improve the learning skills of the students and to encourage positive behaviour like socializing, it uses the location of the player and is only usable if the player is on campus. Our system in contrast, is usable from wherever the player has an internet connection. Moreover, the system of Preston is heavily story-based trying to increase the players' immersion. Our system utilizes other game elements such as highscores or achievements, thus, focussing rather on a game that is enjoyable in short time intervals (without an immersive storyline).

## 5  Summary and Outlook

In this paper, we showed a gamification approach for university education utilizing Bartle's taxonomy and Fogg's Behavior Model and its prototypical implementation as an app for both iOS and Android smartphones. In total, the implemented prototype indicates that the explained concepts are working and there is both a demand for and acceptance of such an application. We already launched a beta phase, where several students participated. Feedback from students and lecturers was generally positive, as the prototype introduced a new source of motivation for the fields of study represented in the game and, thus, created a bigger interest for the material itself. It also indicates that there can exist teamwork along with competition.

However, as our gamification concept is still in the early stages and the prototype is an initial proof-of-concept, there is a lot of work to do refining the game mechanics, designing suitable tasks and rewards, and balancing everything to be used with real-size groups of students. Furthermore, we are going to add more features known from social networks (or even their integration) in order to improve the communication between students and enabling the creation of virtual learning groups. This will also enable novel game modes such as duels, quiz competitions, or even tasks that can only be solved in teams.

**Acknowledgments.** The concept and prototype were developed as part of a second year's bachelor course in computer science. The authors would like to thank Christian Backes, Marius Fiedler, Thorsten Kober, and Benedikt Schmidt for their substantial help with developing the prototype. Furthermore, many thanks go to Laura Lücke for creating the avatars.

# References

1. Deterding, S., Khaled, R., Nacke, L., Dixon, D.: Gamification: Toward a Definition. In: CHI 2011 Gamification Workshop Proceedings (2011)
2. Marczewski, A.: Gamification: A Simple Introduction. Andrzej Marczewski (2012)
3. Kapp, K.M.: The Gamification of Learning and Instruction: Game-based Methods and Strategies for Training and Education. John Wiley & Sons (2012)
4. Bartle, R.: Hearts, Clubs, Diamonds, Spades: Players Who suit MUDs (1996), http://www.mud.co.uk/richard/hcds.htm
5. Zichermann, G., Cunningham, C.: Gamification by Design: Implementing Game Mechanics in Web and Mobile Apps. O'Reilly Media (2011)
6. Fogg, B.: BJ Fogg's Behavior Model (2009), http://www.behaviormodel.org
7. Fogg, B.: A Behavior Model for Persuasive Design. In: Proceedings of the 4th International Conference on Persuasive Technology (2009)
8. Fitz-Walter, Z., Tjondronegoro, D., Wyeth, P.: Orientation Passport: Using Gamification to Engage University Students. In: Proceedings of the 23rd Australian Computer-Human Interaction Conference, pp. 122–125. ACM (2011)
9. Iosup, A., Epema, D.: On the Gamification of a Graduate Course on Cloud Computing. In: The International Conference for High Performance Computing, Networking, Storage and Analysis. IEEE (2013)
10. Preston, J.A.: Gamification of College Life (2013), http://www.spsu.edu/cte/publications/publications2013/cte_publication_06.pdf

All online references in this paper were last accessed and validated in January 2014.

# Social Integration of Stroke Patients through the Multiplayer Rehabilitation Gaming System

Martina Maier[1], Belén Rubio Ballester[1], Esther Duarte[2],
Armin Duff[1], and Paul F.M.J. Verschure[1,3]

[1] Laboratory of Synthetic, Perceptive, Emotive and Cognitive Systems (SPECS),
Universitat Pompeu Fabra, Barcelona, Spain
[2] Parc de Salut Mar. Hospital del Mar / Hospital de l'Esperança, Barcelona, Barcelona, Spain
[3] Institució Catalana de Recerca i Estudis Avançats (ICREA), Barcelona, Spain
paul.verschure@upf.edu

**Abstract.** Stroke is a leading cause of serious long-term disability in adults (Go et al, 2013). The impact of stroke induced impairments goes beyond the mere loss of motor abilities. The psychosocial implications caused by changes in performance of the activities of daily living have to be considered in modern rehabilitation processes since they do influence the potential outcome. From the perspective of traditional rehabilitation it is difficult to directly address these social factors. Here we propose to capitalize on a rising trend in rehabilitation to deploy virtual reality environments in order to overcome this limitation. By creating a multiplayer game that enhances performance of the patient through an adaptive mapping methodology, we compensate for motor impairments and allow the patient to interact with other participants on an equal level. We propose that this approach influences psychosocial dynamics as it changes the participant's mutual perception. We conducted a psychosocial study to gain insight into the patients' social environment and tested the system in two at home experiments. The results suggest that our system is able to equalize a healthy and disabled player and benefits the social interaction.

## 1 Introduction

Stroke leaves survivors mostly with serious long-term impairments that reduce the ability to act, communicate and perform activities of daily living. These physical disabilities also affect the relation and interaction patients have with their social environment (Beth & William, 1999). On the other hand the social environment of the patient plays an important amplifying role in the rehabilitation process (Pellerin, Rochette, & Racine, 2011). Modern rehabilitation attempts should therefore not only focus on physical recovery but also address psychological consequences like social isolation or lower contentment with life. Virtual reality (VR) environments are currently seen to be useful rehabilitation tools to address challenges that could not been solved with previous technologies and methods (Jack et al., 2001; Sandlund, Mcdonough, & Häger-Ross, 2009; Verschure, 2011). Present virtual rehabilitation programs and serious games seem to focus often on regaining the patient's motor

S. Göbel and J. Wiemeyer (Eds.): GameDays 2014, LNCS 8395, pp. 100–114, 2014.

function only and neglect other implications related to the social interaction with the environment. In this study we explore the potential of a VR-system to incorporate the social dynamics into the rehabilitation process (Cameirao, Badia, Oller, & Verschure, 2010). An adaptive mapping diminishes the differences in motor performance between a disabled and a healthy player. Incorporated into a multiplayer game we aim to positively influence the social interaction between stroke patients and their informal caregivers and change their mutual perception.

## 1.1    Importance and Role of Social Environment in Stroke Rehabilitation

Since stroke patients are left with physical and cognitive impairments, they face radical changes in the performance of daily activities and their social roles. These so called life habits or Activities of Daily Living (ADL) ensure the person's wellbeing in society and depend on the social environment the person is in (Di Loreto, Van Dokkum, Gouaich, & Laffont, 2011). After an acquired brain injury like a stroke the social environment needs to undergo a structural change and redistribute the social roles (Ryan, Wade, Nice, Shenefelt, & Shepard, 1996). As post-stroke rehabilitation techniques have improved over the past years and the pressure to reduce public health costs has increased, more patients return home earlier, forcing families to provide follow-up care at home (Ryan, Wade, Nice, Shenefelt, & Shepard, 1996). Therefore therapists prescribe home exercises as part of the outpatient therapy. Unfortunately patients often do not accomplish these home exercises due to lack of motivation and supervision. It is therefore necessary to find new strategies for encouraging and motivating patients to keep on training at home (Alankus, Proffitt, Kelleher, & Engsberg, 2011). The importance of the patients' relatives in the recovery process needs therefore to be considered in rehabilitation (Pellerin, Rochette, & Racine, 2011; Ryan, Wade, Nice, Shenefelt, & Shepard, 1996). A successful rehabilitation is the result of a close interaction between the patient gaining competence in ADL, their abilities, and the social and physical aspects of the environment. Hence, rehabilitation should assist patients in optimizing the use of their physical, mental, and social abilities, in relation to their daily environment (Lilja, Bergh, Johansson, & Nygard, 2003).

## 1.2    The Rehabilitation Gaming System (RGS)

Virtual reality (VR) technologies have proven to be beneficial for a variety of neurological conditions (Lucca, Castelli, & Sannita, 2009). VR-tools can help to enhance velocity and walking distance, attention, speed, precision and timing or provide opportunities for practicing ADLs (Johansson, 2011) and they allow to flexibly deploy scenarios addressing specific needs (Cameirao, Bermúdez i Badia, Duarte Oller, & Verschure, 2010). One of these virtual reality systems is the Rehabilitation Gaming System (RGS), a VR-based rehabilitation tool that integrates a paradigm of action execution and action observation with a number of specific theoretical neuroscience based principles of learning and recovery (Fig.1). RGS includes an interactive interface where the user controls and observes a virtual body (avatar) from a first-person perspective. Execution of goal-directed movement is thus coordinated with observation of the same movement. The rationale for using this action-observation paradigm is the understanding that the observation of action can in turn lead to activation of secondary motor areas such as the so called mirror neurons system (Pellegrino, Fadgia L., Fogassi, Gallese, & Rizzolatti, 1992; Small, Buccino, & Solodkin, 2010). RGS is based on the hypothesis that this link between perception and action, when combined with methods to drive neuronal plasticity, creates optimal conditions for functional recovery after stroke. The usability and effectiveness of RGS for motor recovery of upper limbs has been evaluated in acute and chronic stroke patients, showing that it leads to significant improvements as compared to baseline and/or control conditions (Cameirao, Zimmerli, Duarte Oller, & Verschure, 2007; Cameirao, Bermúdez i Badia, & Verschure, 2008; Cameirao, Bermúdez i Badia, Duarte Oller, & Verschure, 2009; Cameirao, Bermúdez i Badia, Duarte Oller, & Verschure, 2010; da Silva Cameirao, Bermúdez i Badia, Duarte Oller, & Verschure, 2011). In addition, the ability of RGS to drive the mirror mechanisms of the human brain has been validated in dedicated fMRI experiments (Prochnow et al., 2013).

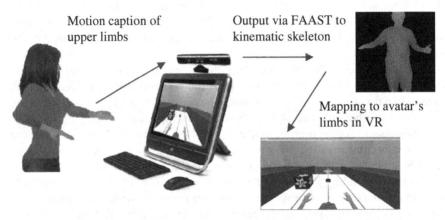

**Fig. 1.** Set up and functionality of the RGS-system. The user's motion are tracked by a motion capture system (Kinect, Microsoft, Seattle) and mapped via the Flexible Action and Articulated Skeleton Toolkit (FAAST) on the virtual limbs of the avatar. By adapting the mapping the user performs different tasks viewing the avatar from a first person perspective.

## 1.3    Adaptive Mapping

RGS incorporates two forms of adaptation. First, it adjusts the difficulty level of the task to the performance of the user optimizing motivation and learning. Second, it can amplify and/or adjust the actual movement trajectory in order to amplify the functionality of the user in the virtual environment. Stroke patients are often unable to perform certain arm movements, thus limiting their range of movements. RGS can be used to enhance the movement of the virtual arms to match them to the patients intended movement, movement goal and its corresponding kinematics. The mapping between the real and virtual limb of the user is modulated by amplifying as well as steering the virtual movements towards the current target to a degree that supports the users in their attempt to reach it. The RGS adaptive mapping assesses the individual performance level of the patient and adjusts the difficulty accordingly, so the task is never too hard nor too easy, ensuring optimal arousal and motivation customized to the patient (Nirme, Duff, & Verschure, 2011).

## 1.4   VR-Based Multiplayer Environments for Rehabilitation

How can the advantages of VR-systems and the need for social interaction in rehabilitation be combined? Studies have shown that playing interactive games may not only lead to improvements in movement quality and mobility but also to a higher motivation, self-efficacy and feeling of social acceptance (Sandlund, Mcdonough, & Häger-Ross, 2009). Multiplayer games in particular offer a shared experience, collaboration possibilities and the reward of being socialized into a community of players (Ducheneaut, Yee, Nickell, & Moore, 2006). These games are especially beneficial for physically disabled individuals as limited mobility causes a lack of social interaction possibilities. They help to form new bonds and bridges by providing social interaction in the virtual space (Trepte, Reinecke, & Juechems, 2011). So far RGS covers only individual physical training of impaired motor functions. By implementing a multiplayer game we explore if such a VR-system can assist patient in overcoming social barriers despite their physical limitations. Through the adaptive mapping we can diminish the motor disabilities of the patients, enabling them to compete on equal levels. Besides lifting their self-efficacy and changing the perception of their own abilities, we assume to influence the valuation that the social environment has of them. To validate and test our hypothesis we analysed the social environment of patients, evaluated the system with healthy subjects and ultimately conducted two at home experiments with patients and their informal caregivers.

## 2   Materials and Methods

### 2.1   The Task

The aim of this study was to explore the potential of the adaptive mapping in RGS to enable a patient and a family member to play together in a multiplayer environment and thus to enhance social functioning and acceptance. For this purpose we designed and developed a gaming scenario that resembles the popular two-player air puck or air hockey game. This game requires speed and precision, two attributes that are also requested in many rehabilitation tasks. The goal of the game is to hit with the hand a puck over a playing field towards the other player. Whenever a player fails to hit the puck back, the opponent player scores and a new puck is spawned. The puck only moves on the horizontal plane over the playing field (maximal range of x-offset: 1.15 m). In addition, players are awarded with extra points when hitting any of the bonus boxes appearing in random locations on the playing field (Fig. 2).

**Fig. 2.** Picture of the two-player network RGS air hockey game. Two players facing each other and tossing a puck with the movement of their limbs over the playing field. The pink bonus box, which appears at random moments and locations in the game, offers 10 extra points to the player.

The adaptive mapping applied to the players facilitates the accomplishment of the goal. The system adapts to the individual capabilities of the patients and learns how much aid the users' movements need in order to achieve the task, thus allowing the patients to perform movements in the virtual environment they otherwise could not achieve. By enhancing their performance we aim to provide the patients with a better match between intended action and observed result. The adaptive mapping applies a gain to the user's virtual movement and partly steers the virtual arm towards the expected target position, which is relative to the current position of the given target, in this case the air puck. The function that determinates the target positions was a result of a pre-test conducted with three healthy subjects using RGS. The subjects were asked to catch spheres arriving at different x-offsets. The target positions and the interpolation between them were calculated as a best fit to the average positions of the hands at five different x-offsets (Nirme, Duff, & Verschure, 2011). The value of the gain applied to the movement of the limbs is the inverse of the reach ratio. The reach ratio is calculated by dividing the vector of the user's real movement towards the target by the vector of the starting position of that movement to the target. The reach ratio sets the modification of the virtual arm for the next arriving target, resp. puck. The gain is then applied to the movement vector as well as to its projection on the vector from the start position to the target position. The interpolation between these two vectors results in the angle of the modulated virtual arm position. The higher the reach ratio, the closer the modulated virtual arm movement is to the real arm movement resp. the less gain and steering are applied. Before the angles are finally applied to the visible virtual arms, they are weighted by blending 80 % of the modified mapping with 20 % of the original mapping. This ensures that the mapping will never help the user too much, keeping a good balance between challenge and help. Although the virtual movements are constantly modulated, the perceived correlation of real and virtual arm movements and the sense of ownership are preserved (Nirme, Duff, & Verschure, 2011). The adaptive mapping algorithm is applied to the movement of both players.

## 2.2    The Setup

The setup for this study consists of two Desktop PCs and two Microsoft Kinects that are placed behind and above the displays. The game is played over a network connection (server and client connection) by connecting the two PCs via LAN. We developed the game scenario in Unity 3D game engine (http://unity3d.com/unity/).

## 2.3    Subjects and Experimental Protocol

**Study 1.** Psychosocial study
We conducted a pre-study to gain a deeper insight into the relation between patients and their social environment. Patient and informal caregiver described and evaluated their relation through two separate questionnaires. This allowed us to understand to which extent a multiplayer game in RGS could be beneficial for the rehabilitation process from a psychosocial point of view.

We interviewed 21 stroke patients (13 male, mean age = 56.6, $SD$ = 14.86) recruited from the Rehabilitation Unit of Hospital de l'Esperança in Barcelona. They were selected through the occupational therapists in charge of their rehabilitation. All subjects had suffered a stroke and displayed different deficits in motor function of varying levels of severity. The patients were interviewed in the hospital during their rehabilitation program. Subsequent to the interview, the patients were asked to pass the questionnaire to their closest informal caregiver. 17 informal caregivers (14 female, mean age = 52.8, years $SD$ = 15.7) filled out the questionnaire. The first set of

**Table 1.** Questions regarding perceived capabilities in performing various ADLs which were answered by patient and informal caregiver on a 6-point scale (very uncertain, moderately uncertain, slightly uncertain, slightly certain, moderately certain and very certain)

| Number | Statement |
|--------|-----------|
| S.1 | How certain are you that you / the patient can continue most of your / his/her daily activities? |
| S.2 | How certain are you that you / the patient can walk 1 km on flat ground? |
| S.3 | How certain are you that you / the patient can lift a 4 kg box? |
| S.4 | How certain are you that you / the patient can perform the daily at-home rehabilitation program? |
| S.5 | How certain are you that you / the patient can perform household chores? |
| S.6 | How certain are you that you / the patient can shop for groceries or clothes? |
| S.7 | How certain are you that you / the patient can engage in social activities? |
| S.8 | How certain are you that you / the patient can engage in hobbies or recreational activities? |
| S.9 | How certain are you that you / the patient can engage in family activities? |

questions in the questionnaires was based on a previous study that analysed the psychosocial variables associated with the informal caregivers' burden of dependent older people in Spain (Garcés, Carretero, Ródenas, & Sanjosé, 2008). The second set of questions was taken from a study that elaborated the Chronic Pain Self-Efficacy Scale (CPSS) which measures chronic pain patients' perceived and their self-efficacy to cope with the consequence of chronic pain (Anderson, Noel Dowds, Pelletz, Edwards, & Peeters-Asdourian Ch., 1995). The patients had to rate how certain they feel in performing various ADL's on a 6 point scale from very uncertain to very certain (see table 1). The informal caregiver evaluated the capacities of the patient through the same questions but from their own point of view. This part was used again in the questionnaire of the at-home intervention. This enabled us to cross-validate the perception of patient and informal caregiver.

## Study 2. System evaluation

In order to validate the RGS adaptive mapping in the RGS hockey scenario, we tested the system on 18 healthy participants (8 female, mean age = 27.72 years, $SD$ = 4.74). The subjects played in pairs one gaming session that consisted of five subsequent rounds of the game. The first round served as a training round and provided baseline data. In the four following rounds the right hand of one player was constrained to the table (each player two rounds) by using a rubber band to simulate a motor impairment, while the other player was able to move freely. The adaptive mapping was alternating switched on and off. All participants experienced four different conditions while playing (Table 2): constrained with adaptive mapping, non-constrained with adaptive mapping, constrained with no adaptive mapping and non-constrained with no adaptive mapping. Through this system evaluation we ensured that the adaptive mapping mechanisms can level out the differences when constrained and non-constrained subjects are playing together.

**Table 2.** Condition scheme of the four applied conditions in one experimental gaming session. All participants experienced all conditions; each player was constrained for two rounds, while the adaptive mapping was alternating switched on and off.

|  | Adaptive mapping | Non-adaptive mapping |
|---|---|---|
| Constraint | 1.    Condition | 3.    Condition |
| No constraint | 2.    Condition | 4.    Condition |

## Study 3. At-home intervention with stroke patients

After the pre-study we tested the system through a home-based intervention, as social interaction between patient and informal caregiver mainly takes place through the daily activities at home. Out of the subjects that were part of the pre-study survey (study 2), two patients (PL, PJ) and their respective informal caregivers (CP, CA) were selected by an occupational therapist. The patients were two male subjects (age 61 and 66). The informal caregiver was in both cases their spouse (age 60 and 65).

In the case of one patient and caregiver pair (PJ and CA), the daughter (CS) conducted one experimental session instead of the caregiver. In order to conduct the experiment the system was stationary set up at the subjects' home.

Over three subsequent days, patient and informal caregiver participated in three gaming sessions. In each gaming session the subjects were asked to play two rounds of three minutes each, but they had the opportunity to play more if they liked to. The limited time intervention period was due to time constraints from patient's side. After each session we applied a questionnaire to detect changes in the mutual perception between patient and informal caregiver. The questionnaire was based on two existing questionnaires: The same set of questions used in the psychosocial study related to the Chronic Pain Self-Efficacy Scale (CPSS), and the Perceived Competence Scale (PCS), which measures the subject's feelings of competence about a particular activity or domain. Besides the qualitative assessment we measured the physical activity and performance of the patient during the gaming sessions.

## 3    Results

### 3.1    Psychosocial Study

The pre-study provided us with new insights about the structure of the social environment of the patient. Most patients that took part in the study live together with their partner and another family member(s). Therefore the informal caregiver was in almost 60% of the cases the spouse. Most patients reported to have frequent contact with friends, followed by the family. Only 5 % stated that they do not have contact with people outside of the caregiving situation. In the majority of the cases the patients receive visits from other persons or they keep up with their social network over telephone or in written form. The lesser part is going out to meet people. The lack of out-of-home social contact could be related to the limited mobility that most stroke patients face due to motor impairments. Further we compared the rating that patient and informal caregiver gave on the patients' perceived capabilities in performing ADLs (Fig. 3 and Table 1). Since not all informal caregivers completed the questionnaire, the statistical analysis included data from only 34 subjects (17 patients and the response of their informal caregivers). In general, patients rated their capabilities higher than the informal caregiver (Fig. 3). Except for the rating pair regarding the rehabilitation at home, all ratings did not differ significantly between patient and informal caregiver (Mann-Whitney test). The patients rating ($Mdn = 5$) on the ability to perform the prescribed daily rehabilitation program at home was significantly higher than the rating of the informal caregiver ($Mdn = 4$), $U = 60.00$, $z = -2.99$, $p < .05$, $r = -.51$.

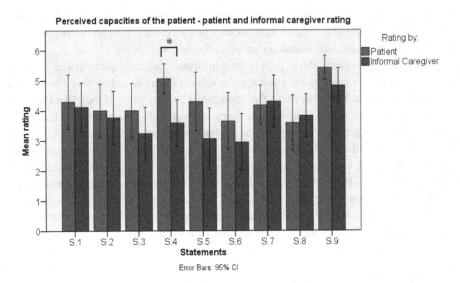

**Fig. 3.** Comparison between the patients self-rating and the rating of the informal caregiver on the perceived secureness of the patients' ability to perform various ADLs

## 3.2    System Evaluation

In order to test the efficacy of the system to level out differences between a handicapped (constrained right hand) and a healthy player (non-constrained) we analysed the 4 different conditions (Table 2).We compared the distance covered with the real non-modulated hand to the distance covered by the virtual modulated hand, steered by the RGS adaptive mapping. As shown in figure 4 the right constrained real hand in condition 1 covered significant less distance than the right non-constrained real hand in condition 2 (paired samples t-test, $p < .05$). The adaptive mapping is overcoming this handicap and converts the movement effectively in the virtual modulated right hand. There was no significant difference in the distance covered between the constraint modulated hand of condition 1 and the non-constraint modulated hand of condition 2 (*ns*). The distance covered by the left hand (modulated and non-modulated) shows no significant difference (*ns*) in both conditions, which suggests that the adaptive mapping is not affecting the non-impaired movement. Regarding the score there is no significant difference (repeated-measures ANOVA test, *ns*) between the points made in condition 1 ($M = 8.75$, $SD = 5.604$) and in condition 2 ($M = 6.81$, $SD = 4.415$). All distances were significantly normal (Kolmogorov-Smirnov test, $D(18)$, *ns*)

## 3.3    At-Home Intervention with Stroke Patients

In order to test the system in a real social context, two at home experiments with patients and their informal caregiver were conducted. Although the subjects were asked to play only two rounds each session, they all wanted to play more. In total both case study groups played 21 gaming rounds with a total of 63 minutes (3 minutes per game round). In the end both groups played 75 % more than they were requested.

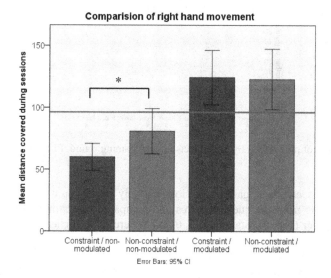

**Fig. 4.** Comparison of mean distances covered with the right hand (non-modulated and modulated) between condition 1 (constraint in red) and condition 2 (non-constraint in blue). The green line marks the grand mean of the movement of left and right hand gained in the test round (baseline).

In order to see how the game affects the patient's motor behaviour we analysed the interquartile range of movement (ROM) of the patients' hand in the horizontal axis (x-axis). This range strongly depends on the ability of the user to perform shoulder adduction/abduction movements. Results suggest that the interquartile ROM in the horizontal axis was higher for the patients' non-paretic limbs ($M = 0.184$, $SD = 0.081$, $p = 0.063$, Wilcoxon rank-sum test) compared to their paretic limbs ($M = 0.138$, $SD = 0.096$). This difference disappeared after applying the adaptive mapping ($p = 0.4812$, Wilcoxon rank-sum test). In addition, we found significant differences between the interquartile horizontal ROM of the patient's paretic limb ($M = 0.138$, $SD = 0.096$) and the modulated paretic limb ($M = 0.217$, $SD = 0.1545$, $p < 0.001$, Wilcoxon rank-sum test). These differences point out the effect of the adaptive mapping over the range of movement covered by the patient's paretic limb.

Further we compared the patients' performance with the caregiver's performance along all rounds by counting the number of pucks they failed to hit back. A Wilcoxon rank-sum test revealed no significant differences between groups in the number of missed pucks ($p = 0.4215$). This result was confirmed by comparing the amount of scores achieved by each group (Fig. 5 and 6).

### Case Study Group PL and CP

This group played nine rounds in total, in which the patient was more successful in gaining points than the informal caregiver (Fig. 5). The patient won five out of nine rounds. The patient's average score was 53.89 ($SD = 16.16$), while his informal caregivers' average score was 40.78 ($SD = 17.39$).

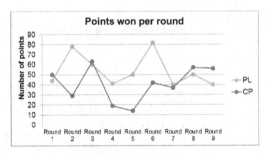

**Fig. 5.** Number of points won by all subjects in each gaming round. PL: patient and CP: informal caregiver.

In order so see if these gaming sessions had any impact on mutual perception, we analysed results from the questionnaires and compared the ratings of patient and informal caregiver (Fig. 6). Statement 2, 6 and 8 were rated higher by both, the patient and the informal caregiver.

**Fig. 6.** Comparison of the ratings of each ADL-statements of PL and CP before and after the at-home intervention

## Case Study Group PJ and CA

Patient PJ was less successful in gaining points and rounds than his informal caregiver, resp. his daughter, who played the second session with him (Fig. 7). Out of the 12 rounds two were won by the patient. The average number of points he made were 39.67 ($SD$ = 12.61), CA average points were 50.14 ($SD$ = 11.54) and the average points made by CS were 51.8 ($SD$ = 11.01).

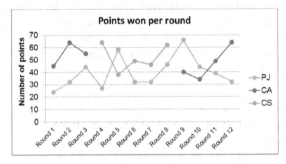

**Fig. 7.** Number of points won by the subjects in each round. PJ: patient, CA/CS: informal caregivers.

Also in this group we compared the ratings of patient and informal caregiver before and after the at-home intervention (Fig. 8). Statement 4, 7 and 8 were rated higher by both, the patient and the informal caregiver. Especially the 2 point increase in the rating of social interaction by the caregiver is of interest.

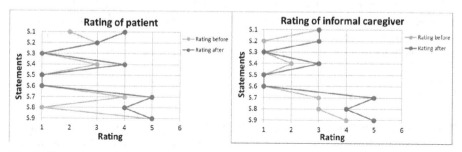

**Fig. 8.** Comparison of the ratings of ADL-statements of PJ and CA before and after the at-home intervention

# 4    Discussion

Combining virtual reality with social interaction through a multiplayer game can lead to new ways to mobilize social actors in stroke rehabilitation and to assist in integrating the patient in their social environment. The RGS air hockey scenario allows patients and their social environment to interact in a playful way and to experience a new common ground for equal social interaction. We hypothesized that this will ultimately lead to a changed mutual perception of roles and capabilities.

The results from both, the system evaluation and the at-home experiments, suggest that the adaptive mapping is capable of levelling out performance differences between two players. The system successfully overcomes the difference in moving distance and range between an impaired / restricted and a healthy / non-restricted limb. This influences the outcome of the game insofar that the status of the player (caregiver or patient) does not determine who will win or lose the game. Moreover, it the game appears to be entertaining since the subjects were willing to play more rounds than requested.

The analysis of the patients' social situation revealed many aspects in favour of a multiplayer rehabilitation game. The majority of patients are embedded into a social network of family and friends. Only a few patients live alone and/or have no frequent contact to other people. Since their disabilities limits the mobility, our system would enable the patients to interact with their social network at home or even online.

In our psychosocial study we found a slight discrepancy in the ratings regarding the patient's ability to perform ADL, although not at a statistically significant level. The patients show a tendency to rate most of their own abilities higher than the informal caregiver. The same trend can be observed in the results from the at-home experiments where both the patients' and the caregivers' reported higher ratings after the gaming sessions.

Our findings suggest that a multiplayer scenario could be beneficial in addressing the requirements of modern rehabilitation with an emphasis on an integrated motor, psychological and social approach. As outpatient therapy will become more important and the involvement of the patient's social environment increases, these kinds of scenarios support the reintegration process, ensuring a sustainable rehabilitation method in the service of enhancing quality of life. Moreover, we believe that further investigation based on our results will shed light on the psychosocial changes stroke patients face and helping to better understand the impact beyond the motor impairment.

## 5     Conclusion

This study evaluated the influence of including social interaction into the VR rehabilitation paradigm Rehabilitation Gaming System. We have shown that the system successfully equalizes the performance differences between a healthy and a disabled player influencing self- and social perception. First observations in this direction could be seen in the change of ratings before and after the at-home interventions. Moreover, the game-like scenarios of RGS provide an entertaining and motivating way to socially interact. Given the relatively small sample, especially in the case of the at home experiments, the preliminary results serve as an initial case study, that shows a trend towards the outlined proposal. Nevertheless we believe that the new multiplayer scenario in RGS is a valuable tool for further investigation of our claims and for assessing its impact on future stroke recovery.

## References

1. Alankus, G., Proffitt, R., Kelleher, C., Engsberg, J.: Stroke therapy through motion-based games: A case study. ACM Transactions on Accessible Computing (TACCESS) 4(1), 1–35 (2011), doi:10.1145/2039339.2039342
2. Anderson, K.O., Noel Dowds, B., Pelletz, R.E., Edwards, W.T., Peeters-Asdourian, C.: Development and initial validation of a scale to measure self-efficacy beliefs in patients with chronic pain. Pain (63), 77–84 (1995)
3. Beth, H., William, E.H.: Family caregiving for patient with stroke: Review and analysis. Stroke 30, 1478–1485 (1999)
4. Cameirao, M.S., Bermúdez i Badia, S., Duarte Oller, E., Verschure, P.F.M.J.: Neurorehabilitation using the virtual reality based rehabilitation gaming system: Methodology, design, psychometrics, usability and validation. Journal of NeuroEngineering and Rehabilitation 7, 48 (2010), doi:10.1186/1743-0003-7-48
5. Cameirao, M.S., Bermúdez i Badia, S., Duarte Oller, E., Verschure, P.F.M.J.: The Rehabilitation Gaming System: A review. Studies in Health Technology and Informatics 145, 65–83 (2009)
6. Cameirao, M.S., Bermúdez i Badia, S., Verschure, P.F.M.J.: Virtual reality based upper exremity rehabilitation following stroke: A review. Journal of CyberTherapy & Rehabilitation 1(1), 63–74 (2008)

7. Cameirao, M.S., Zimmerli, L., Duarte Oller, E., Verschure, P.F.M.J.: The rehabilitation gaming system: A virutal reality based system for the evaluation and rehabilitation of motor deficits. In: Proceedings of the Conference on Virutal Rehabilitation, pp. 29–33 (2007)
8. da Silva Cameirao, M., Bermúdez i Badia, S., Duarte Oller, E., Verschure, P.F.M.J.: Virtual reality based rehabilitation speeds up functional recovery of the upper extremities after stroke: A randomized controlled pilot study in the acute phase of stroke using the Rehabilitation Gaming System. Restorative Neurology and Neuroscience 29(5), 287–298 (2011)
9. Di Loreto, I., Van Dokkum, L., Gouaich, A., Laffont, I.: Mixed reality as a means to strengthen post-stroke rehabilitation. In: Shumaker, R. (ed.) Virtual and Mixed Reality, Part II, HCII 2011. LNCS, vol. 6774, pp. 11–19. Springer, Heidelberg (2011)
10. Ducheneaut, N., Yee, N., Nickell, E., Moore, R.J.: "Alone together?": Exploring the social dynamics of massively multiplayer online games. ACM (2006), doi: 10.1145/1124772. 1124834
11. Garcés, J., Carretero, S., Ródenas, F., Sanjosé, V.: Variables related to the informal caregivers' burden of dependent senior citizens in Spain. Archives of Gerontology and Geriatrics 48(3), 372–379 (2008), doi:10.1016/j.archger.2008.03.004
12. Go, A.S., Mozaffarian, D., Roger, V.L., Benjamin, E.J., Berry, J.D., Blaha, M.J., Dai, S., Ford, E.S., Fox, C.S., Franco, S., Fullerton, H.J., Gillespie, C., Hailpern, S.H., Heit, J.A., Howard, V.J., Huffman, M.D., Judd, S.E., Brett, M.K., Kittner, S.J., Lackland, D.T., Lichtman, J.H., Lisabeth, L.D., Mackey, R.H., Magid, D.J., Marcus, G.M., Marelli, A., Matchar, D.B., McGuire, D.K., Mohler III, E.R., Moy, C.S., Mussolino, M.E., Neumar, R.W., Nichol, G., Padney, D.K., Paynter, N.P., Reeves, M.J., Sorlie, P.D., Stein, J., Towfighi, A., Turan, T.N., Virani, S.S., Wong, N.D., Woo, D., Turner, M.B.: AHA Statistical Update: Heart Disease and Stroke Statistics - 2014 Update: A Report from the American Heart Association (2013), doi:10.1161/01.cir.0000441139.02102.80
13. Jack, D., Boian, R., Merians, A.S., Tremaine, M., Burdea, G.C., Adamovic, S.V., ...Poizner, H.: Virtual reality-enhanced stroke rehabilitation. IEEE Transaction on Neural System and Rehabilitation Engineering 9(3), 308–317 (2001)
14. Johansson, B.B.: Current trends in stroke rehabilitation. A review with focus on brain plasticity. Acta Neurologica Scandinavica 147, 147–159 (2011), doi:10.1111/j.1600-0404.2010.01417.x
15. Lilja, M., Bergh, A., Johansson, L., Nygard, L.: Attitudes towards rehabilitation needs and support from assistive technology and the social environment among elderly people with disability. Occupational Therapy International 10(1), 75–93 (2003), doi:10.1002/oti.178
16. Lucca, L.F., Castelli, E., Sannita, W.G.: The application of robotics in the function motor recovery of the paretic upper limp. J. Rehabil. Med. 41, 1003–1100 (2009)
17. Nirme, J., Duff, A., Verschure, P.F.M.J.: Adaptive rehabilitation gaming system: On-line individualization of stroke rehabilitation. In: 2011 Annual International Conference of the IEEE Engineering in Medicine and Biology Society, pp. 6749–6752 (2011), doi:10.1109/IEMBS.2011.6091665
18. Pellegrino, G., Fadgia, L., Fogassi, L., Gallese, V., Rizzolatti, G.: Understanding motor events: A neurophyxiological study. Experimental Brain Research 91(1), 176–180 (1992)
19. Pellerin, C., Rochette, A., Racine, E.: Social participation of relatives post-stroke: The role of rehabilitation and related ethical issues. Disability and Rehabilitation 33(13-14), 1055–1064 (2011), doi:10.3109/09638288.2010.524272
20. Prochnow, D., Bermúdez i Badia, S., Schmidt, J., Duff, A., Brunheim, S., Kleiser, R., ...Verschure, P.F.M.J.: A functional magnetic resonance imaging study of visumotor processing in a virtual reality-based paradigm: Rehabilitation Gaming System. European Journal of Neuroscience, 1–7 (2013), doi:10.1111/ejn.12157

21. Ryan, N.P., Wade, J.C., Nice, A., Shenefelt, H., Shepard, K.: Physical therapists' perceptions of family involvement in the rehabilitation process. Physiotherapy Research International: The Journal for Researchers and Clinicians in Physical Therapy 1(3), 159 (1996)
22. Sandlund, M., Mcdonough, S., Häger-Ross, C.: Interactive computer play in rehabilitation of children with sensorimotor disorders: A systematic review. Developmental Medicine and Child Neurology 51(3), 173 (2009)
23. Small, S.L., Buccino, G., Solodkin, A.: The mirror neuron system and treatment of stroke. Developmental Psychobiology 54(3), 293–310 (2010)
24. Trepte, S., Reinecke, L., Juechems, K.: The social side of gaming: How playing online computer games creates online and offline social support. Computers in Human Behavior 28(3), 832–839 (2011), doi:10.1016/j.chb.2011.12.003
25. Verschure, P.F.M.J.: Neuroscience, virtual reality and neurorehabilitation: Brain repair as a validation of brain theory. Paper Presented at the Annual International Conference of the IEEE Engineering in Medicine and Biology Society (EMBC), Boston, pp. 2254–2257 (2011), doi: 10.1109/IEMBS.2011.6090428

# Dynamic Difficulty Adaptation
# in Serious Games for Motor Rehabilitation

Nadia Hocine, Abdelkader Gouaïch, and Stefano A. Cerri

University of Montpellier 2, France
{nadia.hocine,gouaich,cerri}@lirmm.fr

**Abstract.** In the last few years, a growing interest has been devoted to improve rehabilitation strategies by including serious games in the therapy process. Adaptive serious games seek to provide the patients with an individualized rehabilitation environment that meets their training needs. In this paper, a dynamic difficulty adaptation (DDA) technique is suggested. This technique focuses on the online adaptation of the game difficulty by taking into account patients' abilities and motivation. The results of the experiment show that the adaptation technique increases the number of tasks, number of successful tasks as well as the movement amplitude during a game session. The technique positively effects the training outcomes of stroke patients, which can help them to recover their functions.

**Keywords:** Adaptation, serious games, stroke.

## 1 Introduction

A stroke is among the major causes of adults' disability and death worldwide. According to the location and the size of the brain lesion, the patients may have different combinations of deficits. This includes for example the inability to move one or more limbs, attention deficits, hemineglect and to understand or formulate speech.

Rehabilitation strategies aim to help patients to regain their functions and to independently perform their daily activities. In particular, upper-limb rehabilitation focuses on the enhancement for example of the range of motion, coordination, motion control and muscle strength. They are based on task-oriented strategies in which the patient is asked to perform reaching and grasping activities. With these repetitive activities, patients often become frustrated and tired and their motivation should be supported by the therapist. Indeed, many studies in motor learning showed that the outcomes of the rehabilitation depend on the quality and the amount of physical activities [1] as well as the patients' active participation and engagement during the therapeutic session [2] [3].

Serious games for rehabilitation (or *rehabilitation games*) can therefore play an important role in providing the patients with a motivating rehabilitation environment in which tasks are adapted to their abilities and training needs.

S. Göbel and J. Wiemeyer (Eds.): GameDays 2014, LNCS 8395, pp. 115–128, 2014.

They also help therapists to support patients' motivation and to simultaneously supervise different patients.

Many researchers have been interested in identifying what can make the game fun and engaging. In this context, we can find different studies that determine the motivational factors e.g. challenge, curiosity and fantasy [5] as well as the notion of optimal experience as first defined by Csikszentmihalyi [6]. The latter is based on the theory of flow which indicates the full immersion in or engagement with an experience. This state may be reached through a successful tradeoff between the players' skills and challenges.

In this paper, we suggest a difficulty adaptation technique for rehabilitation games. The objective is that the patients do not find the game too easy and thus they may feel bored or too difficult and therefore be frustrated. Maintaining patients' motivation may consequently increase their training outcomes during a therapeutic session.

In the following sections, we first introduce related work on difficulty adaptation in serious games for upper limb rehabilitation. In Section 3, we describe the player's profile used to adapt the game. Then, Section 4 deals with the difficulty adaptation technique. After that, we describe the experimental protocol in Section 5. In Section 6, the results of the experiment are discussed. Finally, we conclude this paper by discussing our findings and initiating our future work.

## 2    Related Work

As patients have limited abilities due to stroke, the difficulty of the game has been considered as an important element to adapt [4] [7]. Difficulty adaptation consists in not only assisting the patient when the task is very difficult, but also challenging him/her in order to increase the training outcomes.

The online difficulty adaptation approach has got the interest of many researchers in rehabilitation games [8] [9] [10] [11]. This approach consists in automatically adapting the game in real-time to maintain patient's motivation on the one hand. On the other hand, this makes it possible for the therapist to supervise different patients and remotely when they return home.

For instance, Rabin et al. [8] propose a technique for difficulty adaptation based on an assessment exercise of the player's function that is carried out at the start of each game session. The inputs for adaptation are: the reached zone, wrist weight, grasp pressure and session date. The difficulty can be increased during the game session by making the target area progressively smaller and by adjusting the speed and range of targets. Although the evaluation of the technique included the player's motivation, the latter has not been involved in the decision on adaptation.

Pirovano et al. [10] focus on an intelligent game engine used to adapt games that are based on Wii Balance Board and Kinect. For instance, in Fruit Catcher game the player must catch fruits falling from the top of a tree using the basket. The difficulty is adapted by adjusting the number of falling fruits and baskets, fruit size, fruit weight as well as the falling frequency. The online adaptation

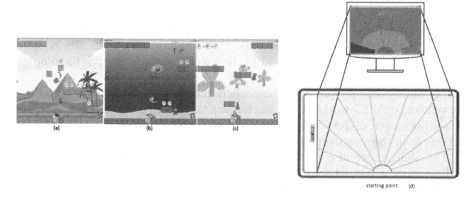

**Fig. 1.** Assessment procedure: patient is asked to cover up all the workspace by going to 9 different directions (d); PRehab game versions: Cat game (a), Turtle game (b) and Rabbit game (c)

is founded on a quest bayesian model that depends on the desired patient's performance (hit ratio in the game). This model was built using empirical data of healthy players' performance. However, as stroke patients performance can highly vary depending on their daily health conditions, this model should also be evaluated by including stroke patients' performance.

In these studies, the adaptation inputs are mainly (i) the player's performance such as his/her final score [10], movement accuracy, range of motion and latency [9], reached zone, wrist weight and grasp pressure [8] as well as (ii) biomechanical measurements such as mean frequency of the position and force of signal [11]. Indeed, most difficulty adaptation techniques in upper-limb rehabilitation games are inspired by motor learning theories. These techniques only focus on the maximization of the effort during the rehabilitation session. However, the patient's motivation and engagement are among the key factors for recovery. In existing rehabilitation games, the patient's fatigue and motivation have been considered only to evaluate the game successfulness, but without including them in the decision on game adaptation [11]. Indeed, most studies attempted to show the utility of the game in increasing the training outcomes (e.g. motor control and shoulder/grasp strength) [8] as well as its usability and acceptability [10]. Only few works, namely Cameirao *et al.* [9], evaluated the effect of difficulty adaptation on patients' training outcomes but without considering their fatigue and motivation.

Our contribution consists in a generic adaptation technique for rehabilitation games. It depends on the generation of adaptive "pointing tasks" which represent the main player's activity in the game. The generation of tasks is based on the player's profile and performance. Unlike the previous works, the proposed technique focuses on the maximization of the effort while taking into consideration the patients' conditions, in particular their abilities, fatigue and motivation.

## 3    Player's Profile

To automatically adapt the difficulty in a rehabilitation game, it is important to have a computational model of patients' motor abilities. The difficulty adaptation module requires the assessment of the current player's abilities to compute this model called the "*ability zone*" [12].

The ability zone represents the area where the patient can effectively carry out movements on a 2D workspace (e.g. graphics tablet). In general, this workspace has a dimension of 1-1.5 m. In fact, patients can be unable to reach very far targets from the starting point position or targets in such side of the workspace.

The ability zone of a patient in a workspace is modelled using a matrix of a dimension $m \times n$, where $m$ represents the number of rows and $n$ the number of columns. Each cell value represents an easiness score for the patient to reach the mapped area of the workspace. In [13] we proposed a bio inspired method to compute the ability zone matrix. Following this model, cells of the matrix contain digital pheromones that indicate whether the corresponding areas of the workspace were reached by the patient and with which quality of movement.

The ability zone is constructed during the assessment step before the play and can be updated during it. During the assessment exercise, the patient is asked to cover up all the workspace by going to 9 different directions as shown in Fig. 1 (d). All reached areas of the workspace are considered attainable and the others difficult. This data is used to compute the ability zone that helps the adaptation process to determine both challenge and assistance areas for the patient. Indeed, we consider all targets placed at areas inside the ability zone easy and the others difficult to reach.

## 4    Difficulty Adaptation Technique

The rehabilitation game is structured as a set of levels. Each game level which corresponds to a therapeutic session ( 20 to 45 min) is defined by an objective that the player may achieve to progress in the game scenario. The level is composed of a set of game scenes. The latter is what the player's perceive during the interaction. Each game scene of the level contain a sequence of targets that the player's may reach to progress in the level. According to the position and range of the target, the patient may find it difficult or easy to reach.

The difficulty adaptation is based on the offline generation of pointing tasks that depends on the player's profile. During the game session, the game level is dynamically adapted according to the patient's performance and motivation. Next, we first describe the offline generation of pointing tasks and then the online adaptation of the game level.

### 4.1    Pointing Tasks Generation

The pointing tasks generator is presented in Algorithm 1. This algorithm takes as an input the player's identifier *playerid* to retrieve the current ability zone (line

---

**ALGORITHM 1.** Pointing task generator

---

**Algorithm** : Pointing tasks generator;
**Data**: *playerid*, the player identifier
**Result**: $S$, a map that contains for each difficulty mode $m$ a sequence of pointing tasks

1  z ← getAbilityZoneForPlayer(playerid) ;
2  img ← buildImageFromAbilityZone(z) ;
3  edge ← detectEdgeFromImage(img) ;
4  *mask* ← getMaskMatrix(edge) ;
   **foreach** $m$ *in Modes* **do**
5  |    $C_m$ ← selectAllPossibleCellsForThisMode($m$, *mask*) ;
6  |    $P_m$ ← generatePointingTasksForLevel($C_m$) ;
7  |    $S[m]$ ← $P_m$;
   **end**

---

1). The obtained image of the ability zone is then used to determine difficult and easy areas of the workspace for the patient (lines 2 to 4). In fact, the edge of the ability zone image is used to compute the mask matrix that helps to determine the difficulty of pointing tasks.

For each predefined difficulty mode, a list of all potential areas is computed (line 5). This list is filtered using a heuristic search defined in Algorithm 2. The heuristic search is based on a Monte Carlo tree search to select the "best" pointing tasks for a game level (line 6). Next, we describe in details the main steps of the algorithm.

**Step 1: Generating Pointing Tasks per Difficulty Mode.** The difficulty adaptation module uses the ability zone of the patient in order to determine the difficulty of pointing tasks. Since the ability zone is a matrix where each cell contains the digital pheromone intensity, we build an image representing this matrix where digital pheromone's intensity is translated to a grey scale color. Fig. 2 (2) is a simple example of the obtained image from the ability zone of Fig. 2 (1). The edge of this image represents the farthest possible area that the patient has reached. In fact, we consider the current abilities of the patient in order to challenge him/her. We assume that this challenge will have a sustainable training effect that can consequently increase the patient's range of motion.

To detect the edge in the ability zone image, a Sobel operator is used [14]. Sobel is an algorithm for edge detection in image processing used for images with high frequency variations. It emphasizes regions of high spatial frequency that correspond to edges. The operator is based on a pair of $3 \times 3$ convolution kernels $k_x = (-1, 0, 1; -2, 0, 2; -1, 0, 1)$ and $k_y = (1, 2, 1; 0, 0, 0; -1, -2, -1)$. These kernels are used to compute the gradient of each pixel of the image vertically ($G_x$) and horizontally ($G_y$). These measurements are used to compute the gradient magnitude on the basis of the following formula : $|G| = \sqrt{(G_x)^2 + (G_y)^2}$.

Using the obtained gradient, we compute the mask matrix $(A)$ that helps the adaptation module to determine challenge and assistance areas as follows:

$$A(i,j) = \begin{cases} true & \text{if } (G(i,j) > t) \\ false & \text{otherwise} \end{cases}$$

Where $t$ is a threshold parameter to determine to what extent the movement frequency is considered. For example, given a gradient threshold $t = 0.4$ the obtained edge of the ability zone image of Fig. 2 (1) is shown in Fig. 2 (3).

The mask matrix is used to determine possible targets in different difficulty modes. These modes are interpreted as follow:

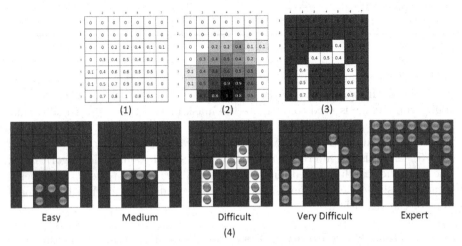

**Fig. 2.** Example of ability zone (1), obtained image (2) and its edge (3); possible targets in the scene according to the difficulty mode (4)

- *Easy*: in this case the target is placed very close to the starting point.
- *Medium*: the target in this case is placed at the nearest bottom area from the edge of the image. The objective is to decrease the difficulty in order that the patient will be able to reach targets.
- *Difficult*: a target is considered as difficult when placed at the farthest reached area by the patient. It is the edge of the ability zone image determined by Sobel operator.
- *Very difficult*: a target is considered as very difficult when placed in the outside of the ability zone.
- *Expert*: the target in this mode is very far from the edge of the ability zone image.

**Step 2: Selecting Pointing Tasks for a Game Level.** The above presented process produces a mapping that links each difficulty mode to the areas of the workspace where pointing tasks with equivalent difficulty can be generated. The set of possibilities is too large and only few pointing tasks should be selected for the level. In [13] we focused on a random selection of pointing tasks. This often results in poor game scenes when for instance rules of symmetry and distribution are not taken into account. Moreover, from training perspective, using random selection for an easy level can produce targets that are very easy to reach. However, it is important in rehabilitation to assist the patient by decreasing the difficulty to the degree that he/she will be able to reach the target. This can help the patient to accomplish tasks with more important amplitude, which may consequently increase their range of motion.

To answer this issue, in this work the decision on the selection of targets is founded on heuristic search. In particular, a Monte Carlo Tree Search (MCTS) algorithm is used to generate the most suitable sequence of pointing tasks that takes into account both training and gaming constraints. The objective is to make a tradeoff between the enhancement of the training outcomes and the playability of the level to maintain the patient's motivation.

MCTS is an anytime search algorithm used to find optimal decisions by building a search tree from random samples in the decision space [15]. The general algorithm of MCTS is based on two policies: (i) *tree policy* to select or create the best leaf node within the search tree and (ii) *default policy* that produces a value estimate following the simulation of the action.

---

**ALGORITHM 2.** General algorithm of tree generation

---

**Algorithm :** treeGeneration;
**Data:** $P_m$, a list of pointing tasks according to a difficulty mode $m$
**Result:** the best sequence of pointing task for the mode $m$
1   create a root node $v_0$ with state $s_0$ ;
   **while** *within computational budget* **do**
2       $v1 \leftarrow$ treePolicy$(v_0)$ ;
3       $\delta \leftarrow$ defaultPolicy$(s(v_1))$ ;
4       Backup$(v_1, \delta)$ ;
   **end**
5   **return** sequence(bestChild$(v_0)$) ;

---

The pointing task generator builds five search trees according to difficulty modes. Each node of the tree represents a state of the game level which is a pointing task. The node contains information about the rewards as well as the number of visits of this node. The search tree involves iteratively building a tree until a *budget* is reached. The latter represents: (i) the given time to find a solution (number of iterations) and (ii) the volume (i.e number of tasks) of the level.

The pseudo code of the tree generation is given in Algorithm 2. This algorithm takes as an input a list of pointing tasks according to a difficulty mode. The first step of the tree search consists in selecting a root node $v_0$ which represent the initial target at state $s_0$ (line 1). Then, within the computational budget the algorithm iteratively build the tree. The tree policy aims to select the best leaf node (line 2). The default strategy is run to simulate the added node (line 3 to 4), where $\delta$ is the reward for the last reached state. The result of the overall search (line 5) is $sequence(\ bestChild\ (v_0)\ )$ which represents the obtained sequence of nodes that leads to the best leaf node from the root node $v_0$. In fact, the result consists in the sequence of all selected best nodes during the search.

The tree search produces a sequence of pointing tasks selected to maximize the reward function. This consists in selecting the best node (i.e. a target) on the basis of Upper Confidence Bounds for Trees (UCT) method. The best node is selected according to its UCT value given by the following formula [16]:

$$V = \overline{R_j} + \sqrt{\frac{2.\log(n+1)}{n_j + \epsilon}}$$

Where $\overline{R_j}$ is the average rewards from node $j$ that are understood to be within $[0; 1]$, $n$ is the number of the times the current parent node has been visited, $n_j$ is the total number of times that the child node $j$ has been visited and $\epsilon$ is a tunable bias parameter.

Indeed, in this formula the reward term $\overline{R_j}$ encourages the *exploitation* of nodes with higher-rewards and the right hand term $\sqrt{\frac{2.\log(n+1)}{n_j + \epsilon}}$ encourages the *exploration* of less visited choices. UCT insures the property of equilibrium between exploitation and exploration. In fact, it is important to suggest to the patient tasks that increase the reward function while checking his/her capability to explore the workspace. This can consequently evolve the patient's ability zone.

The reward value $R$ for a node $j$ is given by the following formula:

$$R = \frac{1}{2}(\alpha.distance(j) + \beta.shift(j))$$

It depends on: (i) the importance of reaching a target in such position of the workspace given by the function $distance(j)$; and (ii) $shift(j)$ function that determines to what extent the child node $j$ is left aligned in the game scene; where $\alpha + \beta = 1$.

## 4.2 Online Difficulty Adaptation

The obtained sequences of pointing tasks are used to generate the game level. In fact, for each difficulty mode a sub-level is created. The next step consists in the online adaptation of the difficulty by suggesting to the patient game scenes of one of the generated sub-levels. This depends on the selected difficulty mode according to the patient's motivation during the game level.

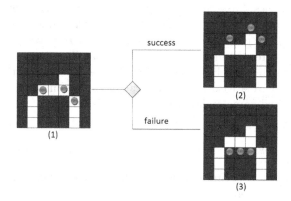

**Fig. 3.** Example of proposed scenes to a player

We focus on a motivation model we introduced in [12]. This model depends on a window of success and failure to make decision on adaptation. The motivation model is inspired by the activation theory [17]. In this theory, stimulation is necessary and the use of an activation level is required in order to make an individual sufficiently motivated to perform tasks. As a measure of the level of activation, we consider the number of successive task success and failure during the level [12]. According to the patient's successes and failures, the motivation model makes the following decisions: (i) decrease the difficulty to avoid putting the player in repeated situations of failure during the game level; (ii) increase the difficulty when the player is in a situation of consecutive successes and finds the game very easy; and otherwise (iii) maintain momentarily the difficulty.

### 4.3    Example

The obtained image of the ability zone of Fig. 2 is used to compute the mask matrix. According to the difficulty mode, the possible targets positions are shown in Fig. 2 (4). Then, for each difficulty mode, a search tree is built in order to find the best sequence of pointing tasks for this difficulty mode. Fig. 3 shows an example of game scenes proposed to the player during the game session. First, the default difficulty mode is *difficult* (1). The window of success and failure $w = 1$. Thus, if the player succeeds the objective of this scene, the next proposed scene is the *very difficult* one (2) otherwise come across the *medium* mode (3).

The adaptation technique has been implemented in a rehabilitation game we developed named PRehab. This game can be played using a computer mouse or a graphics tablet. Different versions of this game have been implemented by varying the aesthetics (ambiances): sea ambiance (Turtle game, see Fig. 1 (b)); desert ambiance (Cat game, see Fig. 1 (a)); and forest ambiance (Rabbit game, see Fig. 1 (c)). In these PRehab versions, the player is asked to eliminate the enemies that constitute the obstacles for the given main character (turtle, cat or rabbit). Besides, the player can collect different coins to increase his/her score points. To free the path, the player has to use objects from his/her virtual box to eliminate obstacles. From motor training perspective, the objective is to reach targets (enemies) that appear at different areas of the game scene.

At the start of the game level, the main character is placed at the first scene of the sub-level corresponding to *the difficult mode*. The game difficulty is then adapted according to the player's performance and motivation during the play. The adaptation in this case focuses on camera move in order to provide the player with adapted game scenes during the game level.

## 5   Experiment

The objective of the experiment is to study the impact of the proposed adaptation technique on patient's motivation and training outcomes. The experiment was conducted in the hospital of Grau du Roi of Montpellier, France.

We focused on a repeated-measures single-blinded design in which each patient is asked to perform an assessment exercise and then play a game version that is randomly selected. Patients play the game versions in different sequences. Only the difficulty strategy that was studied. Three conditions of this independent variable were considered:

- Dynamic difficulty adaptation (DDA): it is the proposed approach based on online difficulty adaptation. The difficulty strategy consists in increasing and/or deceasing the difficulty during the play according to the patient's profile and motivation in Turtle game.
- Incremental difficulty adaptation (IDA): this strategy consists in progressively providing the patient with the easiest to most difficult tasks in Rabbit game. It does not consider the patient's profile and motivation.
- Without a difficulty adaptation strategy (Random) in Cat game.

The objective is to compare the effects of the tree conditions (DDA, IDA and Random) on the player's training outcomes and motivation. The null hypotheses have be defined as follow: *H0. the difficulty strategy has no effect on measures outcomes*. The main measures outcomes were: the number of tasks, number of successful tasks, distance, velocity, perceived game duration and perceived difficulty. Moreover, interviews with therapists and patients have been recorded at the end of the game sessions. In particular, we asked both patients and therapists whether the game is adapted to patients' abilities, whether the objectives are clear and the acceptance of using the games in their daily rehabilitation sessions.

All participants used the same device: a graphics tablet Intus A3. The three versions of PRehab have different aesthetics in order to make it easy to the patient to differentiate the three game versions. The three games are based on the same mechanics and the main activity of the player is to reach targets. In fact, in our previous clinical tests we observed that the patient has difficulties to make distinctions between the different software that are based on the same interface.

Inclusion criteria of subjects were not restrictive. The only criterion was the ability to use the game device (mouse of graphics tablet) and play the game

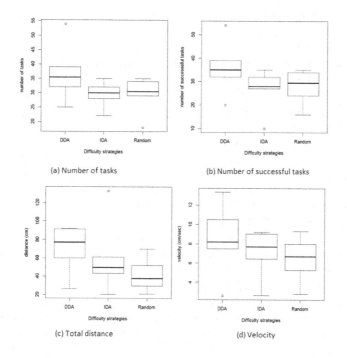

(a) Number of tasks

(b) Number of successful tasks

(c) Total distance

(d) Velocity

**Fig. 4.** Measures outcomes for the three difficulty strategies

(without strong cognitive deficits). Seven post stroke patients aged 38 to 73 years old ($61.57 \pm 12.06$) were provided with the three game versions and were asked to complete tasks using the impaired arm. Only a patient who played the games in bi-manual due to strong difficulties. This group of patients who have limited capabilities due to stroke, was composed of 5 men and 2 women. The number of weeks after stroke was ($15.71 \pm 7.47$).

The experiment was conducted during two weeks in which each participant was asked to perform an assessment exercise and then play a game version during a rehabilitation session (20 min). Each patient carried out three rehabilitation sessions, one each day at approximately the same hour. Each game version generated levels that allow carrying out a bounded number of pointing tasks. After each game session, a questionnaire was proposed to patients to report their experience.

## 6   Results and Discussion

All statistical analysis were performed using R (http://www.r-project.org) version 2.12.0. To analyze the effect of the three difficulty strategies on measures outcomes, a one-way repeated measures ANOVA was used. When an analysis revealed significant differences, post-hoc pairwise comparisons based on Tukey HSD test were used to locate the specific differences, where $p < 0.05$ was accepted as significant. Before the analysis of mean and variance, a Kolmogorov-Smirnov normality test was initially used. In addition, Friedman test was used to reject hypotheses for ordinal measures.

A repeated-measures analysis of variance indicated significant mean differences between the three difficulty strategies for three dependant variables: the number of tasks ($DF_d = 10$, $F = 5.85$, $p < 0.02$, $\eta^2 = 0.53$); the number of successful tasks ($DF_d = 10$, $F = 7.70$, $p < 0.009$, $\eta^2 = 0.60$); and the total distance ($DF_d = 10$, $F = 4.39$, $p < 0.04$, $\eta^2 = 0.46$).

The number of tasks carried out by the patients was significantly more important in the Turtle game (with DDA strategy) compared with the two other games (with IDA and Random strategies). The HSD test indicates a significant difference in number of tasks between DDA and IDA $p < 0,047$ and between DDA and Random $p < 0,058$ and no significant difference has been recorded between Random and IDA (see Fig. 4 (a)). In fact, as DDA is based on the control of patient's motivation through performances, this can increase patients' engagement and prevent their tiredness. Therefore, the patients put more efforts, increasing thus the number of tasks.

The mean differences in the total distance was significant. It was significantly more important in DDA compared with the other strategies, especially the Random strategy with $p < 0,007$ (see Fig. 4 (c)). Therefore, DDA has increased the amplitude of movement which is an important factor in stroke patients' recovery.

Despite the game based on DDA was challenging, the number of successful tasks was more important in this game compared with the other game versions. The difference in the mean of number of successful tasks in the three game versions was statically significant (see Fig. 4 (b)). The differences between DDA and IDA $p < 0,014$ as well as between DDA and Random $p < 0,044$ were significant and no difference has been reported between Random and IDA.

Although the existing differences between the three strategies in terms of velocity (see the graph of Fig. 4 (d)), the ANOVA test was not significant ($DF_d = 10$, $F = 4.03$, $p < 0.051$, $\eta^2 = 0.53$). Moreover, all players have reported their enjoyment when using games in rehabilitation. The perceived session duration for all games was different from the effective one (20 min). Indeed, most patients have reported that the session duration was about 3 to 15 min. Although the existing difference between the strategies, the ANOVA test has not rejected the hypothesis for perceived duration ($DF_d = 10$, $F = 3.54$, $p < 0.06$, $\eta^2 = 0.41$).

Using a scale of five choices (0: not at all, 1: slightly, 2: moderately, 3: fairly and 4: extremely) the patients have reported their perceived difficulty of game tasks. The Friedman test has not rejected the hypothesis for the perceived difficulty as the number of subjects is less than 12 (Friedman chi-squared $= 2.8$; $df = 2$; $p < 0.24$). Nevertheless, the median values show that the game based DDA was moderately difficult (2) as for the other games the difficulty was reported as fairly difficult (3) in IDA and slightly difficult (1) in Random strategy. Hence, we assume that although the game based on DDA was challenging, the patients have perceived that the game was not very difficult. This assumption should be confirmed in future experiments.

Furthermore, interviews with patients have been carried out at the end of the experiment and observations on patients verbal reactions were recorded. All patients have reported their motivation and acceptance of using games in rehabilitation. In particular, some patients who have pains, stressed to continue to play the game as they were motivated. Finally, the patients preferred the game version based on DDA as this game was ranked at the first and second position more times than the other two games.

# 7   Conclusion

Our contribution focuses on a dynamic difficulty adaptation (DDA) technique that aims to increase the patients' training outcomes while maintaining their motivation. The study focused on the evaluation of the effects of proposed strategy on training outcomes and motivation compared with control strategies. The results of the experiment show that DDA has increased the number of tasks, number of successful tasks and total distance in levels compared with the control strategies. This is an important factor allowing to increase the training volume in stroke patients. This study showed the importance of software control and adaptation in the case of serious games, especially for motor rehabilitation. In this area, the adaptation plays an important role to make a tradeoff between the utility of the game and its ability to create an enjoyable game experience.

Finally, some limits of the study have been studied. In particular, the number of subjects we were able to include in the study was limited. Moreover, in order to help patients to make the difference between the three difficulty strategies, we focused on a game with three ambiances. This bias has been considered not important in the study. In fact, the patients have reported the similarity between the three games and we therefore assumed that the bias has not influenced the study outcomes. In our future work, we will increase the number of subjects who should have different profiles. In addition, a particular focus will be in enhancing the difficulty strategy by manipulating time constraints on movements. This can be important for patients who have an advanced recovery stage.

# References

1. Kwakkel, G., Wagenaar, R., Koelman, T., Lankhorst, G.J., Koetsier, J.C.: Effects of intensity of rehabilitation after stroke a research synthesis. Journal of Stroke 28, 1550–1556 (1997)
2. Cirstea, M., Levin, M.: Improvement of arm movement patterns and endpoint control depends on type of feedback during practice in stroke survivors. Journal of Neurorehabilitation and Neural Repair 21, 398–411 (2007)
3. Dobkin, B.: Rehabilitation after stroke. New England Journal of Medicine 352, 1677–1684 (2005)
4. Howcroft, J., Klejman, S., Fehlings, D., Wright, V., Zabjek, K., Andrysek, J., Biddiss, E.: Active video game play in children with cerebral palsy: Potential for physical activity promotion and rehabilitation therapies. Archives of Physical Medicine and Rehabilitation 93, 1448–1456 (2012)

5. Malone, T.W.: What makes computer games fun?, vol. 6, pp. 258–277 (1980)
6. Csikszentmihalyi, M.: Beyond Boredom and Anxiety: Experiencing Flow in Work and Play. Jossey-Bass, San Francisco (2000)
7. Ávila-Sansores, S., Orihuela-Espina, F., Enrique-Sucar, L.: Patient Tailored Virtual Rehabilitation. In: Pons, J.L., Torricelli, D., Pajaro, M. (eds.) Converging Clinical. Research on Engineering, pp. 879–883. Springer (2013)
8. Rabin, B., Burdea, G., Hundal, J., Roll, D., Damiani, F.: Integrative motor, emotive and cognitive therapy for elderly patients chronic post-stroke A feasibility study of the BrightArm rehabilitation system. In: 2011 International Conference on Virtual Rehabilitation (ICVR). IEEE (2011)
9. Cameirão, M.S., Badia, S.B., Oller, E.D., Verschure, P.: Neurorehabilitation using the virtual reality based Rehabilitation Gaming System: methodology, design, psychometrics, usability and validation. Journal of Neuroengineering and Rehabilitation 7, 48 (2010)
10. Pirovano, M., Mainetti, R., Baud-Bovy, G., Lanzi, P., Borghese, N.: Self-adaptive games for rehabilitation at home. In: 2012 IEEE Conference on Computational Intelligence and Games (CIG), pp. 179–186. IEEE (2012)
11. Mihelj, M., Novak, D., Milavec, M., Ziherl, J., Olenšek, A., Munih, M.: Virtual rehabilitation environment using principles of intrinsic motivation and game design. Journal of Presence: Teleoperators and Virtual Environments 21, 1–15 (2012)
12. Hocine, N., Gouaich, A., Di Loreto, I., Joab, M.: Motivation based difficulty adaptation for therapeutic games. In: 2011 IEEE 1st International Conference on Serious Games and Applications for Health (SeGAH), pp. 1–8. IEEE (2011)
13. Gouaich, A., Hocine, N., Van Dokkum, L., Mottet, D.: Digital-pheromone based difficulty adaptation in post-stroke therapeutic games. In: Proceedings of the 2nd ACM SIGHIT International Health Informatics Symposium, pp. 5–12. ACM (2012)
14. Vincent, O.R., Folorunso, O.: A descriptive algorithm for sobel image edge detection. In: Proceedings of Informing Science & IT Education Conference (InSITE), pp. 97–107 (2009)
15. Tavener, S., Perez, D., Samothrakis, S., Colton, S.: A Survey of Monte Carlo Tree Search Methods. IEEE Transactions on Computational Intelligence and AI in Games 4 (2012)
16. Kocsis, L., Szepesvári, C.: Bandit based monte-carlo planning. In: Fürnkranz, J., Scheffer, T., Spiliopoulou, M. (eds.) ECML 2006. LNCS (LNAI), vol. 4212, pp. 282–293. Springer, Heidelberg (2006)
17. Scott, W.: Activation theory and task design. In: Organizational Behavior and Human Performance (1966)
18. Atkinson, J.W.: Motivational determinants of risk-taking behavior. Psychological Review 64 (1957)

# Personalized Adaptive Control of Training Load in Exergames from a Sport-Scientific Perspective

## Towards an Algorithm for Individualized Training

Katrin Hoffmann[1], Josef Wiemeyer[1], Sandro Hardy[2], and Stefan Göbel[2]

[1] Institute of Sport Science, Technische Universität Darmstadt, Germany
kathoffmann83@gmail.com, wiemeyer@sport.tu-darmstadt.de
[2] Multimedia Communications Lab (KOM) Technische Universität Darmstadt, Germany
{sandro.hardy,stefan.goebel}@kom.tu-darmstadt.de

**Abstract.** The following paper addresses the development and first tests of an algorithm for individual control of physical load in Serious Games for Sports and Health. The purpose is to monitor and control the heart rate (HR) as an individual indicator of optimal training load. In the context of the Serious Game "LetterBird", developed by KOM, a playful and yet effective physical training can be realized. In this game the flight of a pidgeon is controlled by a cycle ergometer. The goal is to collect letters approaching the bird at different altitudes.

From the perspective of computer science in sport, the aim was to generate an algorithm that approaches and maintains a defined target HR effectively and efficiently in individuals with different properties (e.g., age, sex, performance and health level) within the game.

For an initial application and testing of this algorithm, a two-part test series was performed with 4 participants. The results are promising: The intended HR could be evoked in all participants. Yet further tests need to be done to improve the adaptations.

# 1 Introduction

The current socio-demographic situation in many countries is characterized by a high prevalence of physical inactivity as one major risk factor for mortality [1], [11]. Therefore, many professional organizations and governmental agencies call for more physical activity (PA), particularly aerobic training. Nevertheless, the recommendations of these organizations to increase the number of burned calories per week are very challenging and hard to fulfill. Hence, motivational issues are a serious barrier to increasing PA.

Serious Games offer a possible option to solve this problem because these games claim to exploit the engaging and motivating effects of computer games to reach serious goals. Concerning the increase of PA level, "Games for Health" or "Exergames" requiring whole-body movements to control the game have been focused by numerous research projects. These studies show that Exergames have the potential to enhance physical fitness, at least at low levels [6], [12]. To improve health and fitness

S. Göbel and J. Wiemeyer (Eds.): GameDays 2014, LNCS 8395, pp. 129–140, 2014.
© Springer International Publishing Switzerland 2014

in a sustained manner, these games need to be designed in a way to ensure that players will be effectively engaged rather than quitting the game because of excessive demand or boredom.

The key problem in physical training is that identical workload (stress, i.e., defined external influences such as power, speed, etc.) can lead to different individual reactions in different organisms (strain). Therefore, the individual control of workload (stress) and strain is the key to an optimal adaptation of the organism during the physical training process.

To neither underchallenge nor overstrain the particular participant, an individual training control is important for an optimal adaptation and therefore essential for the success of the specific training.

The goal is to establish and immediately control individual workload by means of an adaptive algorithm using the example of a game-based endurance training. Hardy et al [3] developed a model addressing the relevant aspects for the development of such an Exergame (see Fig. 1). The model distinguishes between static and adaptive aspects of user and game system.

Based on this model, the game "LetterBird" was implemented. The approach of this study aims at improving the training module, embedded in the adaptive part of the system as highlighted in Fig. 1.

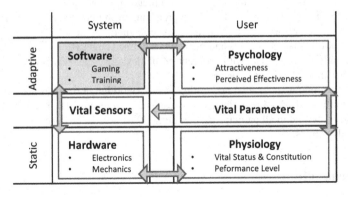

**Fig. 1.** Refined Model of the relevant aspects for the development of Exergames [3] (see text for details)

## 2    Development of the Algorithm

Various requirements from sport science need to be considered to develop an effective and efficient algorithm for the individualized and adaptive control of workload in endurance training.

When exercising, several physiological processes in the human organism are activated, ranging from the brain to the muscles. Therefore, numerous indicators can be used to measure physical workload. Among these, the heart rate (HR) is an often-used valid indicator of individual physiological workload that is easy to measure as compared to other possible indicators that can be applied to controlling a training process like oxygen uptake, hormones or lactate [2]. Different studies (e.g. [10]) show that in the range of submaximal workloads the increase of HR is linearly related to workload (i.e., exercise intensity). So, under certain conditions, the cardiopulmonary strain of the participant can be specifically controlled and an overload can be prevented by the use of submaximal HR.

Concerning appropriate training equipment, the usage of a cycle ergometer has advantages for cardio training. The weight of the participant is supported during the training process and a defined movement constrained by the limited (bio)mechanical degrees of freedom is performed. Therefore, the risk of injuries is reduced and a good comparability of the data is guaranteed [2]. To apply a cycle ergometer as training device in Serious Games, two purposes are required: control of training load and control of the game. In the game "LetterBird", power (P) in W can be adjusted specifically and accurately, e.g., by varying resistance, and was therefore chosen as load parameter. Pedal rate (PR) was chosen for game control.

To ensure accurate control of workload by P, PR should be kept within a range that does not substantially influence workload. In this regard, Löllgen et al. [5] were able to demonstrate that at submaximal workloads (70% $VO_2$ max) the PR on a cycle ergometer ranging from 40 revolutions per minute (rpm) to 80 rpm has only a small and non-significant effect on the HR. However, HR rises considerably at higher PRs (100 rpm). At maximal workload (100% $VO_2$ max) PR has no effect at all. Because the HR is the parameter to be influenced, the game settings need to be adjusted accordingly to ensure that PR is well below 100 rpm.

A major problem with the control of training load via HR is that HR normally shows a delayed response to the onset of training bouts as well as to the change of training load [7], [9].

Based on this evidence and original HR data provided by the Klinikum Darmstadt, an algorithm was developed controlling P of the cycle ergometer relative to the monitored HR of the participant.

The algorithm consists of two parts:

In the first part, the target load evoking the required target HR is calculated using the measured data of the individual HR response at two defined load levels. Therefore, the target HR scope is set submaximal, ranging from 70 to 80 % of the maximal heart rate (HRmax; implemented in the game as target HR scope = 75%HRmax ±10 bpm). In the game, the target HR is calculated as 75%HFmax. The HRmax is calculated using the equation

$$HRmax = 220 - age \text{ [8]}.$$

The second part of the algorithm sets P of the ergometer according to the calculated target load and, after a defined phase of adaptation, controls P depending on the actual HR of the participant. Provided that the target HR is reached or at least approached and due to the delayed response of the HR, control is set to adapt in steps of ±10 W every 30 s, if the HR leaves, i.e., exceeds or falls below, the target range. On the one hand, this procedure prevents an oscillation of the HR caused by the slow adaptation; on the other hand it avoids overloading the participant.

## 3    Method

In this two-phase pilot study participants performed a 4 min calibration phase to measure and calculate data required for the exercise phase. The goal of this study was to test the performance of the adaptation algorithm.

### 3.1    Participants

A convenience sample of four adults (2 men, 2 women, age: range = 26 – 56 yr., $M = 41$ yr., $SD = 13.58$, body weight: $M = 73$ kg, $SD = 14.04$) participated in this study. All participants reported to be healthy and to work out regularly at a non-competitive level. Demographical and anthropometric data is illustrated in Table 1.

**Table 1.** Demographic and anthropometric description of the participants

|  | *Participant 1* | *Participant 2* | *Participant 3* | *Participant 4* |
|---|---|---|---|---|
| **Sex** | male | female | male | female |
| **Age [yr.]** | 53 | 29 | 56 | 26 |
| **Weight [kg]** | 80 | 70 | 90 | 52 |
| **Height [cm]** | 182 | 175 | 180 | 161 |
| **BMI** | 24.2 | 22.9 | 27.8 | 21.6 |
| **Smoker** | no | no | yes | yes |
| **Target HR[1] [bpm]** | 125 | 143 | 123 | 146 |

[1] Formula: *target HR = 0.75 * (220 – age)*

### 3.2    Apparatus

All tests were performed on a cycle ergometer with a flywheel (Daum Ergometer 8008 TRS). Height and distance of the saddle were adjusted to the participant and kept constant throughout the study. The HR was monitored by a chest belt (POLAR, T31) and processed by the ergometer during the whole testing.

After starting the game "LetterBird" the HR data of the participant was logged and saved together with a corresponding timestamp, as well as P in W (measured by the ergometer) and PR (measured at the flywheel of the ergometer).

The ergometer settings only allow a differentiation in steps of 5 W, so the ergometer automatically rounds up or down. The ergometer is directly connected to a computer, where the software controlling the game "LetterBird" runs.

The goal of the game "LetterBird" is to collect randomly occurring letters with an animated pigeon. The approaching letters are differentiated into two types:

- Type 1: slow, score: 100 points
- Type 2: fast, score: 500 points

The altitude of the pigeon is controlled by the PR. With increasing PR the pigeon rises and if the PR is decreased, the pigeon sinks down. The PR range controlling the game is set to a range from 70 to 90 rpm. A higher or lower PR does not influence the game play: Below 70 rpm the pigeon stays at the bottom, beyond 90 rpm the pigeon flies at the top of the screen.

## 3.3    Procedure

The study was divided in two phases: calibration and exercise phase. Four participants passed a first tests series, whereas one participant was tested twice, i.e., repeated the calibration and exercise phase procedure after correction of the algorithm.

*Calibration Phase*
After a short explanation about the game principle, the participants performed a 4 min calibration phase playing the game "LetterBird" at two successive load levels for 2 min each. The two load levels were adjusted depending on the BMI classification of the participant (normal weight vs. overweight):

- Normal weight (BMI $\leq$ 25):

− Load Level 1: 1 W/kg bodyweight (BW)
− Load Level 2: 2 W/kg BW

- Overweight (BMI>25):
   − Load Level 1: 0.5 W/kg BW
   − Load Level 2: 1 W/kg BW


While the measured data was analyzed and the required data calculated, the participant stopped exercising allowing the individual HR to return to pre-exercise levels.

*Exercise Phase*
In the exercise phase the participants again played the "Pigeon game" on the cycle ergometer at four different load levels. The first two load levels matched the load levels in the calibration phase; participants 1 and 2 played for 2 min per load level and participants 3 and 4 played for a shortened time (1 min) per load level

All four participants performed at the third load level for one minute. At this load level, the calculated target load was set at the ergometer. The fourth and last load level represented the automatic load control, in which the ergometer controls and varies the load automatically according to the HR of the participant. The test was stopped after either 10 min or at a stable steady state at the target HR. The procedure is illustrated in Table 2.

## 3.4    Data Processing

First, sex, age, weight, height, sports and smoking behavior were recorded. BMI was calculated using the formula

$$BMI = weight\ [kg]\ /\ height^2\ [m])$$

to classify the participants into normal weight and overweight.

**Table 2.** Illustrated procedure of the exercise phase after onset of the exercise

|  | Timing procedure for participants 1 and 2 [min:sec] | Timing procedure for participants 3 and 4 [min:sec] |
|---|---|---|
| **Load Level 1** | 0:00 – 1:59 | 0:00 – 0:59 |
| **Load Level 2** | 2:00 – 3:59 | 1:00 – 1:59 |
| **Calculated target load** | 4:00 – 4:59 | 2:00 – 2:59 |
| **Automatic load control** | 5:00 – 10:00 | 3:00 – 10:00 |

The target HR was calculated using formula target $HR = 75\% \ (220\text{-}age)$ (see Table 1).

Mean values ($M$) and standard deviation ($SD$) for HR over the last 60 s for every load level were calculated after the calibration phase. This data was used as HR for the corresponding load level. The target load evoking the target HR was calculated using the formula:

$$target\ load = BW * (load\_level\ 2 + \frac{target\ HR - (meanHR\ load\_level\ 2)}{(meanHR\ load\_level\ 2) - (meanHR\ load\_level\ 1)})$$

$M$ and $SD$ for PR were calculated for the whole testing period for all data >0.

## 4　　Results

The algorithm performed satisfactorily in the first two participants, whereas the target HR of the other two participants was reached after a transient increase beyond the tolerance. As an example, the data of one participant of each group (participants 2 and 4) is illustrated.

### 4.1　　First Test Series ($N = 4$)

In the first two participants the target HR was reached as expected at the third load level of the exercise phase (target load) and remained in a region of stable steady state. For participant 1, the target load level even matched load level 2, so the target HR was already reached in the calibration phase.

As expected, the HR showed an initial steep increase after the onset of exercise, followed by a leveling off in the course of the load level during the calibration phase. For participant 2 (see Fig. 2), average values of the HR in the last 60 s of each load level were 118 bpm for load level 1 (70 W) and 135 bpm for load level 2 (140 W). The target load was 2.31 W/kg BW (≙165 W) expecting to evoke the target HR of 143 bpm.

The mean PR for all valid data (values >0) was 80.69 rpm ($SD$=6.37).

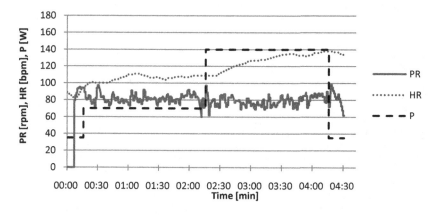

**Fig. 2.** Calibration phase of participant 2

The first minutes of the exercise phase replicated the calibration phase with a less fluctuating increase of the HR (see Fig. 3). Target HR was reached approximately 30 s after starting the target load level. Mean HR of the last minutes was 138 bpm ($SD$=1.098), i.e., slightly beneath the target HR (mean deviation from target HR: -4.87 bpm), but still in the intended training range (72%HFmax). An approach of the target HR "from beneath" was still realized and an overload was prevented.

In the exercise phase mean PR was 80.83 rpm ($SD$=5.99) for valid data (values >0).

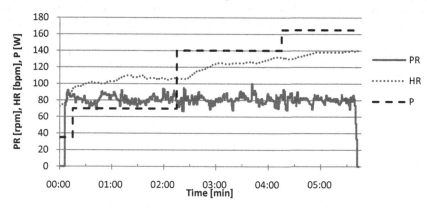

**Fig. 3.** Exercise phase of participant 2

In contrast, the analysis of the HR dynamics of participants 3 und 4 showed a different picture.

For participant 4, a continuous rise of the HR with no clear steady state of HR dynamics was found in the calibration phase (see Fig. 4).

Nevertheless, average values of the last 60 s for each load level were calculated (load level 1: $M$ = 118 bpm; load level 2: $M$ = 152 bpm). This resulted in a target load of 1.81/kg BW (≙94.12 W). A higher PR range than required to control the game ($M$ = 79.35 rpm, $SD$ =9.22) was identified already in the calibration phase,.

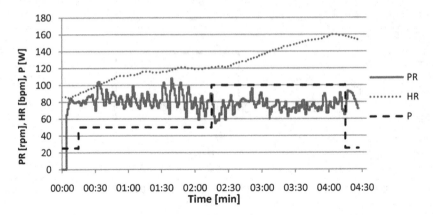

**Fig. 4.** Calibration phase of participant 4

A comparison of HR values in the exercise phase revealed considerable differences between participants 2 and 4. First, the HR recording in participant 4 was interrupted for 5 s (from 2:14 to 2:19) due to technical problems. Nevertheless, PR and P were still logged and due to the constant rise of the HR at this point the missing data could be interpolated.

Additionally, caused by the shortened duration of load level 1 and 2 causing a shortened adaptation time for the HR, the HR response was overshooting (Maximum HR = 161 bpm, corresponding to 82.99% HRmax). A downward adjustment of two steps (in total 20 W) was necessary to reach the target HR of 146 bpm (see Fig. 5)

In participant 4, the exception occurred that the calculated target load was beneath load level 2. Consequently, an approach of the target HR from beneath was rendered impossible.

However, average HR after the target load level (2 min after onset until the end of exercise) ($M$ = 155 bpm, $SD$ = 3.67 bpm) was within the intended training range (79.74% HRmax).

Mean PR in the exercise phase (for data >0) was 79. 51 rpm ($SD$ = 8.86).

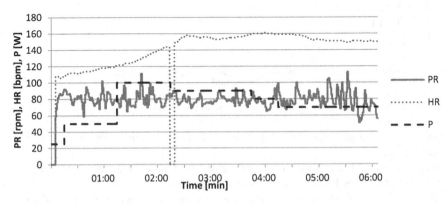

**Fig. 5.** Exercise Phase of participant 4. Note a short period of interrupted recording of HR in the exercise phase.

## 4.2    Adjustments

Before further testing, the following adjustments were made to improve the approach towards the target HR:

- If the calculated target load is lower than load at load level 2 of the calibration phase, this calculated target load is substituted as load at load level 2 in the exercise phase.
- A shortening of the load level duration turned out not to be suitable for the HR adaptation and is therefore set to two minutes. A slow and continuous adaptation to the workload is preferred.
- To minimize the risk of an excessive HR caused by a high PR level, the calculated load in the target load level is subtracted by 10%. Possible efficiency issues, i.e., longer time to reach the target HR, are accepted in favor of the HR approach from beneath.
- The calculation of the average HR in load level 1 and 2 is reduced to the last 30 s of each load level, so the HR has enough time to adapt to the current workload.

## 4.3    Second Test Series (Case Study)

Participant 4 was tested again to validate the adjustments of the algorithm and to test the efficiency.

The calibration phase matched the calibration phase in the first test (see Fig. 6). Maximum HR was lower (148 versus 161 bpm) than the maximal HR in the first test. Average value of the HR in the load level 1 (118 versus 118 bpm) is comparable, but in load level 2 mean HR was lower than in the first test (146 versus 152 bpm). Subtracting 10% of the calculated value resulted in a target load of 1.79 W/kg BW (90 W).

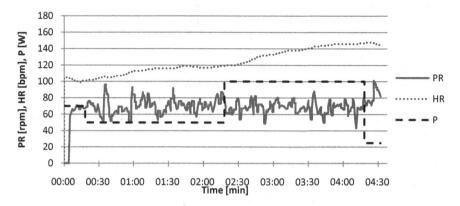

**Fig. 6.** Calibration phase of participant 4 (second trial)

Due to the adjustments the HR followed the expected HR dynamics during the exercise phase (see Fig. 7). A continuous rise of the HR towards the target HR was observed reaching a steady state after approximately four minutes from onset of exercise. Average HR during this steady state was 151 bpm (*SD* =1.61 bpm; range: *Minimum* =146 bpm, *Maximum* =155 bpm). The data also showed a two-step downward adjustment of P. Compared to the first test series this adaptation leads to a steady state of HR. As expected no overshooting or oscillations of the HR can be observed.

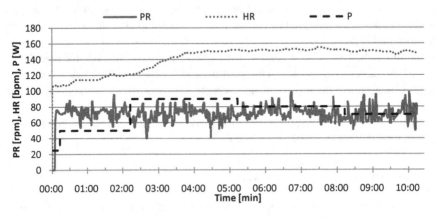

**Fig. 7.** Re-testing of participant 4 with the adjusted algorithm (exercise phase)

## 5     Discussion

The aim of this study was to develop and test an algorithm for individual adaptive control of training load from a sport scientific point of view in the context of the Serious Game "LetterBird". In the first test series, in all four participants average HR was inside the expected target HR range from the beginning of the automatic load control to the end of exercise. Nevertheless, the HR increased beyond the tolerances in two participants causing a successive downward adaptation of the algorithm for more than one step. This demonstrates that the automatic load control algorithm reacted to the increasing HR and adapted the workload as expected; in this regard, the algorithm was working correctly. However, the aim of this research was to guide the actual HR towards the target HR from beneath; this result was not established in two participants. Apparently, the calculation of the target load was not suitable for these two participants.

Compared to participant 1 and 2, participants 3 and 4 show several differences that may have caused the different HR response pattern:

- Smoking behavior:
  Participants 3 and 4 are smokers, whereas participants 1 and 2 did not smoke.
- Target load:
  Although all participants reported to be physically active, the target load of participant 1 and 2 was considerably higher than in participant 3 and 4, indicating a

lower fitness level (participant 1: 180 W, participant 2: 165 W; participant 3: 95 W; participant 4: 90 W). Therefore, the influence of fitness level needs to be considered to adapt the algorithm. Particularly, personal reports on engagement in sports disciplines, average work out time per week and PA level at leisure may serve as indirect indicators of performance or fitness level.

• Shortened length of load level 1 and 2:
  Participants 1 and 2 performed load level 1 and 2 in the exercise phase for 2 minutes, respectively. In contrast, participant 3 and 4 performed for only 1 minute at each load level.

In the adjusted version, technical sources of error leading to an incorrect calculation of the target load were corrected. Using this adapted formula calculating the target load appears to be a reasonable approach preventing an overshooting HR. The target HR was evoked efficiently and effectively in the presented trial.

## 6     Conclusion

The results of the reported tests are promising. The data indicate that the developed algorithm, especially the adjusted version, is a reasonable approach to ensure an individual adaptive control of training load in the game "LetterBird". Of course, the small sample is not representative, so further tests including different age, BMI, cycling experience and performance level (e.g., athletes versus non-athletes) are needed to prove the effectiveness and efficiency of the algorithm.

A problem not yet solved is the influence of PR used to control the pigeon on the HR. Therefore, a further study is required to test the influence of these large short-term oscillations on HR dynamics.

Furthermore, the question has to be addressed, if the preferred PR of the participants has an influence on the HR. Previous studies on preferred PR confirm that the preferred PR exceeds the most efficient one [4].

In the future, the algorithm is intended to be integrated into a long-term training plan, taking into account the current physical condition to enable an optimal and individualized adaptation to training.

## References

1. ACSM: Quantity and Quality of Exercise for Developing and Maintaining Cardiorespiratory, Musculoskeletal, and Neuromotor Fitness in Apparently Healthy Adults: Guidance for Prescribing Exercise. Medicine & Science in Sports & Exercise 43(7), 1334–1359 (2011)
2. Hebestreit, H., Lawrenz, W., Zelger, O., Kienast, W., Jüngst, B.-K.: Ergometrie im Kindes- und Jugendalter. Monatsschrift Kinderheilkunde 145, 1326–1336 (1997)
3. Hardy, S., Göbel, S., Gutjahr, M., Wiemeyer, J., Steinmetz, R.: Adaptation Model for Indoor Games. International Journal of Computer Science in Sport 11(1), 73–85 (2012)

4. Kohler, G., Boutellier, U.: The generalized force-velocity relationship explains why the preferred pedaling rate exceeds the most efficient one. European Journal of Applied Physiology 94, 188–195 (2005)
5. Löllgen, H., Graham, T., Sjogaard, G.: Muscle metabolites, force, and perceived exertion bicycling at varying pedal rates. Medicine and Science in Sports and Exercise 12, 345–351 (1980)
6. Peng, W., Lin, J.-H., Crouse, J.C.: Is playing Exergames really exercising? A meta-analysis of energy expenditure in active video games. Cyberpsychology, Behavior, and Social Networking 14(11), 681–688 (2011)
7. Ricardo, D.R., de Almeida, M.B., Franklin, B.A., Araujo, C.G.S.: Initial and Final Exercise Heart Rate – Influence of Gender, Aerobic Fitness, and Clinical Status. Chest 127(1), 318–327 (2005)
8. Roberts, R.A., Landwehr, R.: The surprising history of the "HRmax=220-age" equation. Journal of Exercise Physiology Online 5(2), 1–10 (2002)
9. Springer, C., Barstow, T.J., Wasserman, K., Cooper, D.M.: Oxygen uptake and heart rate responses during hypoxic exercise in children and adults. Medicine and Science in Sport and Exercise 23(1), 71–79 (1991)
10. Vokac, Z., Bell, H., Bautz-Holter, E., Rodahl, K.: Oxygen uptake/heart rate relationship in leg and arm exercise, sitting and standing. Journal of Applied Physiology 39, 54–59 (1975)
11. WHO: Global recommendations on physical activity for health. Genf: WHO (2010)
12. Wiemeyer, J., Kliem, A.: Serious games and ageing - a new panacea? European Review of Aging and Physical Activity 9(1), 41–50 (2012)

# Creating Age-Specific Interactive Environments about Medical Treatments for Children and Adolescent Patients Diagnosed with Cancer

Carina Gansohr[1], Katharina Emmerich[1], Maic Masuch[1],
Oliver Basu[2], and Lorenz Grigull[3]

[1] University of Duisburg-Essen, Duisburg, Germany
carina.gansohr@stud.uni-due.de,
{katharina.emmerich,maic.masuch}@uni-due.de
[2] Essen University Hospital, Essen, Germany
o.basu@uk-essen.de
[3] Hannover Medical School, Hannover, Germany
grigull.lorenz@mh-hannover.de

**Abstract.** This paper describes the development of an interactive multimedia environment designed for helping young patients to understand cancer-related medical treatments. The application is not intended to replace the medical consultation but to support it by conveying general information about necessary procedures and thus giving doctors more time for individual concerns and fears of their patients. We used a user-centered approach to author the information advisedly to suit different age groups: preschoolers, school-aged children and teenagers. All approaches are combined to an interactive entertainment environment that uses videos, game based interaction and interactive storytelling to make new knowledge easily accessible.

**Keywords:** user-centered design, interactive hypermedia, media for children, learning and knowledge creation.

## 1 Introduction

Being diagnosed with a severe disease is an incisive experience. Besides anxiety and pain, patients often also experience significant uncertainty due to a lack of knowledge regarding their illness and related methods of treatment. In such a situation, providing them with appropriate and reliable information is important to increase patients' understanding, confidence and trust with health care providers and thus also patients' well-being [17]. In practice, it is the doctor's task to explain treatment procedures and consequences in a consultation. As time for these face-to-face conversations is limited and patients may not be able to understand and memorize all important aspects directly, they are usually also provided with additional information material, mostly in form of printed brochures.

S. Göbel and J. Wiemeyer (Eds.): GameDays 2014, LNCS 8395, pp. 141–152, 2014.

While currently available material generally includes a dense bundle of valuable information, the presentation is mainly kept rather simple including formal texts and a limited range of illustrations. These kinds of standard informative explanations are not suitable for all groups of patients, particularly children. Children have to be considered as a target group with specific abilities and information needs due to their limited knowledge, understanding and incomplete development of cognitive skills. Often, information for children is not age-related, either too technical or too trivial. New media technologies like animated videos and digital games provide advanced opportunities to present information in an appropriate way for children and arouse their interest compared to print material [6].

Though information material dealing with cancer itself is prevalent, information referring to certain medical treatments is rather scarce, especially regarding material that is appropriate for children. Thus, in this paper, we present an approach of using interactive digital videos to inform young cancer patients about the diagnostic procedure of a lumbar puncture and its consequences, suggesting that this kind of information presentation fosters knowledge creation and preoccupation with the content. In order to assure that the video application is adapted to the patients' worries, abilities, needs and their complicated life situation, it is developed by following a user-centered design approach.

## 2    User-Centered Design

User-centered design is an established approach to design software applications for clearly defined target groups. The main idea is to focus on the user and the intended usage of the application to ensure a smooth interaction, to avoid misunderstandings and frustration and to decrease the user's learning effort [1]. In general, user-centered design methods are supposed to improve the usefulness and usability of the product and hence the satisfaction of the users [18]. In case of informatory applications for children that are supposed to be used voluntarily – in contrast to software that is institutionally applied at school – it is supposed to become even more important to satisfy the users' needs in order to attract their attention and to keep up their interest.

Since the term was coined in the 1980s by Norman and Draper [14], user-centered design became a widespread practice applied in different fields and disciplines, e.g. website development and software engineering [19]. Related design principles like Shneiderman's eight golden rules [16] and Nielsen's heuristics for usability engineering [13] have been established and are still often referred to in current design practice. As described in [19], it can be differentiated between three main phases in a user-centered design process, including design research, the actual design and design evaluation. The main idea of user-centered design is to involve future users in all these phases in order to get feedback constantly and to be able to iteratively adapt the system. Especially the first phase – design research – is about "understanding users and their needs" [19, p.2] and is focused in the following course of this paper. As the work presented in this paper deals with the special target group of seriously ill children and teenagers, the accomplishment of an understanding of their desires and needs constitutes the basis for an informed design process. Furthermore, design research also includes considerations about already existing related work in order to derive design recommendations. Thus, the following sections outline the user-centered design process giving a detailed description of the needs and characteristics of the target group (based on literature and interviews with pediatric head doctors) as well as an overview of related work and already existing approaches to establish new media applications to inform patients.

## 2.1    Designing an Interactive Information Environment for Seriously Ill Children

The target group of seriously ill children mainly differs from other groups regarding two aspects: characteristics related to the state of health and characteristics related to age. Illness itself, but also medical treatments, are often connected with pain, fear and worries. Recently diagnosed children suffer from the new situation which is full of uncertainty: They are not aware of what happens during the treatments, what the test results will be like and if they can finally conquer illness. Hence, the reduction of those anxieties should be focused. Interviews with two pediatric head doctors indicate that uncertainty is mostly responsible for fears concerning medical treatments, which can be met by honest explanations. Well prepared and briefed children are likely to experience less anxiety, because expected stress provokes less fear than unexpected stress [6]. Therefore, the best way to face anxiety and worries is to describe medical procedures in a detailed and not extenuated way, necessarily adapted to the user's age.

Concerning age, children's perception and understanding of illness differ significantly from those of adults [3]. Furthermore, regarding the group of children there are also important differences regarding the perception of illness and medical treatment between different developmental stages [5, 11]. The target group is therefore subdivided into three different age groups, whose developmental stages are premised on Piaget's theory of cognitive development [15]: Children that belong to the so-called preoperational stage are usually in the kindergarten, while children in school-age can be categorized into the concrete operational stage and teenagers into the formal operational stage. The characteristics and differences of these three stages with reference to [15] are presented in the following.

### The Preoperational Phase: Pre-school Children

The preoperational phase is characterized by a mental stage in which children's thinking is directly linked to the observable environment [5]. Logical skills and hypothetical thinking are not yet developed, thus young children do not make predictions about the future nor do they think about consequences of actions, but just concentrate on the current situation. Due to that, process procedures, such as medical treatments, cannot be captured correctly [11]. It is hardly possible to explain to children in this developmental stage what happens inside their bodies and how medical treatment or diagnostic procedures may actually help them. Furthermore, young children do not see the relation between cause and effect, either. Instead of being able to understand why they are sick, children in this stage attribute their observable symptoms to factors that are directly linked to the environment (e.g. visual stimuli, noises, smell and taste) in order to explain them [11]. Hence, an aching leg may rather be related to the fact that it is bandaged than to the fact that it was operated.

Accordingly, it is suggested to describe medical treatments by mainly focusing on what the child will directly perceive and experience during the procedure. Furthermore, tools and utensils that are used during a medical treatment should be explained regarding their appearance and how the child will experience them (e.g. the gel for a medical ultrasonography is cold on the skin). In this context, it also has to be accounted for the fact that pre-school children often tend to assign simple motives to persons and objects: An injection hurts and thus is regarded as 'mean' [11]. Besides, they are not able to empathize with other persons. Accordingly, for children it is hard to understand that the doctor is not intentionally doing harm. A consequence is the perception of the medical practitioner being a punisher, when he is connected to a painful situation due to generalization effects. As this fear can also be triggered by a doctor's white coat [11], it is suggested to present medical staff and objects in a neutral way, so that no fear will be aroused.

Due to the lack of logical reasoning, when addressing pre-school children it is important to provide understandable explanations of actions and detailed descriptions of procedures, because otherwise children will come up with their own, mostly misleading, interpretations. Such misunderstandings can lead to irrational fears and worries which should be avoided.

**The Concrete Operational Phase: School-Children**
The concrete operational stage is mainly characterized by raising mental abilities such as logical reasoning, realistic argumentations and the recognition of cause and effect relations. All these aspects also lead to the understanding of internal, invisible causes. Due to that, children in this stage can explain illness by referring to internal processes of their bodies [11]. Furthermore, they become able to recognize the time aspect of illness and the variability of stages of illness, so that they increasingly understand it as a process. Due to that, the multi-media concept can refer to inner body processes by using illustrated animations. This can also lead to a better understanding of the cause and effect relation between medicine, medical treatments and the disease. Hence, it can increase the acceptance and compliance to medical treatments. School kids also begin to understand that, although treatments may be harmful for a certain time, they are supporting their long-term recovery [11].

In this stage it is also possible to take other persons' perspectives and thus comprehend their actions to some extent. Therefore, experiences of other patients can also be referred to as an additional information source. Besides, an interactive media environment can be applied by using interactive elements and mini-games to involve the user in a playful way. The self-efficacy that is supposed to be experienced by this can lead to a better understanding of cause and effect relations. On the contrary, hypothetical thinking is an ability that is not yet fully evolved in this developmental stage. Therefore, it is recommended to describe treatments step by step, because otherwise it can lead to misunderstandings [11]. For instance, children assume that a treatment plan, that was once elaborated, has to be met under all conditions without questioning it in case of changed circumstances.

**The Formal Operational Phase: Teenagers**

In the formal operational stage teenagers' abilities approximate those of adults [5]. Complex cause and effect relations, logical thinking as well as hypothetical thinking are established. Additionally, teenagers more often refer to psychological issues and peers become more important. They can express their feelings and spent a lot of time thinking about medical procedures and alternative treatments [11]. They also want to participate in the planning process and prefer to be treated as independent persons who can make decisions on their own due to their high need for autonomy [11].

In order to account for the needs of teenagers, medical treatments have to be explained comprehensively, also including possible alternatives, positive as well as negative consequences and coping strategies. An informative multi-media concept should help to inform young adults, so that they feel enabled to make reasonable decisions about medical treatments and to be prepared for further discussions with their medical practitioners. This may help them gaining a perception of being taken seriously.

## 2.2    Related Work

Besides the analysis of the users' needs and situation, it is also part of a user-centered design process to have a look at related work and concepts that are similar to the planned project. Some of these approaches are exemplarily described in the following and discussed in terms of the fitting between main design aspects and the characteristics of our target group in order to inform the following design process.

On the website of the 'Children and Teenagers Scottish Cancer Network' (CATSCAN) society[1] there are several online information videos provided for children in which a nurse explains in simple sentences what the specific treatment is about and how it is conducted. Furthermore, potentially unpleasant or painful aspects are shortly discussed, explaining the reasons for them and possible coping strategies. Although the content is adjusted to children, there are some design aspects that could be amended. First there is no video or other form of visualization of an ongoing treatment, thus it is explained but not exactly shown what happens. As explained above, this may lead to uncertainty and misunderstandings. Furthermore, the viewer is supposed to empathize with the young patients who are shown in the videos but the role of them is rather minor as they do neither explain the procedure nor report about own experiences. Finally the videos are conventional ones, thus allowing the user to pause, rewind and fast-forward, but not supporting any other interaction or individualization.

---

[1]   http://www.catscan.scot.nhs.uk

The German web portal 'Medizin für Kids'[2] provides a collection of information about health related issues and diseases by presenting it in several forms (e.g. texts, illustrations, animations, field reports and literature recommendations). The preparation of information is adapted to children, for instance metaphors are used to simplify complex aspects or to provide stories that may help children to cope with medical treatment situations by offering distraction from the actual treatment. One application[3] is especially interesting because it presents a more interactive approach of information mediation. On first glance, it is an illustrated video, dealing with the case of a young boy who has to receive bone marrow transplantation. But the linear course of video sequences is interrupted by interactive mini-games several times, in which the user has to fulfill certain tasks related to the treatment, e.g. preparing an intravenous drip. These interactive parts of the application are supposed to increase the users engagement and at the same time may contribute to the need of autonomy, as the user is directly involved in the treatment process and can make own decisions. However, due to the very simple interactive parts and the cartoon-like graphic design, this application is considered to predominantly address younger children.

Finally, there are also digital games which are focused on certain diseases and comprise information about consequences and treatment [10]. One example is the popular health game Re-Mission by Hope-Lab[4], which represents the fight against cancer cells in form of a 3D-ego-shooter. In this playful environment, information about cancer, medicine and several treatment methods is provided. For this and other games it was shown that playing the game contributes to knowledge creation about disease-related aspects and may even increase feelings of self-efficacy [4, 8]. Furthermore, health-related games can be used to initiate informed conversations among patients and between patients and physicians [7]. Games like Re-Mission offer a high level of interactivity and bear the potential to immerse the player for a long time, and it has been shown that the active engagement of children in seeking information supports their adjustment [2]. However, games are at the same time very complex systems that have to be designed carefully. Furthermore, the amount of information that can be integrated well into the game environment and story without interfering with game flow and fun is limited.

## 3    Concept of an Interactive Information Environment

As shown in the previous section, pre-school children, school children and teenagers differ significantly regarding their cognitive development and related characteristics. To comprise all three age groups, three sub-concepts were implemented to meet all age-specific and differing needs. Due to the young children's lack in reading skills, the starting page has to meet the requirements in young children's usability (e.g. by using audio commentary). On this page the user can choose between the three groups

---

[2]    http://www.medizin-fuer-kids.de

[3]    http://www.medizin-fuer-kids.de/kinderklinik/krankheiten/
Krebs/martin_kmt/martin_kmt_content.html

[4]    http://www.re-mission.net/

Hallo und Herzlich Willkommen!

Hier kannst duch dich mit deinen
bevorstehenden Behandlungen vertraut
machen. Du erfährst wieso sie nötig sind,
was dabei geschieht und wo es gemacht
wird. Damit du auch die richtigen
Informationen bekommst, wähle bitte
deine Altersgruppe aus.

Hier gibt's was zu
hören, also
Lautsprecher an!

Vorschulkind    Schulkind    Teenager

**Fig. 1.** Start menu of the interactive environment invites to choose an appropriate age category. The menu can be verbalized to comprise illiterate children.

by clicking on an icon that is representing the age by a drawn young person which will be guiding through the application and is meant to represent the user in the following. Here, the age is not directly mentioned, so that the user is allowed to categorize himself into one of the three groups: Pre-School Child, School-Child or Teenager. Hence, the ability to read is suggested by using the school term (see figure 1).

All of the three sub-concepts have a similar structure and are blended into a story, which allows the integration of the protagonist's feelings and experiences of the protagonist in a way that is appealing to children. Hence, a narrative storytelling can transport the content in a more personalized and less complex way. In the implementation of the concept the story is about the protagonist "Tim", who has not felt well for a long time. In order to check if he has got cancer cells in the neuronal system, he is going through a lumbar puncture. This is a medical treatment, where cerebrospinal fluid is getting off of the lower back by a long injection needle. The multi-media application has the goal to inform the user about the treatment in an honest and realistic way, while decreasing the level of anxiety and worries as well as strengthening the feeling of self-efficacy in order to make the interaction between patient and medical professionals easier. In the following it is shown how this is achieved in each group and what leads to the design decisions.

### 3.1    Concept and Implementation for Pre-school Children

Pre-school children do not have distinctive mental and motoric skills and are not able to read. Due to that, this age-stage has to be designed rather different compared to the other groups [9]. One consequence resulting from the children's lack of reading skills is the menu from which it can choose the kind of treatment it is interested in. Therefore, the implementation provides a cross section of a hospital which enables the user to recognize the rooms and the derived treatments easily. Further, it is believed that children in this age are not sitting in front of the computer alone, but with their parents or other adults, who assist them going through the application. Hence, text can be used to specifically announce the adults to give useful information that can lead to wider interaction in front of the computer or lead to further reduction of anxieties.

Regarding the design, it has to be discussed which form of visual representation is most appropriate for pre-school children. Although the information has to be realistic and honest, a video showing real sequences does not seem to be optimal, because of

**Fig. 2.** The visualization of a lumbar puncture for preschoolers uses a representative character

the mass of details which could be overstraining [12]. Illustrations are more suitable because the abstraction level can be increased while the level of complexity can be reduced. Furthermore, they are able to focus on essential aspects that could otherwise be drowned by other stimuli as well as they can reduce potential distractions. Additionally, animated sequences are used in the implementation to call the child's attention to the most important aspects.

Another advantage of illustrations is the easy and helpful usage of metaphors which can be used in order to explain or to diminish the treatment: E.g. the leaking of the cerebrospinal fluid is often attributed negatively, but it is in fact not painful or terrifying because it is clear as water or clear as tears. Expressed metaphorically, crying is not painful likewise, but it is neither something one like to do.

A further way to diminish potentially terrifying aspects is the usage of the protagonist's teddy bear to show the treatment process. Furthermore, the protagonist is able to see interventions that he could not have seen if the treatment was accomplished on him, e.g. during the lumbar puncture he can comment on what is happening behind the teddy's back (see figure 2). Due to that he is able to reduce the uncertainty that is mostly responsible for anxieties.

After the explanation of the treatment it is also important to discuss how the story should end. A positive result could lead to false anticipations whereas a negative result could be too frustrating. Hence, an open end is preferable because of its ability to explain the consequences in either way (e.g. Tim and his teddy can go home directly or have to withstand some more treatments to get the best therapy available.)

Finally the room in which the treatment takes place has to be presented in order to prepare the child for the upcoming treatment in a clinic specific way. To do so an illustrated design that shows the room and its instruments is implemented in the prototype. Those instruments that are dealing with the lumbar puncture are focused whereas other components are removed. By clicking on objects the user navigates through the room and gets further information about the requested object to become acquainted to the room and the instruments that he will be confronted with during the real treatment.

### 3.2    Concept and Implementation for School Kids

Children in this development stage have extended skills and abilities. Therefore, the explanations can be more complex as in the development stage presented before.

Here the focus will be set on the support of the understanding of cause and effect relations by using more interaction sequences as well as inner-body animations. First, it is necessary to discuss the kind of visual representation. Realistic video sequences or photos will be much more specified and detailed which will lead to a more realistic and credible communication to reduce misleading expectations. It can be used to show the room or the medical treatment. During interviews with pediatric head doctors following points have to be considered:

- On the one hand the video must not show disturbing scenes but on the other hand no decisive elements should be left out since the children will go through the treatment nevertheless. This balancing act can be met by varying the degree of detail or by setting the camera's focus on other aspects (e.g. the patient's face).
- The medical practitioner as well as the patient has to be experienced enough to achieve a situation that is as calm and routinized as possible.
- Both of them should interact and communicate with each other to emphasize the patient's feelings and the doctor's empathy.
- The photo and video material should be hospital specific since the atmosphere, as well as the treatment procedure itself, can be different and can hence evoke wrong expectations. Another advantage of clinic specific material is the personal connection to the hospital's staff.

Still, there are some aspects that can be better explained by illustrations, like cause and effect relations as well as reactions inside the body (see figure 3). Here the usage of metaphors can be especially helpful. Hence, a mixed visual design is most promising. The first part of the implementation tells the protagonist's story and explains the treatment and its effects by using illustrations. Afterwards, the child gets the opportunity to click through a digital representation of the treatment room in a similar manner as in the previous age group, but with the difference that the representation is based on clinic specific photo material. In the following a realistic video is offered showing the treatment in detail, but considering the points given above.

The way in which explanation is given differs between the previous and the given age group as well and can be shown by following example: Since it is important to explain that the extraction is only possible if the patient is bending his back so that the neural spines open, an animated interaction part is used to show this cause and effect relation in the inner body by bringing in explaining metaphors (spiral spring). The interaction part is also useful because it implicates an expected reaction of the patient which could lead to self-efficacy.

Another important point to be explained is the patient's influence on his welfare, e.g. after the lumbar puncture it is necessary to lie still in bed. Here the user is given the choice to lie in bed hearing some music or to play soccer by presenting two interactive buttons. According to his decision the positive or negative reaction is shown.

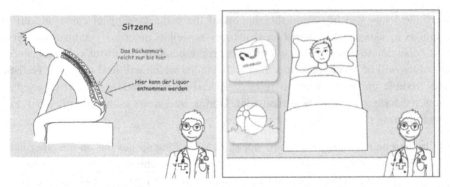

**Fig. 3.** The visualization of a lumbar puncture for school children focuses on inner body processes and explains cause and effect relations by using interactive scenes

### 3.3    Concept and Implementation for Teenagers

The most important distinction in this age stage compared to the other ones is the right to have a say. Teenagers can refuse treatments and due to that it is the highest priority to support the teenager's decision process. Therefore, complete information about the treatment, its side effects, alternatives, coping strategies and solutions have to be presented. Furthermore teenagers have a low tolerance level, referring to a 'childish design'. Although illustrations will be used in the same context as in the school-kid stage, they have to be modified. The design should also be more realistic than child-like and can be compared to illustrations used in senior high school books. Additionally, interaction parts and metaphors should be used with a lower frequency to let it appear more serious and adult. In this way, the teenager is getting a perception of being taken seriously.

Due to that, the presented concept is extended by further information materials where particular attention is paid to the peers, who become more and more important. Hence, the possibility to share personal experiences and information should be given. With regard to the medical background and the sensitive theme, following points have to be considered:

- Experienced patients should have the opportunity to choose between different kinds of ways to express their experiences. Texts, photos, videos and audios can be used, regarding that some teenagers would like to stay more anonymously.
- Experienced patients should be addressed by the hospital's staff because otherwise they may not use the application due to their already existing experience.
- Moderation through the hospital's staff is necessary to avoid terrifying statements.

## 4    Discussion

Among many aspects of the development of an interactive hypermedia environment for teaching knowledge about medical treatments, the core questions were:

**User Centered Design:** The development of the concept was a strict User Centered Design approach. Expert interviews with medical personal and doctors, as well as children and teenagers from different target groups were conducted. This concept is well-known in HCI, we extended it also to the construction of the knowledge spaces. From these the appropriate representation for each age is deduced. It is always difficult to address diverse target groups as exact as possible while keeping the overall effort feasible. We ended up in three versions as a compromise.

**Game-like Interactivity:** In learning environments it is preferable to let learners construct their own knowledge (constructivism). We, however, preferred for this project a hypermedia environment that follows a cognitivism approach as we deal mainly with factual knowledge. Interactivity can preserve engagement and we also allow users to switch between the different explanations at will or to explore different areas at their own pace (resulting in self-efficacy). Whether it is connected to a higher learning effect is subject to a follow-up study.

**Realism:** The use of realism in contrast to graphical abstraction is continuously discussed in visualizations. A mixture allows keeping a general abstract framework, and the possibility to add clinic-specific, individual content (photos, videos etc.). Even doctors were divided about what should be revealed to patients and in what amount of detail. This question is vividly illustrated by the consideration whether to show the punctuation needle to the patient or not.

**Storytelling:** Using a backstory with persona can be beneficial in terms of reception and acceptance, if identification with the protagonist occurs. Due to the obvious link by sharing the same diagnosis this was not an issue for users.

## 5    Conclusion

The main goal of this project was to help patients and doctors alike by fostering the communication process in a difficult situation. Patients face the diagnosis of cancer, doctors struggle with permanent shortage of appropriate face-to-face counseling time. We used a strictly user-centered development to implement an age-specific interactive multimedia environment for young patients. Three target groups were identified. Game-like interactivity and a storytelling approach were used to foster engagement of users in patient education. Though we did not run a formal evaluation, this goal was reached. Reception and acceptance of the solution was very well. If a reduction of anxiety can be achieved and the compliance will be raised significantly will be subject to further research.

## References

1. Abras, C., Maloney-Krichmar, D., Preece, J.: User-Centered Design. In: Bainbridge, W. (ed.) Encyclopedia of Human-Computer Interaction. Sage Publications, Thousand Oaks (2004)
2. Bearison, D.J.: Pediatric Psychology and Children's Medical Problems. In: Damon, W., Sigel, I.E., Renninger, K.A. (eds.) Handbook of Child Psychology. Child psychology in practice, 5th edn., vol. 4, pp. 635–711. John Wiley & Sons Inc., US (1998)

3. Bibace, R., Schmidt, L.R., Walsh, M.E.: Children's perceptions of illness. In: Penny, G.N., Bennett, P., Herbert, M. (eds.) Health Psychology: A Lifespan Perspective, pp. 15–30. Harwood Academic Publishers (1994)

4. Brown, S.J., Lieberman, D.A., Gemeny, B.A., Fan, Y.C., Wilson, D.M., Pasta, D.J.: Educational video game for juvenile diabetes: Results of a controlled trial. Medical Informatics 22(1), 77–89 (1997)

5. Bruckman, A., Bandlow, A.: HCI for Kids. In: Jacko, J., Sears, A. (eds.) The Human-Computer Interaction Handbook: Fundamentals, Evolving Technologies, and Emerging Applications, pp. 793–809 (2008)

6. Dragone, M.A., Bush, P.J., Jones, J.K., Bearison, D.J., Kamani, S.: Development and Evaluation of an Interactive CD-ROM for Children with Leukemia and Their Families. Patient Education and Counselling 46, 297–307 (2002)

7. Gerling, K., Fuchslocher, A., Schmidt, R., Krämer, N., Masuch, M.: Designing and Evaluating Casual Health Games for Children and Teenagers with Cancer. In: Anacleto, J.C., Fels, S., Graham, N., Kapralos, B., Saif El-Nasr, M., Stanley, K. (eds.) ICEC 2011. LNCS, vol. 6972, pp. 198–209. Springer, Heidelberg (2011)

8. Kato, M., Cole, S.W., Bradlyn, A.S., Pollock, B.H.: A Video Game Improves Behavioral Outcomes in Adolescents and Young Adults with Cancer, A Randomized Trial. Pediatrics 122(2), 305–317 (2008)

9. Liebal, J., Exner, M.: Usability für Kids - Ein Handbuch zur ergonomischen Gestaltung von Software und Websites für Kinder. Vieweg+Teubner Verlag, Wiesbaden (2011)

10. Lieberman, D.: Management of Chronic Pedriatic Diseases with Interactive Health Games, Theory and Research Findings. Journal of Ambulatory Care Management 24(1), 26–38 (2001)

11. Lohaus, A., Ball, J.: Gesundheit und Krankheit aus der Sicht von Kindern. Hogrefe Verlag GmbH & Co. KG, Göttingen (2006)

12. Niegemann, H.M., Hessel, S., Hochscheid-Mauel, D., Aslanski, K., Deimann, M., Kreuzberger, G.: Kompendium E-Learning. Springer, Heidelberg (2004)

13. Nielsen, J.: Usability Engineering. Morgan Kaufmann, San Francisco (1993)

14. Norman, D.A., Draper, S.W.: User Centered System Design: New Perspectives on Human-Computer Interaction. Erlbaum Associates Inc., Hillsdale (1986)

15. Piaget, J.: Science of Education and the Psychology of the Child. Orion Press, New York (1970)

16. Shneiderman, B.: Designing the user interface: Strategies for effective human-computer. Addison-Wesley Longman, Amsterdam (1998)

17. Slavin, L.A., O'Malley, J.E., Koocher, G.P., Foster, D.J.: Communication of the cancer diagnosis to pediatric patients: Impact on long-term adjustment. The American Journal of Psychiatry 139(2), 179–183 (1982)

18. Vredenburg, K., Mao, J.-Y., Smith, P.W., Carey, T.: A Survey of User-Centered Design Practice. In: Proceedings of the SIGCHI Conference on Human Factors in Computing Systems, pp. 471–478. ACM, New York (2002)

19. Williams, A.: User-Centered Design, Activity-Centered Design, and Goal-Directed Design: A Review of Three Methods for Designing Web Applications. In: Proceedings of the 27th ACM International Conference on Design of Communication, pp. 1–8. ACM, New York (2009)

# Mobile Learning and Games: Experiences with Mobile Games Development for Children and Teenagers Undergoing Oncological Treatment

Débora N.F. Barbosa[1,2], Patrícia B.S. Bassani[2], João B. Mossmann[2,3,4],
Guilherme T. Schneider[4], Eliseo Reategui[3], Marsal Branco[4],
Luciana Meyrer[4], and Mateus Nunes[4]

[1] Feevale University, Computer Science, Novo Hamburgo, Brasil
{deboranice,mossmann}@feevale.br
[2] Feevale University, Doctored Cultural Diversity and Social Inclusion, Novo Hamburgo, Brazil
{deboranice,patriciab}@feevale.br
[3] Federal University of Rio Grande do Sul (UFRGS), PGIE, Porto Alegre, Brazil
{eliseoreategui,mossmann}@gmail.com
[4] Feevale University, Digital Games, Novo Hamburgo, Brazil
{mossmann,gts,marsal,lucianasmeyrer}@feevale.br,
nuunes3@gmail.com

**Abstract.** The use of mobile technologies enables mobile and connected learning. Working in close association with an institution that helps children and teenagers undergoing oncological treatment, we realized that their main difficulty is that of following school during and after the periods of hospitalization or low immunity. So, our research hypotheses is that mobile technologies and educational games could be used in their learning activities. This article presents a few experiences with the use of tablets and educational games developed with the goal of reinforcing curricular activities for children and teenagers undergoing oncological treatment. The experience of developing the games with an interdisciplinary team had positive aspects, especially in what the challenges of attending to the needs of children under medical treatment is concerned.

**Keywords:** mobile learning, educational games, mobile devices, gamification.

## 1 Introduction

The possibility of the user to take with him/her the object of study or to access it from anywhere, intensifies the use of mobile devices in education, and is called Learning with Mobility (Mobile Learning) [1], [2]. In the region of Vale dos Sinos, in the State of RS, Brazil, the Support Association in Oncopediatrics (AMO) assists children and teenagers in vulnerable social situation with cancer. AMO provides patients with computer workshops and tutoring, besides offering other facilities to patients and their families. One of the difficulties patients have is that of following school classes

S. Göbel and J. Wiemeyer (Eds.): GameDays 2014, LNCS 8395, pp. 153–164, 2014.
© Springer International Publishing Switzerland 2014

during and after the treatment periods, as well as having access to the activities offered by AMO, as the Basic Computer Workshop. Considering this problem and mobile learning possibilities, we are carrying out a research to answer the following research question: how can mobile devices and games be used to assist in school tutoring of students undergoing oncological treatment? In particular, considering the profile of AMO patients, we have been interested in understanding how the use of these technologies can assist in their studies involving the contents of Portuguese and Math between the 4th and 9th year of Elementary School, in Brazil. To answer these questions, it has been important to use motivating and meaningful strategies. In this sense, one of our research hypotheses is that the use of gamification techniques [3] and the structuring of virtual communities [4] could help achieve the goals proposed. Therefore, in a collaborative project involving our university and AMO, we are investigating how tablets, associated with mobile games and gamification techniques, can support tutoring and the development of activities proposed by AMO.

The research has been conducted in face-to-face workshops at AMO, integrating mobile devices in a Basic Computer course. The starting point of the research has been the selection of games available in virtual stores that could assist in school tutoring and teach some basic computer contents. These games were used in the workshops and the research team observed its use by kids and teenagers. From our experience, we identified many applications available that were not adequate in terms of their pedagogical approach, language, usability and the lack of contents associated to school curriculum. In the case of games, many times they were hard to be operated by patients who were, in some circumstances, physically impaired. Because of that, we started developing new games with these students in mind, and also thinking about our research goals. Our focus has been in the contents of the games, also taking into account the computer workshop offered by AMO. The games should also have an interface with good usability so that users would have no problems operating it in the different phases of their cancer treatment.

This paper presents initial results of our research, reporting on our experience with the use of tablets, educational games built by our team and also found in virtual stores. This article is organized in the following way: section 2 addresses concepts involving learning with mobile educational games and mobility. Section 3 presents our game proposal. In section 4 we present the research methodology and initial results. The research methodology involved workshops carried out in three phases. In this article we present our experiences with the implementation of the first two phases. In particular, we focus on the criteria defined for the development of the games, as well as on the contents that had to be included in them. Section 5 presents the conclusions reached so far. We also introduce the last phase that involve the development of a Virtual Learning Community (VLC) with gamification techniques, in which the student gets involved in learning activities in a fun and collaborative way

## 2     Mobile Learning and Games

In Education, mobile learning technologies must be the means, and not the focus of the educational process. They should also be easy to manipulate and comprehend [1]. In our research, we understand that mobile technologies should assist in the activities proposed by AMO to patients and their families. It is important to highlight that the digital resources used in the school tutoring of the target audience should be involving, meaningful, and should address contents from the current curriculum in the schools, and consider distinct ergonomic aspects (since many times the patient are debilitated). The artefacts and methods should also be challenging and allow the collective construction of knowledge.

There are studies that have as a main goal to determine whether games may be useful in improving health outcomes, as in [5] and [6]. According to these studies, games can help patients to improve their health in some aspects, and they may also help doctors and care takers to better understand the illnesses and patients' needs for psychological and physical therapy. Based on that, our research hypothesis is that games are an appropriate way to assist students to overcome psychological difficulties faced because of their cancer treatments [7], [8]. Games, as well as mobile devices, have a new language, applied successfully in the communication with the younger generations [9]. The mastering of this technological language enables the association of traditional contents and actions that enrich experience and experimentation [10]. Experiences with the use of games [11], [5], [12] with children undergoing cancer treatment are also being developed. Combat [11] is a Brazilian game inspired by an American game, in which the user is a hero and uses powerful weapons to destroy cancer cells. Based on the same idea, the game "Re-Mission" [5] was developed to get young people with cancer to learn about the illness and its treatment. The Brazilian game called "Corrida da Saúde" (Health Course) [12] aims at getting people to become aware of the importance of healthy eating and practicing physical exercise to prevent the development of cancer. Research works about the use of games with people undergoing medical treatment concluded that games can be an effective resource for health education, specially for children, teenagers and adults with chronic illnesses such as cancer [11], [5], [12]. According to these works, patients who use that type of resource feel more confident during the entire treatment.

In Brazil, previous work has reported on the benefits of the use of mobile devices in Education [13], [14], [15], and also for students undergoing oncological treatment [16]. In this last paper it has been shown the use of mobile technologies may facilitate tutoring activities, as teachers can use multimedia presentations, videos and other resources with their students. Another relevant aspect is the cleaning of the digital equipment, which is easier with tablets and other mobile devices.

In our research, we have been interested in understanding how the use of mobile devices, collaboration and games technologies can assist students undergoing oncological treatment in their studies. Our focus has been to help students with contents related to Portuguese and Math, for Elementary School courses.

According to [1], learning is a process that involves the interaction between the subject and the knowledge (object), as well as between subjects. In this sense, in this work we have focused on the development of educational games that had interaction as a central design aspect. The games developed had as an important goal to enable collaborative learning between the different participants of AMO. This way, we also wanted to create a collaborative space that could strengthen the development of a Virtual Learning Community (VLC) [4].

With that in mind, we thought of introducing in the project the concept of Gamification, defined by Zichermann and Christopher [3] as the use of gaming characteristics, such as thought processes and mechanics, as a means to involve the user in other activities. Therefore, considering that the participants of this research are children and teenagers, our research hypothesis is that the inclusion of Gamification techniques in the VLC would be a promising approach.

## 3     Game Development

### 3.1     Requirements for the Development of Educational Games

The research group has defined the strategy for the development of games. Thus, one of the goals of this research is to develop educational games with the perspective of "Digital Learning Construction" [10] that is related to the development of artefacts in a multidisciplinary way so as to assist players to build or re-arrange their knowledge. To define the features of the games that were selected previously, especially considering the patients' learning needs in the different phases of their cancer treatment, the research group established a set of criteria:

- Process of incremental development based on prototyping: While the computer system of the game is built and validated, another step happens simultaneously, taking artistic/design aspects into account;
- Appropriate language: The game should provide a suitable language to the level of expected knowledge, as well as the profile of the participant - who is in a vulnerable situation. This should be coupled with the aspects of recreation and entertainment inherent to games;
- Involvement of multidisciplinary teams and constant validation with AMO's staff: Using "Digital Learning Construction" concepts, the development of the game involves the research group, programmers, designers, content providers and AMO to validate the concept of the game;
- Multi-platform game: With this in mind, the player has the ability to play both in web platform as well as in mobile platforms. This is important because there are moments in which the subjects may be away, in treatment and unable to attend the workshops at AMO. This also allows them to keep using with game anywhere, even without the use of a tablet. Therefore, regarding the construction of the computer system, Unity 3D engine from Unity Technologies has been used in the development of the games. This technology allows the games to run in different platforms using the same source code. Adobe Illustrator and Adobe Photoshop were used in the design of the game's graphics;

- Several possibilities for gameplay: As the subjects can be in distinct treatment stages and may present different types of cancer, it is important that the game allows a diverse gameplay choice. With that in mind, the players may choose how to play according to their capabilities at any particular moment;
- Content easily modified: It is important that content changes be easily implemented in the games, without the need for structural changes. Furthermore, depending on the type of scenario, the possibility of working with multiple contents in a single game should also be considered;
- Appropriate feedback: As the goal of the game is to provide users with a good learning experience, if the player makes a wrong move, the game should display an incentive message and the correct answer. At the end of the game, tips should be displayed with links showing where contents can be revised;
- Levels of increasing difficulty: Games must present several stages, with levels of increasing difficulty. The idea here is to motivate players to use the game as well as to reinforce the contents covered. Furthermore, it is possible to include different content levels in the same game;
- Gamification concepts that integrate the game to VLC: The game and the learning community should be connected, keeping players connected. It is understood that the kind of recognition, reward or incentive for competition must be decided upon according to the type of game developed. This aspect facilitates the sociability of the players who are away from school or from AMO, for instance patients who may be in intense treatment. Even away from home, patients can interact with the communities and play the games using web technologies.

From these requirements, we defined our game development process. These elements guided the work of the programming, the design and the contents teams. Thus, the games were developed in an incremental format. Through a discussion with the group, a survey was made about games that could be adapted to provide some sort of educational content in its gameplay. Based on this scope a prototype was developed to evaluate issues of gameplay and contents. It has also been our goal to identify specific places in which educational could be inserted in the game, and to understand how gameplay motivation occurs. Together with the prototype construction, game concepts were conducted to create its visual identity, based on the same scope principles. After adjustments and approval of the prototype, the game went to the stage of production and art integration, being finished and made available to the target audience.

### 3.2    Gaming Development: "Corrida Gramatical" and "Navegática"

One of the games developed was titled "Corrida Gramatical", in English *Grammar Race*. The goal is to enhance contents of Portuguese related to verbs, nouns and adjectives, focusing on 5th-7th year of elementary school. A Portuguese language teacher who worked in collaboration with the research group developed the game content.

The scenario of the game is the school itself, with its indoor and outdoor spaces. Our choice in each scenario was due to one of the aspects that we wanted to strengthen, the students' attachment to school, as well as their identification with the school environment. As mentioned earlier on, because on their disease, the students often need to withdraw from school and sometimes end up by quitting the school year. Therefore, a scenario involving the school tends to reinforce the need for social interaction in this space. We also decided to strengthen the relationship between the student and AMO. The game represents the grammatical challenges with a big star, referring to AMO's logo.

Another problem faced by the research participants is that in the school environment, sometimes they are excluded. Since, they often have restrictions to physical exercises and, depending on the stage of the disease, they present a "different" physical appearance, these students end up by going through a certain seclusion process, which may involve other students and even teachers. As a way of addressing the differences of acceptance and accessibility aspects, the game's characters, a boy and a girl, are in wheelchairs and have attached to their wheelchairs a rocket that allows them to fly. So, to start the game, the player chooses one of the characters. Figure 1 shows the game's opening screen.

**Fig. 1.** Main Screen

Once the character has the ability to "fly" with his wheelchair, the player must avoid the obstacles, collect items to score, as well as collect other items that may increase his/her points when the student answers correctly questions that address grammatical knowledge. During the first few minutes the player learns to use the rocket and becomes familiar with the environment that is always moving forward. As the other students are also present in the scene, the player must find his/her way to avoid colliding with them. If the player hits the other students three times, the round is finished. Besides, the player learns to collect the small stars to score. Figure 2 shows the game environment.

After that, the player learns to gather larger stars (the ones with the heart in the middle), with grammatical challenges, as shown in Figure 3. When completing the challenge, points already earned are duplicated. If the player makes a mistake, a brief explanation associated to the question is presented.

**Fig. 2.** Environment of Corrida Gramatical

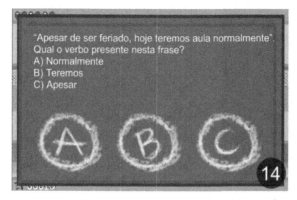

**Fig. 3.** Original screen of one of the game's challenge[1]

The second phase is currently being developed, where the player then is in the scene of the schoolyard and the contents have a higher degree of difficulty. Thus, to reach this stage, the player has passed and scored the first phase (inside the school).

Another game in development by the team is called "Navegática". The goal of the game is to strengthen mathematics contents related to the four basic operations, focusing on 4th to 5th year of elementary school. Its contents were based on exercises proposed in the Brazilian Teacher's Portal (http://portaldoprofessor.mec.gov.br/). A math teacher will join the research team in the near future to analyse the proposed content. On the initial screen of the game, a mathematical operation is chosen. The player can then switch operations during the game. In other phases, the operations are shuffled automatically.

The main concept of the game can be defined as puzzle top-view, in which a ship must avoid obstacles and get answers to the questions involving mathematics (initially related to the four basic operations). A more ludic artistic theme has been chosen for this game, taking into account the health issues of the students. To beat cancer and

---

[1] "Translation of the screen's contents: "Although today is a holiday, we will have classes normally". Which of these is a verb in the sentence above: (A) Normally; (B) Have; (C) Although"

economic difficulties, it is important to persist and to overcome obstacles. The scenario also has challenges (questions) related to the contents of his/her course curriculum. Figure 4 presents the scenario of "Navegática".

The game is geared towards learning mathematics. However, as one of the requirements of the games was that they could be adapted to any educational theme, it has also been a goal that the contents of the game could be changed. Questions about Basic Mathematics that were used for the development of this project are modular and do not require knowledge about programming languages. As for the gameplay, depending on the profile of the student, we have considered the possibility of operating the game by using one single hand. Thus, the phone gyroscope functions were used in the development of this game. As a result, individuals who are unable or have a motor difficulty can play the game by moving the mobile device to displace a little boat within the scenario. However, it is also possible to operate the boat by using touchscreen functions.

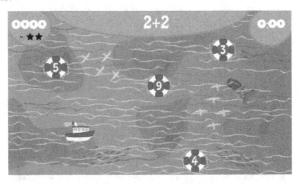

**Fig. 4.** Initial screen of the Navegática

## 4    Research's Methodology

### 4.1    Participants

Twelve students in the age rage of eight to sixteen, as well as their families, participated in this research, which also involved the AMO Association. Seven participants of the workshops were patients, while the others were family members. The patients were undergoing medical treatment for cancer problems such as leukemia, lymphoma and bone cancer. One of the patients was going through oral chemotherapy, while the others were in a stable phase of the disease. The patient with bone cancer had difficulty in moving his right arm.

### 4.2    Methods and Research Actions

We have classified our research work as exploratory, involving case studies and informal interviews methods. The organization of the workshops involved the setting up of the technological resources and labs, the creation of a specific virtual learning community, and the selection and development of educational games. Regarding the selection of mobile games available at the online store, the main requirements were related to the games' contents and cost.

The research was carried out through face-to-face workshops at AMO, integrating mobile devices and a Basic Computer course. The workshops were developed in three phases [17], namely: (1) Digital Literacy: free workshops for the use of mobile devices targeted to the entire community served by AMO; (2) Knowledge Appropriation: workshops to use the applications related to the teaching Mathematics, Portuguese, entertainment, as well as basic computer and office tools; (3) Knowledge Production: exploring communication tools such as Forums, Blogs, Chats and site building. Gamification techniques will also be incorporated in the development of the activities in this stage. The two first phases are the focus of this paper. The third phase will be developed during the year 2014.

The research described here began in August 2012. Twelve workshops focused on the use of mobile devices were given during the year 2013, in addition to the 5 technological workshops that were held in 2012. From 2012 until March 2013 we held the "Island of Technology", a space where the tablets were used by patients and their families during social events at AMO. Currently, we are finishing the Knowledge Appropriation phase. Throughout the five workshops we used the games developed by the group. In the first workshop, the research proposal was presented to the subjects. Some "contracts" were established, the most important of which was that the main idea of the workshops was to learn and have fun. Therefore, oriented activities took place in each workshop, involving the games aimed at strengthening school contents. There were also moments in which the participants could use the tablets freely, with any of the apps installed in it. However, we've always kept in mind that our first focus was on the development of contents related to Portuguese and Mathematics, using both applications found in the virtual store as well as games developed by the group.

During the workshops, data are collected through the observation of the subjects and the application of unstructured interviews. This phase takes place within the workshops, where two subjects are selected for the interviews at a time. In each workshop, photos are taken and videos are recorded. After the collection of data, it is analyzed through an initial categorization, including data about the tutoring and the articulation of that with educational games. Each category also considers the age group, the education level and the type of cancer of the student, among other information. From the data collected, we evaluate how games and others technologies are employed by the participants, and how they may support tutoring learning. In the case of this research the tablet devices are shared. Thus, the observation regarding the use of devices by each participant is the responsibility of the team involved in the research.

## 4.3     Results

Children and adolescents have no difficulty using tablets. One initial explanation is usually enough to make students understand how to select a game and use the main tablet menu. After that, they discover naturally how to operate these devices on their own.

According the subjects, the fact the "Corrida Gramatical" (Grammar Race) has the identity of AMO (the biggest star with the challenges) and that it uses a school environment has been positive. Another aspect that they liked was the fact that the character is in a wheelchair, flying with the help of a rocket. When the researchers asked the students about this aspect, one of them said: *"I liked the wheelchair because at AMO we have some friends who use a wheelchair. I think that they also will like that the wheelchair can fly with a rocket".* As the game was under development during the first workshop, the participants identified elements that could be improved, such as the need for a pause button; the availability of new challenges and scenarios. So, the game was changed according these suggestions and it was used in 3 subsequent workshops. The fact that the contents of the game were presented in a ludic way helped the participants to understand certain concepts that were considered difficult. For instance, one of the subjects said: *"it was only after I played the game that I understood verb tenses, and the different types of nouns. My teacher at school has explained this sometimes, but I did not understand".* Another aspect observed by the researchers was that participants between 5th-6th year of elementary school found the characters in the game more interesting. The participants who were in the 7th year of elementary school (age range between 14-15) did not identify so much with the characters.

The "Navegática" game was used in the workshops with the students, a game to support Math learning. The participants' feedback has been very positive, and the students understood contents without any problem. Interacting with the game either using the gyroscope function or touchscreen buttons has been well accepted by the participants. The group has also demonstrated its appreciation for the scenario created for the game. An interesting aspect was that the students frequently organized themselves in pairs to help each other. One of subjects, who had difficulty in moving one arm because of bone cancer, did not have any problem to use the game by employing the gyroscope function: *"using the gyroscope function is easier than using the buttons".*

During the informal interviews with the group, participants were asked about some criteria defined by the research group as important aspects in game development for educational purposes (see section 3.1). Specifically, we were interested to know about: (A) Several possibilities for gameplay; (B) Appropriate language; (C) Content change; (D) Appropriate feedback; (E) Levels of difficulty. All participants (100%) considered gameplay (A) and appropriate language (B) as important aspects to be taken into account in the development of the games; 80% considered the possibility to change contents of the games (C) as a relevant feature, noticing that during workshops they played the same game with different contents and challenges; 90% of the participants also expressed that appropriate feedback (D) and increasing level of difficulty are important aspects to be considered in the development of educational games.

## 5    Conclusions

This paper presented some initial results regarding the use of games for mobile devices with patients undergoing oncological treatment, as a way to help them face some of their difficulties related to having to be away from school for certain periods of time. Results obtained in a workshop carried out with twelve participants (7 patients and 5 family members) demonstrated that the game development criteria defined by the research group was relevant. When the two games developed in the project, namely "Corrida Gramatical" and "Navegática", were used in the workshops, we observed that participants were very receptive, even the youngest ones who sometimes were not aware of the complexity of the games' challenges. In the workshops, sometimes it was necessary to help students go through game challenges that were somewhat hard. In this type of situation a staff member was always available to help the students overcome the problems faced.

Currently we are continuing the workshops, the study of available games at the online store, and the improvement of the games "Corrida Gramatical" and "Navegática". Because of the game development methodology, it has been possible to work with different contents with the same game engine. That makes it easier to have a good portfolio for users. Thus, we will provide students with more specific games to match their needs in the future. Additionally, we will begin to apply the concepts of gamification to the VLC. The use of stamps or badges according to the player's level of expertise is also under evaluation by the group. The goal is to engage the communities in activities that are both meaningful and fun. In the VLC students will be able to discuss about the game, to exchange experiences and knowledge.

**Acknowledgement.** This work has been partially supported by the National Council for Scientific and Technological Development - CNPq.

# References

1. Roschelle, J., Roy, P.: A walk on the WILD side: How wireless handhelds change computer-supported collaborative learning. In: Int. Conf. on Computer-Supported Collaborative Learning, Colorado, January 7–11 (2002)
2. Saccol, A., Schelemmer, E., Barbosa, J.: M-learning e U-learning: Novas Perspectivas da Aprendizagem Móvel e Ubíqua, vol. 1, 162 p. Pearson Prentice Hall, São Paulo (2010)
3. Zichermann, G., Cunningham, C.: Gamification by Design - Implementing Game Mechanics in Web and Mobile Apps. O'Reilly (2011)
4. Pallof, R., Pratt, K.: Construindo comunidades aprendizagem no ciberespaço. Artmed, Porto Alegre (2002)
5. Kato, P.M., Cole, S.W., Bradlyn, A.S., Pollock, B.H.: A Video Game Improves Behavioral Outcomes in Adolescents and Young Adults With Cancer: A Randomized Trial. In: Pediatrics, vol. 122(2), pp. e305–e317 (2008), doi:10.1542/peds.2007-3134
6. Primack, B.A., Carroll, M.V., McNamara, M., Klem, M.L., King, B., Rich, M., Chan, C.W., Nayak, S.: Role of video games in improving health-related outcomes: a systematic review. Am. J. Prev. Med. 42(6) (2012), doi: 10.1016/j.amepre.2012.02.023
7. Bittencourt, J.R., et al.: Aprendizagem baseada em Jogos Móveis e Ubíquos. In: Omar, N., Lopes, R., Silveira, I. (Org.), (eds.) Minicursos do VIII SBIE (Disponível em CD-ROM), vol. 1, pp. 1–20. Editora Vida & Consciência, São Paulo (2007)
8. Branco, M., Max, C.: Ludemas. Lógica da Sedução nos Games. In: X Simpósio de Games e Entretenimento, Salvador (2011)

9. Mattar, J.: Games em educação: como os nativos digitais aprendem. Pearson Prentice Hall, São Paulo (2010)
10. Bez, M., et al.: Dimensões dos jogos de ensino. In: ICECE 2013 - Congresso Internacional em Educação em Engenharia e Computação, Luanda, vol. 1, pp. 1–6. COPEC, São Paulo (2013)
11. Combate. Jogo pode estimular crianças com câncer a reagir contra a doença, http://www.isaude.net/pt-BR/noticia/21458/ciencia-e-tecnologia/jogo-pode-estimular-criancas-com-cancer-a-reagir-contra-a-doenca (accessed in: January 25, 2011)
12. Corrida da sáude, http://www.accamargo.org.br/corrida-saude/ (accessed in: January 20, 2014)
13. Merino, A., Rirvas, P., Diaz, F.J.: Mobile Application Profiling for Connected Mobile Devices. IEEE Pervasive Computing, 54–61 (January-March 2009)
14. Silva, M., Moreira, G., Consolo, A.T.: Mobile learning – uso de dispositivos móveis como auxiliar na mediação pedagógica de cursos a distância. In: REUNIÃO ANUAL DA SBPC, 60, Campinas Anais eletrônicos, SBPC/UNICAMP, São Paulo (2008), http://www.sbpcnet.org.br/livro/60ra/resumos/resumos/R4675-1.html (accessed in: January 25, 2011)
15. Barbosa, J., et al.: Computação Móvel e Ubíqua no Contexto de uma Graduação de Referência. Revista Brasileira de Informática na Educação 15, 53–65 (2007)
16. Escola Móvel: Tecnologias melhoram escolas móveis, http://www.educacionista.org.br/jornal/index.php?option=com_content&task=view&id=9905&Itemid=32 (accessed in: January 2011)
17. UNESCO. Padrões de Competência em TIC para Professores (2009), http://unesdoc.unesco.org/images/0015/001562/156209por.pdf (accessed in: June 20, 2013)

# Evoking and Measuring Arousal in Game Settings

Jeltsje Cusveller[3], Charlotte Gerritsen[1], and Jeroen de Man[2]

[1] Netherlands Institute for the Study of Crime and Law Enforcement
De Boelelaan 1077a, 1081 HV, Amsterdam, The Netherlands
[2] Vrije Universiteit Amsterdam, Department of Artificial Intelligence
De Boelelaan 1081a, 1081 HV, Amsterdam, The Netherlands
[3] Vrije Universiteit Amsterdam, Department of Criminology
De Boelelaan 1077, 1081 HV, Amsterdam, The Netherlands
j.j.cusveller@student.vu.nl, cgerritsen@nscr.nl, j.de.man@vu.nl

**Abstract.** Serious games seem to be more effective if the participant feels more involved in the game. The participant should experience a high sense of presence which can be obtained by matching the level of excitement to the level of arousal a participant experiences. The level of arousal should be measured at runtime to make the game adaptive to the participant's physiological state. In this paper an experiment is presented that has as main goal to see whether it is possible to evoke arousal during different types of computer games and to monitor the physiological response. Using three online games, participants reported different levels of stress and understanding between games. Furthermore, an increase of skin conductance was found as well as a decrease in heart rate for the most difficult to understand game.

**Keywords:** experiment, physiological measurements, stress, serious gaming, virtual environment.

## 1    Introduction

Serious games are games that do not have entertainment as primary purpose. They are mainly used to for training or education purposes [8]. Examples are simulations of real-world events or processes designed for the purpose of solving a problem (e.g. Flood Sim [21], CyberCIEGE [16], Flight Gear [18]). Although serious games can be entertaining, their main purpose is to train or educate users, though it may have other purposes such as marketing or advertisement [2].

Serious games seem to be more effective if the participant feels more involved in the game. The participant should experience a high sense of presence (indicating a strong involvement of the user in the virtual environment) [13], which can be achieved by dynamically adapting the (affective) content of the game to reach a desired level of arousal [1,12]. We use the term arousal to indicate a physiological reaction to stimuli, i.e. increased heart rate and blood pressure. To obtain the 'optimal' level of arousal it is necessary to measure arousal at runtime and to make the game adaptive to it, meaning that the game should become more challenging or exciting if the level of arousal is too low and vice versa if arousal is too high [12].

S. Göbel and J. Wiemeyer (Eds.): GameDays 2014, LNCS 8395, pp. 165–174, 2014.

There already exist research projects in which arousal is measured during games [6, 11]. In this paper we build on the existing research by measuring skin conductance during three different types of games to obtain the level of arousal of the participants and investigate differences in physiological responses between games with various levels of difficulty and stressfulness. The results will be used in future research to relate changes in physiological measures to the player's mental state and develop an adaptive game for learning to deal with aggression.

In this paper, Section 3 provides some background on the research presented here and Section 3 discusses related work. In Section 4 the methods used are discussed, and in Section 5 the results are presented. Finally, Section 6 concludes the paper with a discussion.

## 2     Background

The research presented in this paper is part of a larger project. This project is called STRESS [14] and is joint work between the VU University Amsterdam - department of Computer Science and the Netherlands Institute for the Study of Crime and Law Enforcement.

The STRESS project [14] has as the main goal to develop an intelligent system that is able to analyse human decision making processes, and analyse the causes of incorrect decisions and inadequate emotion regulation (e.g. distress, aggression). The system will be incorporated in an ambient electronic training environment, based on Virtual Reality (VR), cf. [7, 17]. In this environment, trainees will be placed in a virtual scenario, in which they have to make difficult decisions, while negative emotions are induced. Modern Human Computer Interaction (HCI) techniques will be applied to measure aspects of their mental state (among others, stress level, emotional state, attention, and motivational state) during the scenario. This information will then be used as input for the ambient system, to determine why the trainee made certain less optimal decisions and to advise him/her how to improve this.

An important asset of the ambient approach is that the system can adapt various aspects of the training (e.g., scenarios, difficulty level, feedback) at runtime on the basis of its estimation of the trainee's mental state. In this way, both of the training goals can be fulfilled: 1) by selecting training scenarios with an appropriate context in terms of difficulty level, and providing useful feedback, the system can improve the trainee´s decision making behaviour, and 2) by selecting training scenarios with an appropriate context in terms of stress level, the system can improve the trainee´s emotion regulation skills.

## 3     Related Work

The work presented in this paper focuses on the physiological response in gaming. Therefore, the current section covers some related literature in the field of physiological measurements and serious gaming.

*Physiological Measurements*

Measuring the physiological and emotional reaction to different kinds of computer generated stimuli has been done in other research projects. In Gerritsen et al. [4] the physiological and subjective response to injustice is measured. In this work the authors performed an experiment in which the respondents had to perform a task in a virtual environment. They had to determine which of two pictures showed the more happy/sad face. If they chose correctly they moved on to the next picture combination, if they made a mistake they were set back three steps. The experiment contained two sets and in the second set the system purposely misjudged the answers. The participants were set back three combinations even if they had answered the question correctly. During the experiment the physiological responses were measured. The results showed that the level of skin conductance increased during the second set while the heart rate remained stable, indicating an increased level of arousal when feeling unjustly treated.

In the work of Brouwer et al. [3] a combination between a virtual environment and bio-neuro-feedback to help treat stress related disorders is investigated. An experiment was performed in which participants had a surveillance task in two cities. To induce stress the researchers used a bomb explosion and negative feedback. Physiological measurements were performed (heart rate variability, cortisol level and EEG) and the results indicate that the general levels of stress correlated between the participants. Besides that also associative stress was reflected in the measurements.

*Serious Gaming*

In the field of serious gaming the (physiological) reaction to games has been studied as well. Nacke et al. [9] present an approach to formalize evaluative methods and a roadmap for applying these mechanisms in the context of serious games. They discuss user experience (UX) and player experience models, based on which they propose a three-layer framework of GX. For each layer, they list a number of measurement methodologies and their focus is put on physiological and technical metrics for game evaluation. Their conclusion is that it depends on the kind of serious game that should be tested, which evaluative UX measure is chosen, but they do recommend affective measures for evaluating the effectiveness of motivation to play game-based learning applications or games for sports and health. While these measures might focus on emotional assessment, the authors assume that a link between positive emotion and long-term storage and recall of information in the brain exists.

In Nacke et al. [10] the authors propose a classification of direct and indirect physiological sensor input to augment traditional game control. They conducted a mixed-methods study using different sensor mappings. The results of their study show that participants have a preference for direct physiological control in games. This has two major design implications for physiologically controlled games: (1) direct physiological sensors should be mapped intuitively to reflect an action in the virtual world; (2) indirect physiological input is best used as a dramatic device in games to influence features altering the game world.

## 4     Methods

A computer task has been designed to measure the level of arousal in different situations while physiological measurements are registered. In the following sections, the experimental design, the participants and the hypotheses will be described.

*Experimental Design*

In the experiment the participants had to play three (off the shelf) computer games. These games were separated by a break. A message was presented to the participants indicating that they could continue when they felt ready. The first game (Tetris) lasted approximately four minutes, the second and third game (respectively Grid16 and Guitar Maniac) two minutes each. This of course depended on the results of the player. These games were chosen based on the anticipated pressure they would bring about.   The games were presented to all of the participants in the same order.

The first game that the participants played is Tetris [20]. Tetris is a well-known puzzle game in which blocks in different shapes move from top to bottom on the screen (Figure 1). The player has to adjust the blocks so that lines will be made. A full line (from left to right) will disappear and gives the player points. If the blocks are not adjusted correctly, lines will not be made and the blocks will stack. When the blocks reach the top of the screen the game ends. Before the game started the participants received an explanation of the game and the instruction to play only the first two (easy) levels and to stop after those levels. This game was used as a baseline game. We wanted the participants to play a game which was relatively easy to do. The first two levels of Tetris are not yet very demanding and can therefore provide a baseline level in heart rate and skin conductance. The next two games were expected to be more demanding leading to a physiological response.

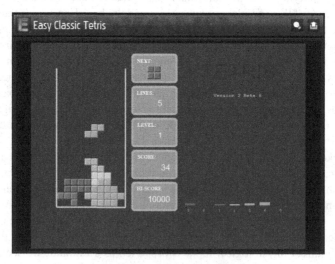

**Fig. 1.** Screenshot game 1: Tetris

The second game the participants played is called Grid16 [22]. In this game the participants had to play different games of skill without any explanation (see Figure 2 for a screenshot of 4 different games from Grid16). For example, in these games the participants had to avoid obstacles or had to make sure an object would not fall. The player played a game for 10 seconds and then automatically switched to another game. Meanwhile the pace increases, the games go faster and the system switches faster from one game to another game. The system continued to switch between the games until the player was *game over* in all games. The participants were instructed to play the entire game twice.

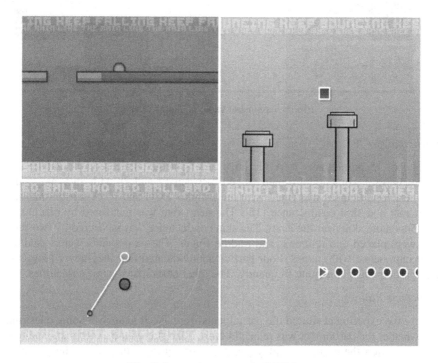

**Fig. 2.** Screenshots game 2: Grid16

The third game is called Guitar Maniac [19]. The player had to press the correct key on the right moment (Figure 3). On the screen the participants saw arrows move from right to left. The arrows were accompanied by numbers 1, 2, 3 or 4. When the arrows (and numbers) reached the grey part of the screen the participant had to press the key on the keyboard that corresponds to the number on the screen.

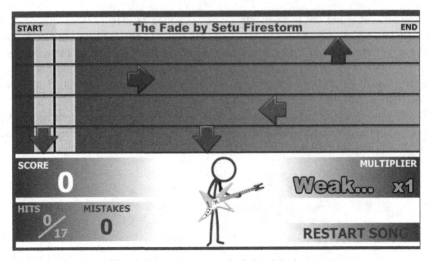

**Fig. 3.** Screenshot game 3: Guitar Maniac

*Participants*

A total of 15 participants were recruited among acquaintances of the authors. The age of these 9 women and 6 men ranged between 17 and 28 with an average age of 20.8. Each participant was fitted with the Bioplux ECG and EDA sensors measuring heart rate and skin conductance [15]. The heart rate was measured by placing three sensors on the skin near the heart. The skin conductance was measured by two sensors that were placed on the index- and middle finger. The participants were asked about their experience with games. Four participants indicated that they never play games, five participants game quite frequently. The other participants game sometimes.

*Subjective Ratings*

Before the experiment started the participants were asked to answer some questions to see whether the participant was relaxed before (s)he started the experiment and to find out how often the participant plays games. After each of the games the participants were asked if they understood the game, if they found the game difficult to play and if they found the game stressful to play. The answers to these questions were rated on a 7-point scale, with 0 being indicated as never/not at all and 6 as very often/very much.

*Hypotheses*

The expectation was that the participants would feel stress during the faster and more complicated games. It is expected that this will show in the subjective ratings of stress with a significant increase between game 1 and games 2 and 3. For Guitar Maniac, an increase in reported difficulty of the game is expected, while for Grid16 a lowered understanding is hypothesized as well. Furthermore, it is hypothesized that this increase in stress would lead to an increased level of skin conductance in game 2 and game 3. For heart rate, stating a hypothesis is more difficult, as the increase in arousal due to stress is associated with an increased heart rate. However, as stated in Section 3, similar work did not always find any changes in heart rate.

# 5    Results

The following sections describe the main results of the experiment. It is divided in three sections. First the results regarding the subjective questions following each game are described. Afterwards, the measurements of both skin conductance and heart rate are presented and finally correlations between the subjective and physiological results are considered.

*Subjective Questions*

After each game, participants answered a number of questions regarding their understanding of the game, how easy the game was to play and how stressful they experienced the game to be. Figure 4 shows for each game the average response for all 15 participants, including the standard deviation. As can be seen, Tetris was well understood and easy to play, accompanied by a low stress score for that game. Participants had more trouble understanding Grid16, found it less easy to play and also rated the game to be more stressful. Guitar Maniac was understood by the participants, but was also found difficult to play and scoring high for stress.

Statistical analysis underlines these results. A repeated one way ANOVA showed significant differences for each aspect; understanding with $F(2,28) = 56.031$, $p<0.001$, $\eta_p^2 = 0.80$, easy to play with $F(2,28) = 26.793$, $p<0.001$, $\eta_p^2 = 0.66$ and using the Greenhouse-Geisser values due to violation of the assumption of sphericity yields $F(1.44,20.22) = 26.793$, $p<0.001$, $\eta_p^2 = 0.66$ for stress. Post-hoc tests using the Bonferroni corrections shows all differences to be significant at the 0.05 level, except for the scores on easy to play and stress between Grid16 and Guitar Maniac. Further analysis has shown that there is a correlation between how easy each game was to play and how stressful participants rated the game ($r = -0.571$, $p=0.029$; $r = -0.651$, $p=0.009$; $r = -0.584$, $p=0.022$). A similar correlation was found between understanding and stress, except for guitar maniac ($r = -0.60$, $p=0.018$; $r = -0.62$, $p=0.013$; $r = -0.15$, $p=0.598$).

*Physiological Measurements*

Besides subjective questions, skin conductance and heart rate were measured to gain insight into the arousal of the participants. Repeated measures ANOVAs with Greenhouse-Geisser corrections showed statistical differences for both skin conductance ( $F(1.266, 12.660) = 13.916$, $p=0.002$, $\eta_p^2 = 0.58$ ) and heart rate ( $F(1.437, 15.802) = 7.818$, $p=0.008$, $\eta_p^2 = 0.42$ ). Post-hoc tests using a Bonferroni correction showed all differences in skin conductance to be significant at the 0.05 level, while the heart rate only significantly differs between Tetris and Grid16 as well as between Grid16 and Guitar Maniac.

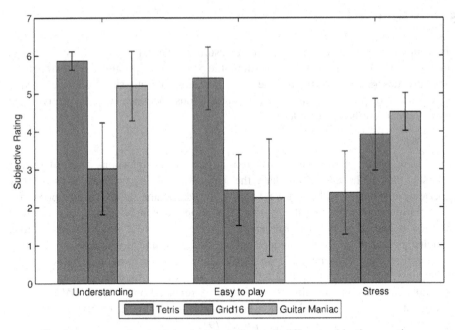

**Fig. 4.** Average rating (and standard deviation) to 3 different subjective questions

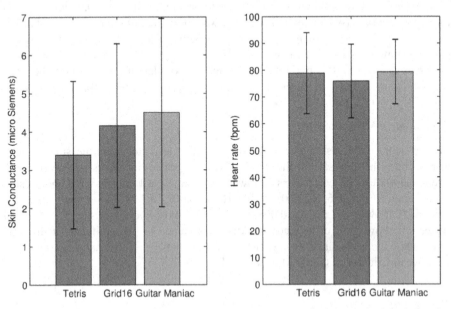

**Fig. 5.** Average skin conductance (left) and heart rate (right) including standard deviation for each game

*Correlations between Subjective and Physiological Measurements*

Finally, it has been investigated whether there were any correlations between the subjective and physiological measures. Tetris was taken as a baseline game, providing both a subjective and physiological baseline. For each of the subjective aspects and both physiological measures, the difference between Grid16 and Tetris as well as the difference between Guitar Maniac and Tetris was calculated. Spearman's rho was calculated for each combination of subjective question and physiological measurements, but resulted in no significant correlations.

# 6    Discussion

In the previous section, subjective and physiological results from playing three different games were discussed. Regarding the subjective questions, playing Tetris was, as expected, less stressful for the participants. Both Grid16 and Guitar Maniac were more difficult to play, making it plausible that the easier a game is to play, the less stressful it is to the participants. For Grid16, it was found that participants had trouble understanding the game, which could have caused stress. Guitar Maniac was well understood by each participant, but nonetheless hard to play and stressful. Statistically, not understanding the game did not cause a difference in the stress experienced, but on visual inspection there is a trend towards lower stress levels when this stress is (partly) caused by incomprehension.

It was hypothesized that both the skin conductance and heart rate would increase with the more stressful games. However, this was only true for the skin conductance. The heart rate dropped significantly when playing Grid16 and no differences were found with Guitar Maniac. There is some literature showing anger to be related with a decrease in heart rate [5], but it is unclear whether this applies to the situation at hand.

In the end, there was no correlation found between the answers to the subjective questions and the physiological responses. It could be that the heart rate here reflected some different aspect than stress, as it did not show the expected increase over the three games. For the skin conductance however, the increase shows a similar pattern to the increase in stress experienced by the participants, but a significant correlation between the two variables could not be found. At this point in time, it is unclear whether the skin conductance is indeed not directly correlated with the stress experienced, or that a weaker correlation between the two variables is obscured by a low number of participants.

Another aspect not considered in this work yet is personality traits. Each participant undertook a personality tests and initial analyses show some correlations between personality traits and the participants' physiological responses. A more in-depth analysis of these personality traits might reveal underlying correlations between stress and physiological responses.

**Acknowledgement.** The authors are grateful to Tibor Bosse for his feedback and fruitful discussions. This research was supported by funding from the National Initiative Brain and Cognition, coordinated by the Netherlands Organisation for Scientific Research (NWO), under grant agreement No. 056-25-013.

# References

1. Baños, R.M., Botella, C., Alcañiz, M., Liaño, V., Guerrero, B., Rey, B.: Immersion and Emotion: Their Impact on the Sense of Presence. CyberPsychology & Behavior 7(6), 734–741 (2004)
2. Bergeron, B.P.: Developing Serious Games. Charles River Media, Massachusetts (2006)
3. Brouwer, A.M., Neerincx, M.A., Kallen, V.L., van der Leer, L., ten Brinke, M.: EEG alpha asymmetry, heart rate variability and cortisol in response to virtual reality induced stress. Journal of Cybertherapy & Rehabilitation 4(1), 21–34 (2011)
4. Gerritsen, C., de Man, J., van der Meij, J.: Physiological and subjective response to injustice: the effects of unjust evaluations on physiological responses and subjective experiences. In: Proceedings of the Seventh International Workshop on Human Aspects in Ambient Intelligence, HAI 2013. IEEE Computer Society Press (2013) (to appear)
5. Hassett, J.: A primer of psychophysiology. WH Freeman, San Francisco (1978)
6. Kotsia, I., Patras, I., Fotopoulos, S.: Affective gaming: beyond using sensors. In: Proceedings of the Fifth International Symposium on Communications, Control and Signal Processing, ISCCSP 2012 (2012)
7. Marsella, S., Gratch, J.: Modeling the influence of emotion on belief for virtual training simulations. In: Proceedings of the 11th Conference on Computer-Generated Forces and Behavior Representation, Orlando, FL (May 2002)
8. Michael, D.R., Chen, S.L.: Serious Games: Games That Educate, Train, and Inform, Muska & Lipman/Premier-Trade (2005)
9. Nacke, L.E., Drachen, A., Goebel, S.: Methods for Evaluating Gameplay Experience in a Serious Gaming Context. International Journal of Computer Science in Sport 9, 2 (2010)
10. Nacke, L.E., Kalyn, M., Lough, C., Mandryk, R.L.: Biofeedback Game Design: Using Direct and Indirect Physiological Control to Enhance Game Interaction. In: Proc. CHI 2011 (2011)
11. Nacke, L.E., Mandryk, R.L.: Designing affective games with physiological input. Proceedings of Fun and Games (2011)
12. Nogueira, P.A., Rodrigues, R., Oliveira, E., Nacke, L.E.: Guided Emotional State Regulation: Understanding and Shaping Players' Affective Experiences in Digital Games. In: Proceedings of the Ninth AAAI Conference on Artificial Intelligence and Interactive Digital Entertainment, pp. 51–57. AAAI (2013)
13. Steuer, J.: Defining virtual reality: Dimensions determining telepresence. In: Biocca, F., Levy, M.R. (eds.) Communication in the Age of Virtual Reality, pp. 33–56. Lawrence Erlbaum Associates, Hillsdale (1995)
14. http://stress.few.vu.nl/
15. http://www.biosignalsplux.com/
16. http://www.cisr.us/cyberciege/
17. http://www.ehow.com/list_5982829_benefits-police-trainingsimulators_.html
18. http://www.flightgear.org/
19. http://www.kongregate.com/games/shinki/super-crazy-guitar-maniac-deluxe-3
20. http://www.newgrounds.com/portal/view/235136
21. http://playgen.com/play/floodsim/
22. http://www.spelletjes.nl/spel/Grid-16.html

# Serious Games for Solving Protein Sequence Alignments - Combining Citizen Science and Gaming

Martin Hess[1], Josef Wiemeyer[3], Kay Hamacher[2], and Michael Goesele[1]

[1] Department of Computer Science, Technische Universität Darmstadt, Germany
[2] Department of Biology, Technische Universität Darmstadt, Germany
[3] Department of Human Science, Technische Universität Darmstadt, Germany

**Abstract.** A fundamental task in computational biology is the identification of similarities between multiple protein sequences, to get insight into their functional, structural and evolutionary relationships. These similarities can be revealed by aligning the sequences. This alignment is a NP-hard problem.

In this paper, we present an improved game approach to solving large protein sequence alignments with the concept of citizen science. We abstract the alignment problem into a kind of puzzle, that can be solved even by non-expert players. Due to the early stage of development our approach is primarily focused on usability and game experience. We evaluated our game prototype by a user study with a convenience sample of 20 persons. This study showed, that our prototype is already capable to elicit fun and to deliver a true game experience despite its early stage. Some issues have been revealed requiring further improvement.

**Keywords:** Serious Games, Bioinformatics, Multiple Sequence Alignments, Protein Sequences, Citizen Science, Game Experience, Game Evaluation.

## 1 Motivation

One of the most fundamental tasks in computational biology is the identification of similarities between a set of DNA, RNA or protein sequences. These similarities provide insight into functional, structural or evolutionary relationships between the sequences, which forms the basis for many important biological applications like evolutionary heritage [1].

The similarities are usually revealed by aligning identical or similar parts of the sequences and thereby adding gaps into the sequences. The quality of such an alignment is determined by an evolutionary model, which „rewards" matching regions in the sequences and penalizes mismatching areas and gaps.

To get a reliable similarity analysis of the sequences for a given evolutionary model, it is necessary to find a good alignment. However the alignment of multiple sequences (MSA) is computationally expensive and an NP-hard problem

S. Göbel and J. Wiemeyer (Eds.): GameDays 2014, LNCS 8395, pp. 175–185, 2014.

[2]. Therefore many MSA algorithms like ClustalW [3], MUSCLE [4], Probcons [5] and MAFFT [6] rely on heuristics to find a good alignment [7].

Due to this probabilistic approach, the quality of the resulting alignments is questionable. One approach to improve the quality is to refine the alignments by hand using the human pattern recognition capability. Humans can easily detect visual patterns, e.g. by applying Gestalt principles or other organization principles of visual perception [8].

One concept to use human capabilities in solving scientific problems or improving their results is called *citizen science* [9]. In this concept, research tasks are outsourced to a volunteer crowd of amateur or non-professional „scientists". Due to the large number of potential volunteers, this concept of doing research can be very useful for computationally expensive problems. Examples for successful citizen science approaches are Galaxy Zoo [10], Fold it [11] and Phylo [12].

In this paper, we present an improved game approach to solving large protein sequence alignments (currently up to 50 sequences of variable length) by using the concept of citizen science. Inspired by Phylo [12], a computer game for solving DNA sequence alignments, we implemented a computer game prototype in order to enhance game experience by improved game mechanics. In our game prototype, the players have to solve puzzles of colored spheres, which are related to protein sequences alignments. The usability and the game experience of our prototype game was evaluated by a user study with a sample of 20 persons.

The main contributions and application benefits of the paper are:

1. Our approach is capable of dealing with a large number of protein sequences (i.e. up to 50) with variable length. The playing field is not restricted in its dimensions, which enables players to handle the sequences with a high degree of freedom. According to Self-Determination Theory [13], increased options for self-regulation enhance intrinsic motivation, well-being, and consequently game experience.
2. Our computer game prototype is designed to be visually appealing and to deliver a true game experience to the player. In addition, our game runs natively on many platforms like Windows, Mac, Linux and Android devices and can be played using mouse and keyboard as well as touch interfaces. These aspects allow to involve a huge amount of possible players, which ensures a high „human computing power".
3. Inspired by Phylo, we abstract sequence alignments to puzzles of colored spheres, which enables non-experts to solve alignments without further information or experience.
4. Analogous to Phylo, we use a high score system to ensure that the game is challenging and is capable of refining alignment solutions to get the best results.

## 2   Related Work

Our work aims at combining the principles of citizen science and computer games. The main idea is to bundle the strengths of both approaches, i.e., exploiting the capabilities of many people and the fun of gaming.

A well-known example of a successful citizen science approach is *Galaxy Zoo* [10]. Galaxy Zoo aims at identifying and classifying galaxies in millions of pictures by using the human visual pattern recognition. The users determine the shapes of galaxies presented to them and classify certain features.

*Fold it* is another citizen science approach, that deals with protein folding problems [11]. Unlike Galaxy Zoo, Fold it utilizes multiplayer game concepts to attract more volunteer „scientists". In Fold it, the players see the structure of a protein in a 3D rendered context. The players can manipulate the 3D structure to optimize the computed energy using direct manipulation tools and a collection of algorithms. In addition, Fold it features the creation of interaction macros [14]. These so called recipes are collected in a cookbook and are available to all Fold it players. Recent results show, that some solutions found by Fold it players using these concepts outperformed their computer-based counterparts [15,16].

*Phylo* is a citizen science approach for solving DNA multiple sequence alignments [12]. Analogous to Fold it, Phylo features a multiplayer game approach. In Phylo the players solve puzzles of colored squares. Each square corresponds to a nucleotide inside a DNA sequence, while the color represents its type. The players improve the alignments by dragging squares inside their row. The puzzle states are scored by an evolutionary model, that penalizes gaps and misaligned squares, whereas matching regions are rewarded. A puzzle is solved, if the player beats a given minimum score. Unlike Fold it, Phylo hides more of the scientific context from the player allowing even non-expert users to produce good results.

This promising approach also has some limitations. Phylo is only capable to deal with DNA or RNA sequences and supports only 10 sequences at once. The size of the playing field is fixed, which constrains the players in their movements. They also have few help mechanics supporting them during the game such as a consensus view of the columns.

## 3   Approach

Our prototype facilitates the alignment of large sets of protein sequences. A single amino acid is represented by a colored sphere inside the puzzle (see Fig. 1). Each amino acid has its own unique color. As a first approach to distinguish the different amino acids, we selected 20 different colors from the whole color spectrum related to the Windows Phone 8 accent color palette (see Fig. 2). We note, that the selection of the colors is arbitrary and may change in the future for a better discrimination.

On the top left side of the screen, the player can see all relevant information about the current progress. The four icons on the left show the score rewards and penalties for the current level (see [1] in Fig. 1). Matching spheres in each column are rewarded, mismatching spheres and gaps are penalized. In the example level in Fig. 1, each matching sphere is rewarded by one point, mismatching spheres are penalized by one point, and gaps are penalized with 5 points and one additional point for each length unit but the first. This gives the player direct information about the current scoring scheme. We note, that for reasons of simplification, our prototype does not take into account any mutation probabilities of the amino acids, as they are, e.g, represented in the BLOSUM matrices [17]. Two spheres are therefore only considered as a match, if they have exactly the same color. We will change this scoring scheme in the future to represent evolutionary models used in real applications.

Next to the penalties, the high score and the player's current score are shown (see [2] in Fig. 1). A puzzle is solved, if the player has beaten the high score at least once by improving the alignment.

To improve the alignment, the player has to align identically colored spheres in each column. On the other side, the player should minimize the amount of differently colored spheres in the columns and the number of empty cells.

By clicking and holding the left mouse button, the player can drag a sphere within its row (see Fig. 3). On touch devices, the player can drag a sphere with the finger. The currently selected sphere is highlighted with a white ring for an easy identification (see [3] in Fig. 1). If the sphere collides with other spheres, these will be moved too. It is not possible to switch spheres within a row due to the constraints of sequence alignments. Each moving step enforces the recalculation of the current score. The player can use this feature to determine if the movement results in a score improvement or not.

To grant the players full control over their movements, we implemented an undo/redo functionality. By clicking the arrow buttons on the top right of the screen (see [4] in Fig. 1), the player can revert each movement step done so far, as well as redo a reverted movement. In addition the player can save and load different puzzle states via the game menu, which can be accessed by clicking the monitor button on the upper right of the screen (see [4] in Fig. 1).

As mentioned above, the size of the alignment can be very large. To support the player in handling large alignments, the player can zoom the alignment by rotating the mouse wheel as well as scroll the current view by clicking and holding the right mouse button. On touch devices, the zoom feature is bound to a two finger multi touch gesture. If the distance between the two touches is reduced, the view will be zoomed out, otherwise the view will be zoomed in. For scrolling the view, the player can make a wipe gesture on the screen edges.

To support easy learning of the game mechanics and controls, we implemented a short stepwise tutorial. In each step, the player learns a new aspect of the game mechanics and can directly try out the learned content inside the tutorial level.

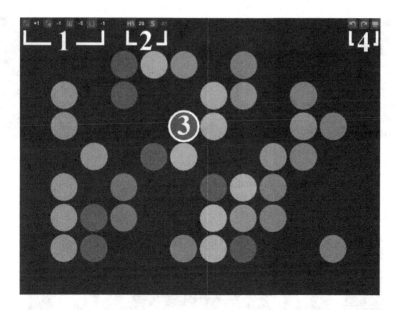

**Fig. 1.** Game prototype: Ingame view of the tutorial level. Each sphere corresponds to a single amino acid. The color indicates the acid type. [1] shows the scoring scheme, [2] the high score and current score, [3] a selected sphere, and [4] the undo/redo and menu buttons.

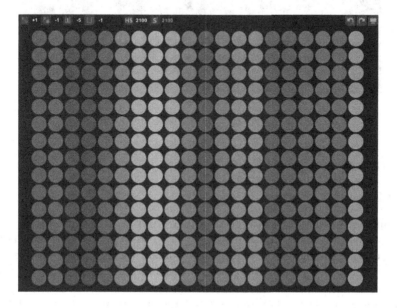

**Fig. 2.** Color scheme for the 20 different amino acids represented as a game level

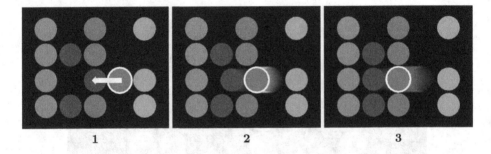

**Fig. 3.** Aligning by drag and drop. The green sphere with the white outline is dragged one position to the left. It collides with the neighbored red sphere which is also moved one position left.

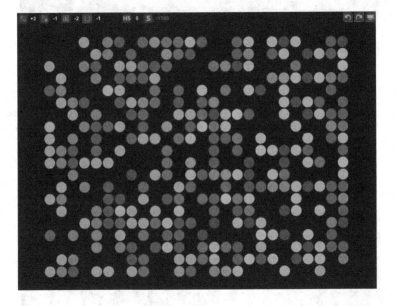

**Fig. 4.** One of the larger levels played in the user study

## 4    Evaluation

### 4.1    Methods

We evaluated our game prototype in a user study with a convenience sample of 20 persons (6 women and 14 men; age: 22 to 34 yrs). The participants were colleagues and students from the biology domain ($n$=11), from the computer science domain ($n$=8), and from the educational science domain ($n$=1). Five participants had no prior experience in computer games.

The purpose of the evaluation was to test the prototype concerning the quality of the tutorial, the game mechanics, and the game experience.

We implemented 10 different puzzles with increasing difficulty on basis of artificial sequence alignments. With each difficulty step, the number of sequences and their length were increased. On the other hand, the similarity of the sequences was decreased and the scoring scheme changed with each level. For practical reasons, the biggest levels had 20 sequences with a length of 16 amino acids (see Fig. 4).

Each test person had a maximum of one hour to play. There were no further restrictions, therefore playing the tutorial or specific levels were completely optional as well as the minimal playing time. Each participant was encouraged to report her or his immediate game impressions and to identify issues while playing the game. After playing, the participants had to answer a questionnaire consisting of 38 items based on a Likert scale. Each item had 5 possible answers, ranging from „fully disagree" to „fully agree".

The first 14 items represented a short version of the Game Experience Questionnaire (GEQ)[1] [18]. The GEQ measures game experience on seven categories: Immersion, Flow, Competence, Tension, Challenge, Positive and Negative Affects. In the short version (ingame GEQ; iGEQ), each category is measured by two items.

The items 15 to 29 were related to usability aspects regarding the design of the user interface and the controls according to the ISO 9241/(1)10 norm. These items were designed in correspondence to the Isometrics Questionnaire [20]. The last 9 items addressed the usability and helpfulness of the tutorial.

We analyzed the different items by coding their correspondent answers with a integer value between 0 (fully disagree) and 4 (fully agree). The results shown in the following sections correspond to the mean value of the coded answers.

### 4.2    Results

**Game Experience** The results for the GEQ categories are represented in Fig. 5. Our prototype performed very well in the category of positive affect with a mean of 3.03. The players had fun playing the game and felt pleased. They also had a substantial feeling of competence (2.6) and challenge (2.65) in the game. The majority of the participants reported a loss of their sense of time during the play, which relates to a considerable flow (2.55).

In the immersion category, our prototype performed moderately with a mean value of 2.22. While the majority of the participants were aesthetically pleased by the prototype (2.7), they were only moderately impressed (1.74).

Relating to negative impressions, our prototype showed also very good results. The majority of the players were neither bored nor found the game tiresome, which results in a mean of 0.57 in the category of negative affect. They experienced only a very low level of tension (0.61).

---

[1] Unfortunately, the original GEQ document [18] is no longer available. The GEQ can be found in [19].

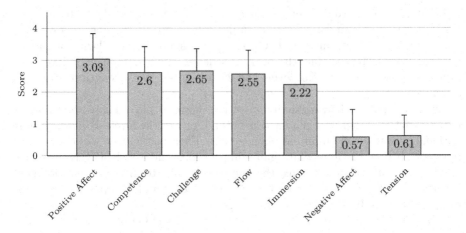

**Fig. 5.** Results for the GEQ items. The bars indicate the mean values for the single categories. The error bars represents the corresponding standard deviations.

**Tutorial.** The evaluation of the tutorial showed also reasonable results (see Fig. 6). All but one participant used the tutorial. The majority found the tutorial comprehensive (3.3), well structured (3.06) and helpful (2.79). They had the feeling, that they learned all relevant parts of the game (3.06). The possibility to instantly practice the learned content inside the tutorial level was also considered very positive (3.5). Some participants rated the tutorial length as too long (0.97) and would appreciate a shorter version with fewer text components.

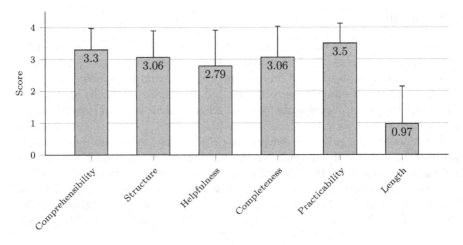

**Fig. 6.** Results for the tutorial items. The bars indicate the mean values for the single categories. The error bars represents the corresponding standard deviations.

**Usability and Game Mechanics.** The results of the usability study and the game mechanics are represented in Fig. 7. The design of the graphical user interface (GUI) was rated very well with a mean of 2.95. The participants were very pleased with the screen layout and they estimated the graphical user interface very comprehensive.

The controls showed even better results with a mean of 3.37. The participants stated, that the controls were very intuitive, easy to learn, good to memorize, and precise.

Contrary to the tutorial, the comprehensiveness of the scoring system received only moderate ratings (1.95). Some of the participants had problems identifying the reasons for an increase or decrease of the score, especially with gaps involved. This was primarily due to a lack of transparency of the interdependency of matches, mismatches and gaps and the different scoring schemes per level.

Another problem reported by some test users was the discrimination of some sphere colors like different types of green. Due to this issue, the rating for the color discrimination was only moderate with a mean of 2.2.

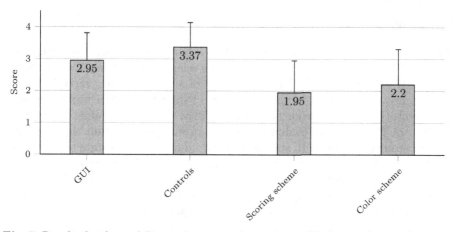

**Fig. 7.** Results for the usability and game mechanic items. The bars indicates the mean values for the single categories. The error bars represents the corresponding standard deviations.

## 5   Discussion and Future Work

As mentioned above, our prototype already performed reasonably well regarding usability and game experience. However, there is no 'ground truth' available because game experience was not measured directly in previous studies. Furthermore, comparing our game to a purely entertaining game or sequence alignment applications would be equally unfair. However, the results of this first study can serve as a reference for follow-up studies. Some major issues are the comprehensiveness of the scoring scheme and the discrimination of the sphere colors, especially in alignments with twenty different amino acids. According to flow theory [21], a negative effect of these issues on game experience would have been reflected in low flow and high tension scores. As illustrated in Fig. 5, this is obviously not the case.

In addition some participants felt a little constrained in their game control due to the lack of a multi-selection feature. The players' immersion should be also improved in the future.

To address these issues, we are planning to implement several new features. We will change the scoring scheme to take into account biologically derived mutation probabilities (e.g, the BLOSUM matrices [17]). Further, we will implement highlighting techniques to improve the understanding of the new scoring schemes. The sphere colors will also be rearranged to improve their discrimination. Another intermediate task, is the development of improved interaction techniques.

On the long run, we are planning to improve the prototype by adding sound, a more game like visual design and multiplayer features. We are also planning to integrate the game into a story context to improve the players' immersion.

## 6    Conclusion

We presented an improved game approach to solving protein sequence alignments using an integration of the concepts of citizen science and gaming. Our approach is capable of dealing with a large number of sequences with variable length without any restrictions on the playing field dimensions. We implemented a game prototype with a major focus on usability, visually appealing appearance and fun of gaming. The evaluation of our prototype regarding these aspects showed promising results. In spite of the early developmental state of our game, the players already had much fun in playing it, especially in large levels. They rated the game prototype as visually appealing, controllable, and challenging. In the future, we will improve our game concept and will evaluate, under which conditions the players are able to solve real alignments.

**Acknowledgment.** The authors are grateful for a FiF (Center of Interdisciplinary Research) grant by Technische Universität Darmstadt supporting this study.

## References

1. Mount, D.W.: Bioinformatics: Sequence and genome analysis, 2nd edn. Cold Spring Harbor Laboratory Press (2004)
2. Wang, L., Jiang, T.: On the complexity of multiple sequence alignment. Journal of Computational Biology 1(4), 337–348 (1994)
3. Higgins, D.G., Sharp, P.M.: Clustal: a package for performing multiple sequence alignment on a microcomputer. Gene 73(1), 237–244 (1988)
4. Edgar, R.C.: Muscle: multiple sequence alignment with high accuracy and high throughput. Nucleic Acids Research 32(5), 1792–1797 (2004)

5. Do, C.B., Mahabhashyam, M.S., Brudno, M., Batzoglou, S.: Probcons: Probabilistic consistency-based multiple sequence alignment. Genome Research 15, 330–340 (2005)
6. Katoh, K., Misawa, K., Kuma, K.I., Miyata, T.: Mafft: a novel method for rapid multiple sequence alignment based on fast fourier transform. Nucleic Acids Research 30(14), 3059–3066 (2002)
7. Notredame, C.: Recent evolutions of multiple sequence alignment algorithms. PLoS Comput. Biol. 3(8), e123 (2007)
8. Wagemans, J., Elder, J.H., Kubovy, M., Palmer, S.E., Peterson, M.A., Singh, M., von der Heydt, R.: A century of gestalt psychology in visual perception: I. Perceptual grouping and figure–ground organization. Psychological Bulletin 138(6), 1172–1217 (2012)
9. Hand, E.: People power. Nature 466(7307), 685–687 (2010)
10. Land, K., Slosar, A., Lintott, C., Andreescu, D., Bamford, S., Murray, P., Nichol, R., Raddick, M.J., Schawinski, K., Szalay, A., Thomas, D., Vandenberg, J.: Galaxy zoo: the large-scale spin statistics of spiral galaxies in the sloan digital sky survey. Monthly Notices of the Royal Astronomical Society 388(4), 1686–1692 (2008)
11. Cooper, S., Khatib, F., Treuille, A., Barbero, J., Lee, J., Beenen, M., Leaver-Fay, A., Baker, D., Popović, Z., et al.: Predicting protein structures with a multiplayer online game. Nature 466(7307), 756–760 (2010)
12. Kawrykow, A., Roumanis, G., Kam, A., Kwak, D., Leung, C., Wu, C., Zarour, E., Sarmenta, L., Blanchette, M., Waldispühl, J.: Phylo: A citizen science approach for improving multiple sequence alignment. PLoS ONE 7(3), e31362 (2012)
13. Ryan, R.M., Deci, E.L.: Self-determination theory and the facilitation of intrinsic motivation, social development, and well-being. American Psychologist 55(1), 68–78 (2000)
14. Cooper, S., Khatib, F., Makedon, I., Lu, H., Barbero, J., Baker, D., Fogarty, J., Popović, Z., Foldit Players: Analysis of social gameplay macros in the foldit cookbook. In: Proceedings of the 6th International Conference on Foundations of Digital Games, FDG 2011, pp. 9–14. ACM, New York (2011)
15. Khatib, F., Cooper, S., Tyka, M.D., Xu, K., Makedon, I., Popović, Z., Baker, D., Foldit Players: Algorithm discovery by protein folding game players. Proceedings of the National Academy of Sciences 108(47), 18949–18953 (2011)
16. Khatib, F., DiMaio, F., Cooper, S., Kazmierczyk, M., Gilski, M., Krzywda, S., Zabranska, H., Pichova, I., Thompson, J., Popović, Z., Jaskolski, M., Baker, D.: Crystal structure of a monomeric retroviral protease solved by protein folding game players. Nature Structural & Molecular Biology 18(10), 1175–1177 (2011)
17. Henikoff, S., Henikoff, J.G.: Amino acid substitution matrices from protein blocks. Proceedings of the National Academy of Sciences 89(22), 10915–10919 (1992)
18. IJsselsteijn, W., Poels, K., de Kort, Y.: The game experience questionnaire: Development of a self-report measure to assess player experiences of digital games, TU Eindhoven, Eindhoven, The Netherlands (2008)
19. Nacke, L.: Affective ludology: Scientific measurement of user experience in interactive entertainment (2009)
20. Gediga, G., Hamborg, K.C., Düntsch, I.: The isometrics usability inventory: an operationalization of iso 9241-10 supporting summative and formative evaluation of software systems. Behaviour & Information Technology 18(3), 151–164 (1999)
21. Csikszentmihalyi, M.: Beyond boredom and anxiety. Jossey-Bass (2000)

# Serious Game Mechanics, Workshop on the Ludo-Pedagogical Mechanism

Theodore Lim[1], Sandy Louchart[1], Neil Suttie[1], Jannicke Baalsrud Hauge[2],
Ioana A. Stanescu[3], Francesco Bellotti[4], Maira B. Carvalho[4], Jeffrey Earp[5],
Michela Ott[5], Sylvester Arnab[6], and Damian Brown[7]

[1] Heriot-Watt University, Riccarton, Edinburgh EH14 4AS, Scotland, UK
[2] Bremer Institut für Produktion und Logistik (BIBA), Germany
[3] National Defence University "Carol I", Bucharest, 50662, Romania
[4] University of Genoa, 16145 Genova, Italy
[5] Consiglio Nazionale delle Ricerche (CNR), 16149 Genova, Italy
[6] Serious Games Institute, Coventry University, Coventry CV1 2TL, UK
[7] Serious Games Interactive, 2100 Copenhagen, Denmark
{t.lim,s.louchart,n.suttie}@hw.ac.uk, baa@biba.uni-bremen.de,
ioana.stanescu@adlnet.ro, {imartinez,pablom}@fdi.ucm.es,
{franz,Maira.Carvalho}@elios.unige.it, {jeff,ott}@itd.cnr.it,
s.arnab@coventry.ac.uk, djb@seriousgames.net

**Abstract.** Research in Serious Games (SG), as a whole, faces two main challenges in understanding the transition between the instructional design and actual game design implementation [1] and documenting an evidence-based mapping of game design patterns onto relevant pedagogical patterns [2]. From a practical perspective, this transition lacks methodology and requires a leap of faith from a prospective customer in the ability of a SG developer to deliver a game that will achieve the desired learning outcomes. This workshop aims to present and apply a preliminary exposition though a purpose-processing methodology to probe, from various SG design aspects, how serious game design patterns map with pedagogical practices

## 1    Organisers

T. Lim - Heriot-Watt University, Riccarton, Edinburgh EH14 4AS, Scotland, UK
S. Louchart - Heriot-Watt University, Riccarton, Edinburgh EH14 4AS, Scotland, UK
N. Suttie - Heriot-Watt University, Riccarton, Edinburgh EH14 4AS, Scotland, UK
J. Baalsrud Hauge - Bremer Institut für Produktion und Logistik (BIBA), Germany
I.A. Stanescu - National Defence University "Carol I", Bucharest , 50662, Romania
F. Bellotti - University of Genoa, 16145 Genova, Italy
M. Carvalho - University of Genoa, 16145 Genova, Italy
J. Earp - Consiglio Nazionale delle Ricerche (CNR), 16149 Genova, Italy
M. Ott - Consiglio Nazionale delle Ricerche (CNR), 16149 Genova, Italy
S. Arnab - Serious Games Institute, Coventry University, Coventry CV1 2TL, UK
D. Brown – Serious Games Interactive, Copenhagen, Denmark

S. Göbel and J. Wiemeyer (Eds.): GameDays 2014, LNCS 8395, pp. 186–189, 2014.
© Springer International Publishing Switzerland 2014

## 2      Length

The proposed workshop will last a day and will run as follow:

1. Invited talk on Serious Games Design  - (45mn)
A short introduction to the main elements in SG design from a technical perspective will be given by Damian Brown (SGI, Denmark), whereas Dr Sylvester Arnab (Serious Game Institute, UK) will explain different pedagogical methods which support the game design process.

2. Short Introduction to Serious Games Mechanics (SGMs) - (15mn)
SGMs are seen as the relationship between pedagogical patterns and game design patterns [3]. The process of investigating the links between the two lies between the instructional design requirements and the actual game/game-play design. This is not obvious and direct links between the low-level game implementation aspects and high-level instructional design aspects of SGs remain obscure. This session will provide a definition of SGM and suggest a purpose-processing methodology (PPSM) to identify the link. This talk will also introduce the use of the PPSM towards identifying the role of narrative as a motivational and reflection tool in SG design. The PPSM could then be used as a design tool or an evaluation tool for SG design.

3. Game play session - (1 hour 30min)
During this session the participants will try out the presented methodological approach and framework. Participants will be divided in groups working with two different aims: 1) to analyse (and provide suggestions to improve) existing games; 2) to design new gameplays. The organizers will provide a set of state of the art SGs to be played and analysed. Participants, who would like to apply the framework to a specific game, must provide the organizer access to the game before March, 1. 2014

4. Game SGM analysis – (1 hour)
This is a two-step approach – 45mn for identifying SGMs from the game perspective and 15mn to generalize these SGMs away from a particular topic or game.

5. Mapping SGMs (45 min)
Groups exchange their set of SGMs and are provided with the SGMs identified in the Year 3 case study. Groups are then asked to comment on the sets provided to them. We will need a good questionnaire there. At the end of the exercise, the groups will be asked to link, map, SGMs collectively on a board.

6. SGM card game (1 hour)
This activity is based on the board game "cards against humanity".

7. Filling questionnaire (40 min)

8. Expert panel (Games and Pedagogy) – (45 min)

Based upon the result of game play session, the expert panel will analyse, discuss and show how different aspects of the proposed methodological approach and framework can effectively support the design process, increasing the quality of the outcome and decreasing the time to market. The panel will also discuss typical challenges in the design process as well as challenges in finding the right SGMs for specific purposes.

## 3     The SGM Approach

Serious Games, like games in general represent a complex system of intertwined experiences influencing on one another so as to motive a player not only to play and engage with a proposed experience, but also to express and reflect on a gaming activity during and after experiencing it. In this context, game activities, various levels of Game Mechanics, motivational elements, competition, challenge etc.. are all inter-related elements through which a gaming experience can be defined. Purposeful learning is in itself an aspect specific to Serious Games. The methodological approach towards identifying SGMs is a simple approach which focuses on the nature of Game Mechanics associated with the specific aspect of purposeful learning. All of these elements can be described in terms of Purpose, Process and Structure, in the sense that SGMs elements are designed for a reason and have a purpose with regards to a gaming and learning experience. This purpose is generally achieved through a process in which activities, information or events represent the structural tangible elements of the overall element described (Figure 1).

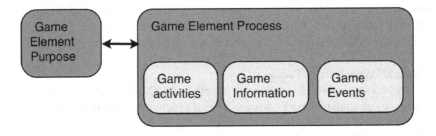

**Fig. 1.** SG element methodological approach

Example

The element of competition for instance could be defined at an abstract level as a process into which a player is provided with a task (score goals, collect things), presented with a challenge (score more goal than an opponent, collect things in a defined period of time) and ultimately made to review his/her performance (leader board, final score results). From a structural perspective, there are many elements determining the actual nature of the challenge and specific GMs can be identified as clear patterns for defining competition. For instance, a player Vs player competition will require specific elements that are not necessarily present in other types of competitions related games. For instance a player vs player approach could be looking at mechanics related to a duel or a direct competition. A massively on-line multiplayer game will, however, implement different elements such as a leaderboard for instance. A leaderboard would serve no purpose in the player Vs player approach but would act as an essential mechanic in a multiplayer game. Finally each game or SG element has to have a purpose bounding the actual gaming system framework and set of activities to the player experience. In the case of a player Vs player approach, the purpose would be to provide a safe competitive environment for friends to interact or a framework to support social connection (i.e. the concept of party games etc.).

**Acknowledgments.** This project is partially funded under the European Community Seventh Framework Programme (FP7/2007 2013), Grant Agreement nr. 258169 and EPSRC/IMRC grants 113946 and 112430.

# References

1. Karagiorgi, Y., Symeou, L.: Translating Constructivism into Instructional Design: Potential and Limitations. Educational Tech. & Soc. 8(1), 17–27 (2005)
2. Kelle, S., Klemke, R., Specht, M.: Design patterns for learning games. IJTEL 3(6), 555–569 (2011)
3. Suttie, N., Louchart, S., Lim, T., Macvean, A., Westera, W., Brown, D., Djaouti, D.: Introducing the "Serious Games Mechanics" A Theoretical Framework to Analyse Relationships Between "Game" and "Pedagogical Aspects" of Serious Games. Procedia Computer Science 15, 314–315 (2012)

# QuizeRo -
# Recipe for a Successful
# QR-Code Scavenger Hunt

Marcus Birkenrahe and Kai Erenli

FH des bfi Wien, Film-, TV- und Medienproduktion, Maria Jacobigasse 1/3.4,
1030 Wien, Austria
kai.erenli@fh-vie.ac.at

**Abstract.** QuizeRo is a scavenger hunt game that aids any educational scenario using QR-Codes. Whether students are new to a campus or city, employees get introduced to the process management of their company or organizations want to increase team building, QuizeRo has proven to increase engagement. How to design a QuizeRo is described in this paper.

## 1    Introduction

This short paper aims to support people who want to install their own QuizeRo-Scavenger Hunt as described in a paper published in 2013 (Erenli 2013). The reader should refer to Erenli (2013) for information on the intentions and history of the project. QuizeRo is a location-based scavenger hunt using QR-Codes. It was developed to engage learners or people new to a city or topic and impart knowledge in a fun way. After having installed a number of QuizeRo Scavenger Hunts since the method was first introduced, this paper describes a step-by-step guideline based on the experience of the QuizeRo project team and the feedback received by the "players". It should enable readers to design their own QuizeRo game. However, this "recipe" is just a guideline: readers are invited to adapt, develop and change the method. The authors greatly appreciate any input or feedback that aids the purpose. As in any recipe we have to start with the ingredients before we give directions. Those ingredients are:

## 2    Ingredients

- 1 Smartphone
- APP/Software to scan QR Codes
- 1 QR-Code generator
- 1 Computer
- 1 Scenario (QuizeRo will do for ANY Scenario)
- Ability to tell a story
- A planning horizon of (at least) a day
- Optional: 1 Camera, 1 Mapping tool, books to cover background story

How to use these ingredients will be described hereafter.

S. Göbel and J. Wiemeyer (Eds.): GameDays 2014, LNCS 8395, pp. 190–194, 2014.

## 3    Directions

### 1. Develop a (good) Story

Developing a good background story is the key to success. Other research projects using scavenger hunts to engage learners have failed because no storyline has been provided. But what makes a good story? And how can a scavenger hunt story be developed from a real life situation?

Good stories consist of three elements: a plot (something happens over time with a sense of causality), characters (people represented in the plot), and a theme ( meaning of the plot). If we assume that our target group (the people who play QuizeRo) is a group of exchange students who is visiting the city of Berlin to study at our school. The goal is to help them get oriented on campus. Berlin is "noir": in the Cold War, it was a city of spies (our characters!) who smuggled dissidents and secrets across the Wall that once separated East and West Berlin.

One possible background story could start with: *"We're deep in the Cold War. Upon your arrival in Berlin, you're charged with a mission. If you choose to accept it, you will save lives. If you fail, lives may be lost. Though you're a team of spies, you assume the cover of regular students. To pull this off, you need to find out..."* and so on. We have now defined a fact-finding rescue mission. The story needs more work of course: what type of spy work are we going to do? The answer to this question provides the climax, the penultimate part of the plot before the actual ending (which coincides with the end of our quiz). Since we do not want to write a thriller, we only need simple story elements, but it is still important to have a sense of climax as we approach the end. We could, for example, bring in an antagonist or enemy spy half way through the action. The questions could become more difficult or time elements could be introduced. A good example would be: *"You must get to the office of the registrars exactly 5 minutes before it closes, or the enemy will uncover your identity."*

### 2. Define the Playing Field

When defining the playing field, the gamemaster should ensure that it is closely connected to the background story. This could also be done before you start developing the story. The size of the playing field is highly variable. It can be the whole city, the university campus, or just a single building, even a (virtual) QuizeRo around the world is possible. As soon as you have determined the borders of the playing field (e.g. use a mapping tool like Google Maps to do the "homework" online), it is time for some field work (offline). You have to lay out a path for the riddle as this is a scavenger hunt where participants progress from stage to stage. At each stage the participants have to answer a question, solve a riddle, and perform a certain task. Whatever they should do is decided by the gamemaster. In order to keep the motivation and engagement level high a QuizeRo Hunt should neither exceed 1½ hours or 10-15 stages. The distance between the stages should be approximately the same. Nevertheless it is also possible to have a "power-stage" with multiple

**Fig. 1.** A "QuizeRo-Map"

tasks/questions. As stated, gamemasters should connect the story to each stage. If you have a Cold-War-Spy-Story taking place in Berlin, you could establish a stage where the Berlin Wall once stood or you could assign a "conspiratorial" meeting at a place where they serve a good "Currywurst". These stages would not work in a city like Vienna, of course, since there are different places of history and traditional food. In Vienna you would most probably have to send a "spy" to a good coffee house, a historical building or to the city sewers.

If the gamemaster discovers an interesting spot, he/she should decide if the spot is worth being adapted to the story or not. A short walk within the playing field should help to find to discover possible spots that could not be seen "online". After this task is completed it is time to design the quiz.

### 3. Use Software to Design the Quiz/Riddle/Scenario

In short, you can link the QR-Code to any item such as an URL, a calendar event, contact information, geolocation, email address, short message, text or even a WIFI network. The gamemaster can mix these items user-defined. Usually the gamemaster links a QR-Code to an URL which opens up another extensive range of possibilities. In the QuizeRos played so far, the QR-Codes were linked to Google forms. The advantage of this choice is that many gamemasters are already familiar with the toolset and one can create a riddle without sophisticated IT skills. Moreover, answers are stored in a spreadsheet aiding the process of administration and evaluation. The forms are also available for smartphones.

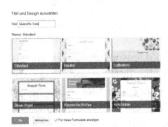

### Choosing the Right Template

In Google forms, the gamemaster can choose the best template for the QuizeRo, adding a graphical mood to the background story.

**Fig. 2.** Choosing a template

## Designing the QuizeRo

The gamemaster should create one form for each stage. Each form may ask one or more questions and may mix question types. Since it is important to guide the players to the next stage, the confirmation message should contain a hint where the next QR-Code is hidden. This is a key element!

**Fig. 3.** Designing the quiz

## Copy the Link

Since it is crucial to link the QR-Code to an item, the gamemaster needs to produce a link. By using Google forms this can be done easily. Simply use the built-in tool as seen in Fig. 4.

**Fig. 4.** The Link

## 4.     Create     QR-Codes     and     Link     to Quiz/Riddle/Scenario

Any QR-Code generator will do (e.g. http:// zxing.appspot.com/generator). Some may provide a selection of linkable items as stated before, some will add advertisement to the link. In the end you should get a QR-Code that looks like this.

**Fig. 5.** QR-Code-Generator

## 5. Find Hiding Spots for Your QR-Codes

This is tricky since there are already many QR-Codes out there. The gamemaster should customize the QR-Code (e.g. link it to Corporate Design). This will help to distinguish the QuizeRo-Code from one of the local pizza restaurant. It will also help to prevent frustration, if players have to scan multiple wrong QR-Codes before finding the QuizeRo-Code. This part is indispensible in urban areas. Additional specific hints should be given where the QR-Code is hidden (e.g. "under the message board", "in the upper right corner", etc.). The codes should be valid long enough during the playtime. Therefore spots should be picked wisely. Any hidden place is a good place, but the gamemaster should bear in mind that scanning the QR-Code is still possible (The surfaces should not be too curved, hidden etc.). Also, the gamemaster should not get into trouble with public authorities and/or facility management. Attaching a QR-Code to a cultural heritage site or obstructing an emergency phone number might not be the best idea.

## 6. Beta-Testing Is Key

Test-run your game (or ask someone to do it) at least once to locate errors in the story, riddle or technical part of the QuizeRo. If an unfinished QuizeRo is started it may result in major frustration of the players, giving the game a bad name and demotivating players.

## 7. E-Mail Can Help

In the event of a QR-Code loss the game would be over, since players could not advance to the next stage from this point. Teams who cannot find the QR-Code or solve problems where the QR code is not scannable/torn apart can be supported by mail addresses with auto-responder. QuizeRo can be continued. If the team is not successful at finding the right spot, it is possible to give penalty points. The gamemaster just has to take a look at the inbox of those addresses (forwarding those messages also helps since the gamemaster knows right away if something is wrong when mails come pouring in.) Using the "mail-system" can also help to play the game when it is not possible to attach QR-Codes anywhere (legally). In this case, the gamemaster may ask the teams to send a pic with the right location to the given stage mail address.

## 8. Share the Experience

We are most interested what gamemasters have to say about QuizeRo, and how other QuizeRos do look like. So far users have told us the following:

- *"Take your time, especially to design the game"*, Lennart B.
- *"Game is particularly suitable for open-minded people who have no problems or friction points with new technology"*, Christos N.

Happy hunting!

**Acknowledgments.** Thank you for the valuable feedback sent by QuizeRo Players and Developers so far: *"Keep up the spirit, because you are born to hunt"*.

# Reference

1. Erenli, K.: Gamify Your Teaching - Using Location-Based Games for Educational Purposes. International Journal of Advanced Corporate Learning, iJAC 6(2), 22–27 (2013)

# StoryTec and StoryPlay as Tools for Adaptive Game-Based Learning Research

Laila Shoukry[1], Christian Reuter[1], and Florian Mehm[2]

[1] Multimedia Communications Lab - KOM, TU Darmstadt, Germany
[2] Hessisches Telemedia Technologie Kompetenz-Center e.V.
Rundeturmstr. 10, 64283 Darmstadt, Germany
{florian.mehm,christian.reuter,
laila.shoukry}@kom.tu-darmstadt.de

**Abstract.** In this session we will present different ways in which the StoryTec framework can be helpful for researchers in the field of Adaptive Game-based Learning. From initial prototyping stages of complex, adaptive learning adventure games to authoring, cross-platform-publishing and evaluation of such projects, StoryTec offers a range of useful research-based tools which make the process faster and team collaboration easier. Interested researchers will be able to get guided hands-on experience with the authoring and evaluation tool.

## 1 Objectives

The authoring of adaptive learning games is not an easy task as it integrates several expertise fields. Moreover, researchers in this field often have the desire to create good educational games on the one hand and to effectively use them for research purposes on the other hand. Only few tools are available which can be used to facilitate this complex and time-consuming process. In this session we will present the StoryTec[1] environment which was specifically created for this purpose and demonstrate the ways in which it can support research on adaptive game-based learning.

## 2 Intended Audience

This workshop is primarily targeting researchers in the field of game-based learning but will also be of benefit to developers of serious games or educational software in general as well as educators.

## 3 Agenda

The workshop will be comprised of two elements, an introduction by the developers of StoryTec on the overall structure of the authoring tool and its application to game-based learning, followed by a hands-on session in which the audience works with StoryTec. The following topics will be presented:

---

[1] Available for an open community for free at http://www.storytec.de

S. Göbel and J. Wiemeyer (Eds.): GameDays 2014, LNCS 8395, pp. 195–198, 2014.
© Springer International Publishing Switzerland 2014

### 3.1 The Authoring Process of Educational Games

During the creation of an educational game, an interplay between different disciplines (technical, including especially game programmers on the on hand; pedagogical, for the learning aspects of the game on the other hand). The various phases and roles in the production of digital educational games are discussed, along with challenges frequently faced and the solutions offered by StoryTec.

### 3.2 Creation of Adaptive Narrative Learning Games with StoryTec

We will discuss how StoryTec makes it easy to build adaptive learning games based on the theoretical model of Narrative Games based Learning Objects. Using this model, authors can specify how an adaptive system included in StoryTec will influence the game based on the input of the player.

### 3.3 Rapid Prototyping and Iterative Authoring with StoryTec

A specialized version of the StoryTec player called "StoryPlay" (see Figure 2), allows researchers/testers to play a created game while simultaneously analyzing context information about game flow, logging and game logic update. We will present how this can be used for evaluation purposes. Figure 1 shows the workflow resulting from this approach: Intermediate game versions are created in StoryTec. Based on playtests of these game versions, authors can change and improve the games.

**Fig. 1.** Iterative Authoring with StoryTec and StoryPlay

### 3.4 Example Projects and Discussion

We will present some projects where StoryTec was used and discuss patterns and solutions found in these projects. Examples include the publicly available demo game "Favourite Places" included in StoryTec as well as the game "Der Chaos-Fluch" [2], a local tourism and culture serious game.

---

[2] Available at http://darmstadt-marketing.de/fileadmin/spiel/

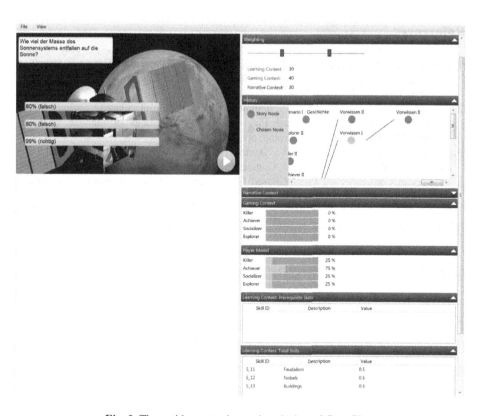

**Fig. 2.** The rapid prototyping and analysis tool StoryPlay

## 3.5    Hands-on Training

The participants of the workshop will be provided with a guided hands-on experience of building their own game in StoryTec. For this purpose, participants are invited to prepare the workshop by trying out the public version of StoryTec and assembling content they might require for a game. Suggestions are travel photos for an interactive travel journal-game or assets for a simple educational game. Assets for the hands-on training will also be provided for participants without own assets.

## 4    Equipment Requirements

Participants are asked to bring a laptop with Microsoft Windows installed.

# References

1. Mehm, F., Göbel, S., Steinmetz, R.: Authoring of Serious Adventure Games in StoryTec. In: Göbel, S., Müller, W., Urban, B., Wiemeyer, J. (eds.) Edutainment 2012/GameDays 2012. LNCS, vol. 7516, pp. 144–154. Springer, Heidelberg (2012)
2. Reuter, C., Mehm, F., Goebel, S., Steinmetz, R.: Evaluation of Adaptive Serious Games using Playtraces and Aggregated Play Data. In: Proceedings of the 7th European Conference on Games Based Learning, pp. 504–511 (2013)
3. Mehm, F., Wendel, V., Göbel, S., Steinmetz, R.: Bat Cave: A Testing and Evaluation Platform for Digital Educational Games. In: Bente, M. (ed.) Proceedings of the 3rd European Conference on Games Based Learning, pp. 251–260. Academic Conferences International, Reading (2010)

# Author Index